The Management of Trade Marketing

The Management of Trade Marketing

Arthur Lawrence

Gower

Published by
Gower Publishing Company Limited
Aldershot, Hants, England

Lawrence, Arthur
The management of trade marketing.
1. Marketing
I. Title
658.8 HF5415

ISBN 0-566-02395-4

Typeset by
The Letter Box Company (Woking) Limited

Printed and bound in Great Britain
at The Pitman Press, Bath

Contents

Illustrations

Figures

Tables

Preface

The prospective reader will want to know what this book is about. It has been written from a conviction that the whole process of putting goods and services into the market place, as a means of getting them through to the consumer, deserves to be thought of as a strategic process, whose component actions should fall into place, as part of a logical sequence. Put in this way, the concept is certainly part of marketing strategy; and to distinguish it from other aspects of marketing, it seems appropriate to call it 'trade marketing'.

Marketing generally has taken on the emphasis of being a response to the needs, attitudes and beliefs of consumers. Obtaining the necessary distribution to the consumer through trade channels is often relegated to the function of selling, with the implication that this is essentially a reactive operation, doing the best it can to fulfil the plans of other people, using what opportunities it can find. Trade marketing assumes instead that the strategic aims of achieving distribution through the trade must be made an integral part of the overall strategy of the business. Indeed one could go further. There is little or no point in promoting products to the consumer which cannot be obtained through his or her chosen outlet – probably owned by one of the dominant retail chains. So securing distribution at acceptable trade discounts becomes the core of the marketing effort and of the protection of hard-won brand loyalties. Modern advertising increasingly accepts that multi-million pound budgets must be devoted to this end.

In developing this theme, the book deals in turn with the issues which go to make up a selling, or a trade marketing, strategy. However, this is not a book which is limited to philosophical concepts. At each stage, the practical considerations involved in dealing with each issue are examined, choices reviewed, methods of implementation described and, where applicable, the best practice recommended. Starting with the need to secure distribution in the market place, the sequence proceeds logically through the rational selection of appropriate trade channels for the purpose; coping with ever more monopolistic distributors; maintaining control over trade remuneration and consumer pricing; the provision of selling and supply services in the field and the detailed methods for planning and implementing these services; the organisation of management information; the handling of promotions; and the combination of all of these into one coherent strategy.

The book is therefore intended for all who are concerned with the effectiveness of the trade marketing effort of a business, which would include senior management on the lookout for fresh insights into familiar problems, as well as all managers and operators in selling forces interested in the broader scope of their activities, and in practical methods of operation. To the student of business practices it will also provide, I believe, a different perspective on some marketing issues.

Basics are dealt with where necessary to the comprehensiveness of the sequence, and however familiar these issues may be in practice to more experienced readers, they may still find material for reflection in the application of them to strategic thinking.

Fundamentally, the same principles of securing trade co-operation apply to all businesses which make any use at all of third party distribution in getting their products through to the user – and very few businesses do not. The issues discussed are therefore as relevant to the marketing of industrial as of consumer items, and to services as well as to goods. Trade marketing is sometimes thought of as being confined to the mass retailing of domestic supplies; in fact, the concept is as wide as is the use of distributors, stockists and agents in all types of business. Industrial sellers may have something to learn from the sophisticated techniques coming into use among suppliers of consumer products; but the latter may derive insights from the more varied approaches and the more diverse problems of industrial marketing. Equally, the principles apply to all types of markets, whether economically advanced or still developing, even though the applicable methods may vary greatly. Instances have been chosen by way of illustration to show this relevance to overseas markets, as well as to the uniquely British, or even European, environment.

The book follows the logical sequence of the development of a selling strategy, to the point where each chapter broadly represents the issues which would merit a section in a written selling strategy document. On the assumption that most readers will be associated in one way or another with a currently operating business, each chapter ends with a checklist inviting reflection on the topics discussed, as they would apply to that business. While all businesses are different and there can be no rigid pattern either for review or for implementation, almost every business should find topics that are relevant, and which give cause for some new thinking.

The book should be read first as a whole, following the suggested sequence of strategic planning, to be used as a starting point either for the revision of an existing selling strategy, or as an initial attempt at producing one. Thereafter, the division of the book into sections will, I hope, render it valuable for reference to specific issues as they come up for review in the course of a company's operations.

Finally, a word in self-defence: in my experience, the most effective and certainly the most persuasive members of a sales force are frequently female. It is a matter of regret that there are not more female sales managers. It has not been apparent to me that these women in the front line derive much satisfaction from being referred to as sales persons. In totally unregenerate fashion, therefore, my text throughout refers to salesmen, in the hope that this honourable title will be acceptable to female readers, and especially to those who aspire to have influence in the management of trade marketing.

Arthur Lawrence

1

Getting market distribution

The saying is that the world will beat a path to the door of the inventor of a better product. In practice, the inventor would do well to lay out the path himself, and put up a few signposts; otherwise he may find that the world is making its way to the inventor next door. This necessity to get his product through to the consumer lies heavily on every producer, whether of goods or services, in developing markets as well as in sophisticated ones. Whether the product is aimed at the general public, or intended only for a limited number of specialist users in commerce or industry, the same problem arises – achieving an efficient method of moving the product through to those users in sufficient numbers. In very many cases, the producer will find that he cannot do this unaided using only his own resources, and that he has to have recourse to whatever facilities are offered by the existing market distribution system. Such distribution facilities exist practically everywhere, in markets large and small, and for nearly every kind of trade and speciality; but the participation of distributors in the marketing of a product can by no means be taken for granted. While addressing himself primarily to the needs and wishes of his users, the producer must simultaneously ensure that his chosen channels of distribution function effectively in delivering his goods to his users. This last sentence would serve to sum up the theme of this book.

In exploring all the considerations that arise in achieving market distribution, the logical starting point must be the question whether the services of the market have to be used at all. The option to do otherwise is quite often a valid one, at least for some part of a producer's business.

Selling direct to the user

In the simplest of all situations, the producer merely sells his output himself to the potential users who come to him. If he is a peasant farmer in a simple community, he may take his produce to the market place to do so, but once he is there he is still dependent on buyers finding him and making their purchases direct from him as the producer. Even in modern, highly commercialised markets there are still plenty of specialist artisans and craftsmen continuing to operate in exactly the same way. Indeed, the more sophisticated the market, the more of a cachet there is to the business which can make the boast 'Made by craftsmen on our own premises'. In these circumstances the producer, whether a simple village ironworker or high class goldsmith, saves the cost of using middlemen and his customers probably feel that they are getting a bargain by dealing with him direct.

At least, the producer may believe that all his customers are buying for their own use, but he has no means of knowing whether or not some of them are buying to resell at a profit elsewhere. Sooner or later, he may be propositioned by a trader asking to buy a bulk quantity at a special price, for distribution to markets which he as producer cannot normally reach. However determined the producer may be to retain all his distribution in his own hands, he may be unable to control it, or else may find himself obliged to deal through traders if he is to reach all the customers he needs.

Some producers however, in a variety of markets, have determined not to give special prices to intermediary traders, so that they can simply increase the price and gain the profit from the sale but to try to make all their sales directly to users, while still achieving the widest market coverage possible. This can hardly be achieved from only one static selling point, and so it is necessary for the producer to have either outlying branch selling points, or travelling salesmen, or perhaps both. These methods of operation lend themselves well to producers of specialist or industrial items; on the one hand, they have only a limited number of potential users, with whom it is easy to make personal contact; and on the other hand the more specialist or 'tailor-made' the product or the service, the more reason there is for wanting to deal with all one's users oneself, or at least, through one's own employees. Thus direct selling to the user is largely the norm for those producers who provide raw materials, manufacturing equipment and specialised services to industry.

Going direct to the public

Even when the potential user of the product is the general public itself, selling direct may sometimes remain a valid option for the supplier. There have been successful instances of this being done on a national scale using travelling salesmen, aiming at no less than every household in an entire country. A familiar example in Britain some years ago was the ice cream man, in his van or on his tricycle, with the 'Stop Me and Buy One' slogan. Originally, this operation, employing literally thousands of salesmen, was carried out directly by the national manufacturers of ice cream; nowadays, the ice cream vans that one sees patrolling the suburban streets are all operated by independent franchise-holders and the great national direct selling operations are no more. There have also been numerous door-to-door selling campaigns for products

A case study

The larger the number of potential users for a product, the more questionable is a direct selling policy. Within particular trades and industries it may sometimes be found that one group of producers is vehemently in favour of direct selling to users, while their competitors are equally strongly convinced of the opposite. An interesting instance of this existed in Britain in the 1960s, among the manufacturers of animal feeding stuffs. Animal feeds are compounds of grain and other commodites, ground down and compressed. Millions of tons are manufactured annually in huge mills and sold to farmers for their livestock. At the time, there were estimated to be well over 100,000 significant livestock-raising farms in Britain, and several of the largest feeds manufacturers had a policy of selling to all these farmers direct. This meant each of them maintained local sales offices in practically every county, and employed hundreds of salesmen whose task it was to call regularly on every worthwhile farmer they could find. The supplies ordered were despatched direct from the mills to the farms using elaborate national transport systems.

As time went on, the costs of providing all the services needed for the direct sale and supply of just one item out of the farmer's complete range of purchases became increasingly hard to bear. For their other needs farmers are in the main served by a network of agricultural merchants, supplying everything from farm machinery to seeds and fertiliser and rubber boots. One transaction can frequently cover a whole range of supplies, delivered by the same transport. One by one the direct supplying manufacturers of animal feeds had to concede that it would be more economical to sell through merchants at prices which would allow the latter to resell and deliver to farmers locally at sufficient profit. The transition was painful but inevitable. Nowadays, animal feeds have been added to the range of commodities which reach the farmer through the intermediary of merchants and stockists, and the vast armies of feed manufacturers' salesmen have been disbanded. In this instance, the efficiency of the existing market distributive system has won out over the merits of selling direct to the user.

as various as cosmetics, brushware and encyclopaedias. Fifty years ago, vacuum cleaners were sold to the British housewife in this way. But more commonly nowadays, direct selling to the public has come to mean mail order, either based on the direct mailing of offers and catalogues to individual addresses, or on media advertising. In the 1970s, both in the USA and in Europe, sales by mail order accounted for less than one per cent of total retail sales, so that clearly this method of distribution makes no great impact in total. However, for the particular types of merchandise to which the system lends itself, and in those markets which can provide the reliable mail service and money transfer systems necessary to support it, mail order can still be a possibility for the producer which should by no means be overlooked.

Future technology

If the public responds only marginally to shopping by post, it is intriguing to wonder how well it may respond to shopping by a combination of television, telephone and the credit card. This futuristic scenario is already perfectly feasible technically, and provided the enormous capital investment in multichannel telephone lines can be justified, it could become a reality in the United States and Europe at any time.

In essence this new system works by linking the telephone to the television set so that pages of text can be transmitted down the telephone line from a central bank of information and displayed on the television screen, while other information can be sent back. Experimental 'teletext' systems of this type are already in operation. The system merely needs development to send high quality pictures as well as plain text. The potential will then exist for suppliers to use the central information bank as a kind of electronic mail order catalogue, allied to their existing television advertising campaigns. The viewer will be able to call up on his screen any catalogue 'page' he wants, see for himself the entire range of items that is available, and send in his order simply by pressing a few keys on his push-button telephone. His credit card number can also be keyed in, or perhaps the credit card companies will provide everyone with a slot-machine in his own home, also connected to the telephone, so that the card can be popped in and read automatically against each transaction.

All of this gives a glimpse of a possible future society which is not only 'cashless' but less and less dependent on the kind of retail distribution network with which we are familiar at present. Suppliers of goods and services may again find it possible to communicate with and sell directly to individual consumers on a very large scale rather than having to achieve distribution anonymously through the retail market as at present. Manufacturers planning their distribution strategies into the next century should perhaps bear this in mind.

Own retail outlets

Another option for the producer who does not wish to use the existing market is to open his own chain of shops throughout the country. Clearly this can only be done by the producer whose product is in sufficient demand to justify a whole shop to itself. This is unusual, but it does occur: in Britain the multiple tailoring firms in their heyday maintained their own retail shops as outlets for their central mass-production factories, and to some extent still do. Remembering that distribution is as essential to services as to goods, the building societies in Britain provide an example of the establishment of wholly owned retail outlets. Building societies (for the non-British reader) are in effect co-operative, real-estate banks, attracting investment from the small saver and making loans to the private house buyer. The product they are most concerned to sell is the attractiveness of their savings plans; and having found other agencies inadequate for this purpose they have, at great expense but presumably cost-effectively, established their own retail shops in every high street throughout the country. The small saver is attracted by the convenience, and happily pays over his money in return for an intangible service – that of security, accessibility, and a good rate of interest.

The state as distributor

The ultimate instance of the producer setting up his own retail distribution is where the state itself, already the sole producer in a state-owned industry, also operates the retail outlets through which the product is sold exclusively. This is the objective of all 'managed' economies, and is by no means the sole prerogative of the Communist bloc. Many developing countries in Africa and elsewhere have found it advantageous to set up state trading agencies for state controlled manufactures, produce, or imports, for which they are the sole distributors and retailers. Even in Britain an example may be found in the retail shops operated by the state owned gas industry. These exist to sell, not gas, but gas appliances, of which they have a near monopoly; and since you cannot use gas unless you have an appliance such as a cooker or a heater to use it in, the retail distribution both of the gas itself and of the ancillary equipment is effectively controlled through these retail outlets set up for the purpose.

Using the existing market

For the majority of producers, however, neither making direct contact with all possible consumers, nor establishing their own chain of selling points will be viable options. For them, the requirement is to use the facilities of the existing distribution system to get their product through to the ultimate consumer, while keeping the maximum of profit for themselves. As a general rule, the existing market can spread its overheads over the multitude of products which it handles and therefore should be able to provide distribution for any one product more cheaply than it would cost to provide unique services for that product alone. The question is, can the existing market provide the know-how necessary to get this particular product through to its potential consumers, in terms of understanding it, being able to explain it, recommending it or installing it correctly? In short, however inexpensive the market system may be, is it cost-effective for the purpose?

The answer is likely to be that very few producers will find themselves able to make absolutely all the sales they want to make directly to the actual consumers in every case. Very many producers, especially of goods for domestic consumption, will have no direct contact with their public at all. Those who can advantageously deal direct with some proportion of their users will nevertheless find it worthwhile to use the market to reach certain other classes of user, who are either too small or too distant or too undemanding to justify contacting direct. The manufacturer of industrial supplies will typically sell direct to his major user customers, each of whom will demand personal attention and, no doubt, the keenest prices, while providing a volume of business that justifies the cost. But there is nearly always an interesting volume of additional sales to be made to some other sector of users, which cannot be obtained economically directly, but which trade distribution is adequate to supply. Across the whole range of alternatives, nearly every producer finds it necessary to make some use of the trade distribution system; and it is to the producer in that situation that this book is addressed.

The marketing concept

The art or science of marketing, as applied to products, consists essentially of making explicit the processes which have always taken place in the successful launching of a product on the market. The newness of the marketing concept is not so much in the things done as in the recognition of them for what they are, and the attempt to achieve them methodically. Marketing as a process comprises a circular chain of events:

1 Assessing or predicting a need for a particular kind of product
2 Creating or designing the concept of such a product, in line with the resources and abilities which are available to produce it
3 Appealing to the potential users and so stimulating the latent need and demand for the product
4 Re-assessing the need, and so on.

Being circular, this process can in practice be commenced at any point, and different degrees of emphasis can be given to the various stages. Many products have been successfully launched that were thought of first, and the demand for them discovered afterwards. When 200 years ago James Watt invented the condensing steam engine, he was not thinking of the Industrial Revolution, but of how to make a machine that would work better. Nevertheless having invented it, he was not slow to appeal to potential users, and to strike a latent demand which went on to transform the world. The real summit of the art of marketing lies in detecting a need which no one else has ever thought of, which can be met from the resources that happen to be available, and where the success of the appeal creates a demand where no demand existed before. The antithesis of marketing, still sadly to be met with in some industries, is to go on manufacturing a product and trying to sell it, without either making an effective appeal to the consumer, or trying to find out what the consumer wants, or can be persuaded to want.

Marketing, in the sense of product marketing, is nowadays given a great deal of attention. To be effective, the complete marketing concept must also include the requirement of moving the product to the user or consumer, thereby completing the deal and actually achieving the profit. Regrettably, there is a tendency to confine attention to the purely product-consumer relationships in the marketing concept, and to imply that once these have been taken care of, all that remains to be done is simply to sell the product through the usual channels. This unconscious attitude is often reflected in the way manufacturing businesses organise themselves and in the titles they use to describe their internal functions. Frequently a marketing director and a marketing department take charge of product concepts, market research and consumer advertising; leaving a sales department to look after what is deemed to be the straightforward job of bringing in from the trade the orders that are warranted by the product marketing plans. Marketing must include selling, in the sense of getting the product through to the user, making use of trade distribution where necessary. It is immaterial whether the two functions of product marketing and trade selling are controlled by one marketing director, or shared by marketing and sales colleagues; what is essential is that both functions are accorded an equal degree of importance in the strategic thinking of the business.

Market distribution

Achieving market distribution is as much an art as product marketing, and the two processes are totally interdependent. Market distribution is concerned with how the market works; what functions the various sectors perform; which of those sectors could provide the kind of distribution required; and in what ways could they be induced to co-operate, since they cannot be directly controlled. It has to be remembered that the distributive market is not 'organised' but responds only to the normal forces of supply and demand. The situation is unlike that in product marketing, action cannot be commissioned directly, simply by paying someone to carry it out, but it has to be achieved indirectly by processes of cause and effect.

The processes involved in market distribution are of general application, very largely irrespective of the type of product or the market environment; whether material goods or intangible services; for the individual consumer or the industrial user; in sophisticated markets or in the developing regions. No apology is made for trying to find the general rule where this exists. It is often positively helpful to stand back and look at an operating situation from first principles, rather than remaining obsessed with the specific detail of one particular market or type of trade. To do so may put a particular problem in a better perspective, or give a better understanding of some evolution which is taking place.

Levels of distribution

One such generalisation is the definition of the number of *levels* which are made use of in the distribution system. If the producer in fact sells only directly and at first hand to actual users, then he is using no market distribution at all, and thus no levels. The next simplest situation is where the producer sells all his output to distributors or traders at one level, who in turn sell on to consumers. The most common example of this would be a manufacturer of, say, a domestic consumer item, making all his sales in the first instance to retail shops, who resell to the public. Note that it is immaterial that some of these retail shops might be huge supermarkets, while others might be tiny one-man businesses; despite the discrepancy in size, both are performing the same function of acting as a single level intermediary between the producer and the product user.

Exactly similar would be the case of a manufacturer of an industrial commodity making all his sales to specialist merchants who in turn supply the actual industrial users. This situation occurs quite frequently; steel mills sell to specialist steel stockholders who resell to users; cement manufacturers sell to builders' merchants, who sell to construction firms; and, as we have already seen, manufacturers of animal feeding stuffs sell to agricultural merchants, who supply farmers. Again, in every case, only *one* intermediary level of distribution is being used, and the specialist merchant performs a function entirely comparable to the retail shop, to his own specialist customers.

A more complicated situation is where the producer makes use of *more than one* level of distributor to reach his ultimate consumer. This would be the case where, for example, a manufacturer of a domestic commodity sells only to wholesale distributors in the first instance; the wholesalers resell to retail shops which finally sell to the public. Thus two levels of distributor are involved in providing distribution. It is not necessary to limit the number of levels to two. Motor manufacturers for instance have been known to sell their output to 'main agents' who supply 'distributors' who supply 'dealers' who in turn sell to the public. In developing countries, often with great distances to cover, it may be almost impossible to trace the number of levels of distribution through which a product passes in finding its way from the manufacturer via large and small traders, local transporters and dealers, until it reaches the ultimate consumer in some village market place.

The use of words to describe exactly how levels of distribution are being used can often be confusing. We sometimes speak of selling 'directly' to users or of selling 'indirectly' through distributors. The term indirect selling does not of course define how many levels of distributor are involved. In continental Europe, perhaps because of the greater distances involved, manufacturers of consumer supplies tend to make more use of wholesalers than do their counterparts in Britain, who sell, wherever possible, to the retail shops. On the Continent, 'selling indirectly' has come to mean specifically selling through wholesalers; while 'selling directly' means selling to retail outlets – not selling to consumers themselves. Because of this risk of misunderstanding, reference to direct versus indirect will be avoided as far as possible, and the actual distributor level defined instead.

Selling to different levels

What is of importance is whether the producer is content to make all his sales only to distributors in the top level, or whether he feels obliged to try to make some sales to other, lower, levels as well. For example:

1. A producer of industrial supplies who mainly sells through specialist merchants may also wish to deal direct with some of the largest industrial users himself;
2. A manufacturer who normally supplies only to wholesalers may wish to sell direct to some of the larger retail outlets, such as supermarkets, because of their need for special terms and service;
3. A manufacturer in a developing country may sell all his output to large traders at the factory gate, but from time to time would like to send his own sales vans to sell direct to consumers in remote market places, in order to publicise the product.

In all these cases the producer is in the position of selling to buyers who are already the potential customers of his own principal distributors; in other words he is competing with his own existing customers. This of course raises a most fundamental conflict, and a totally insignificant volume of sales made over the heads of the first level of distributor – whether prices are undercut or not – may easily have the effect of wrecking an entire distribution system. Alternatively, a producer faced with powerful distributors may feel that he is being needlessly prevented by them from doing business directly with users, in ways which could not possibly harm the distributors' interests. This question of reconciling the interests of distributors with the manufacturer's need to retain some direct contact with lower levels of buyer arises again and again, and we shall be returning to it later.

Exclusive arrangements

Whichever combination of distribution levels is chosen there may be a further choice between making sales unrestrictedly to all comers in any particular level of the market, or of limiting sales to a more or less select group of distributors, chosen because of their superior ability to handle and promote the product properly. Thus, a motor manufacturer will wish to sell his vehicles only through distributors who have invested in spare parts and special tools, and who can provide a proper level of specialist service. This issue is one where questions of fairness to all distributors conflict with the need to ensure active distribution and to protect it against unfair competition. Some national legal systems are more sensitive than others on this issue and it may be quite a complex matter to ascertain what is permissible before charges of unfair discrimination arise.

Strategy for distribution

In an ideal market, there would exist what the economists call 'perfect competition', that is to say, such a large number of mutually competing traders in each segment of the market that what any one trader will not handle, another will. As a result every product could be sure of finding an outlet to its consumers, at a price; and that price would be its true market value, as determined by supply and demand in the market place. Needless to say, such ideal markets exist only in economic theory and never in reality, although some of the vast market systems in Africa must come pretty close to the ideal. However, for most of us, there is no assurance at all that our product will automatically obtain complete distribution and exposure to consumers, at its true market value. With a product which is in strong consumer demand, and in a market in which there are in fact very large numbers of independent distributors available, then it is true that the distribution of the product can very largely be left to free market forces. All classes of traders in the market will be only too eager to 'get their hands on' the product in order to get some share in the profits of distribution. But as markets become more sophisticated, small independent traders fail to compete and are swallowed up or superseded by their larger neighbours; the markets become dominated by a much smaller number of larger, more powerful distributors, who between them will be interested in handling only a limited range of items in any given product field. Thus the producer begins to require a positive strategy whereby he can be assured of distributor co-operation, and of getting an outlet in the market place.

Getting trade distribution, therefore, is an aspect of a company's operations which ranks in importance with its strategies for product marketing, for product development, for manufacturing efficiency and for financial planning. A company should no longer be content to leave to a subordinate 'sales department' the task of achieving the sales throughput for which the market is assumed to be ready to provide a channel. Developing a strategy for successful trade distribution must be based on accurate knowledge:

1 Knowledge of the consumer population for the product, who it consists of, and where it is located;
2 Knowledge of the distributive trade for the type of product, how it operates, and how it is made up;
3 Knowledge of competitors and how they operate;
4 Knowledge of one's own business, what are its strategies, its strengths and its weaknesses.

Subsequent chapters discuss in detail the topics which go to make up an operating strategy, but before this can be embarked on it is essential to be sure that all the facts are available. At the end of each chapter in this book will be found a checklist relating to the topics covered. The checklist at the end of this chapter is intended as a set of headings for self questioning. It is not intended to be in the form of a questionnaire to which one line answers can be given; but rather as topic questions which would serve as paragraph headings to be used when writing operating strategies for a market oriented business. Looking at these information headings, the reader might ask himself whether he could write such a report in respect of his own business. If information is lacking in any of these areas, the task should be to set about discovering it as quickly as possible.

Checklist 1

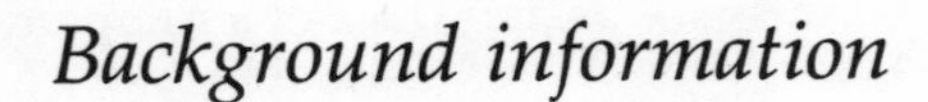

Background information

1.1 The product range

(a) How should the product(s) or service(s) be defined?
(b) Who are the intended product users? (This should be clear from the product marketing strategies)
(c) What are the numbers of potential users, and (as far as is known) of actual users?
(d) How are users located geographically, if this is significant? (e.g. all in towns, more in south than in north, etc.)

1.2 The distributive system

(a) What types/classes of trade act as distributors for this product group?
(b) How many levels are there in the distributive system, what functions and relationships?
(c) What are the approximate numbers per size grouping,and their geographic spread?
(d) Within each class of trade, who are the big traders, who owns whom?
(e) What are the prospects for growth, and longer term potential in these trade sectors?
(f) How does each class of trade operate, how is it financed, what are its needs, attitudes and beliefs?
(g) What are its profit margin expectations for this product group?
(h) What is its policy on stockholding in this product group, and its need for credit?
(i) What level and type of servicing is required from suppliers?
(j) How active is the trade in selling? in displaying/promoting/canvassing?
(k) What exactly are the existing arrangements/dealings/terms between the company and the trade?
(l) What are the current arrangements between the trade and their customers?

1.3 Competitors

(a) Who are the competitors per product type, what are their relative sizes and market shares?
(b) What distribution methods and arrangements do they employ?
(c) What terms and deals do they offer to the trade?
(d) What other selling/distribution resources do they employ?

2

Trade marketing

The distributor function

When we talk of the *trade,* we mean of course the distributive trade, that which subsists by buying and selling and living off the difference; as distinct from productive *industries* which create or physically transform things. If the distributive trade did nothing else beyond physically moving merchandise closer to the buyer, it would still perform a useful role as a channel of supply. Its main function however is to do more than this – it is to bring together for the consumer as wide a range of items as possible from a great diversity of sources, and make them available from a single source. Thus, not only can the user's convenience be served, but his purchasing power can thereby be concentrated, and so rendered more valuable both to his trade supplier and to himself.

The distributor's job is to provide the maximum degree of service to his customers, whether this be in the form of product availability, or delivery service, or credit facilities, or even comfortable, attractive premises. Of all these, product availability at competitive prices is likely to be the overriding factor. None of the other facilities will compensate for the plain fact that the distributor cannot supply what the customer wants. Knowing what it is that the customer wants, from what is available, is the distributor's main purpose. The distributor is in business for his own account, not to further the interests of the supplier. Where the distributor has some kind of special relationship with a supplier, such as being his exclusive agent for a territory, his interests and the supplier's coincide to a large extent. But it is still his own money which the distributor is investing in the supplier's stocks, and he will go on doing this only for so long as his commercial judgement tells him that this is the best stock investment he can make with a view to meeting his own customers' needs. Loyalty from distributor towards supplier is strictly short term and changeable. One has only to look at the frequency with which motor car distributors change their agencies, as market demand alters between the different makes.

Buyers or consumers?

The distributor's objective is to strengthen his own identity in the minds of his customers and so develop their loyalty to him rather than, or in parallel with, their loyalty to a producer. In doing this, the distributor will appeal to his customers in their capacity as *buyers,* in contrast to the manufacturer, who must appeal to them as *consumers.* That is to say, the distributor will tend to address himself to their 'purchasing behaviour' rather than their 'consumption behaviour', which is all that the manufacturer can concentrate on. The retailer to the general public sets himself out to capitalise on the public's behaviour as shoppers, its susceptibility to atmosphere, to display, to impulse buying; as well as to the more rational factors of availability, pricing policy, opening hours and general convenience. The wholesaler or specialist supplier to industry does exactly the same thing; but in terms of frequency of attention, speed of delivery, the fact that a whole range of supplies can be covered by only one invoice, and so on. As far as the larger industrial consumer is concerned, it should not be forgotten that the buyer and the user are very often two quite different people. The user of the product in some industrial process will be the production manager on the factory floor, or a white coated chemist in a back room; whereas the buyer of the product will be the person in charge of buying as a function in the corporation. If the users are satisfied with any one of a choice of alternative products, the buyer will decide the purchase on the basis of the commercial considerations of price, credit, reliability of supply and so on – and not least on any remaining considerations of convenience, personal relations and attention from the supplier.

The two approaches, to the customer as buyer and as consumer, can and should be complementary. There is room for partnership between the producer and the distributor, in making a joint appeal to these two distinct halves of the customer's nature, each reinforcing the other. Wary though this partnership may be on both sides, and on occasion more like an armed truce, there is still every advantage to the producer in cultivating it and trying to achieve it in however imperfect a form, rather than treating the distributive trade as an antagonist to be overcome.

A case study

For the producer, the great danger is that the distributive trade may usurp his function of appealing to the customer as consumer, and take on this function as well as that of responding to the customer's buying behaviour. One of the largest retailing chains in the Netherlands, the Albert Heijn supermarkets, has been particularly forthcoming and articulate in public about what they see as their role in the changing relationships between manufacturer and distributor. The attitude that they have made public is representative of the fundamental policy of many large retailers. First of all they are perfectly clear about seeing themselves not just as retailers, but as a marketing-minded institution developing and selling their own 'product'. This product is the whole *store concept;* i.e. the store as something saleable in itself, rather than just the physical collection of merchandise which the store happens to contain. In the Albert Heijn philosophy, the store concept is based on what they call the '8Ps':

1. Products and assortment
2. Pricing
3. Promotional activities
4. Place: i.e. the location of the store
5. Personnel
6. Physical distribution and handling
7. Presentation of stores and products
8. Productivity

Using store concepts of this kind, the modern retailer ceases to be merely a passive distributor of suppliers' products. In the past, in Albert Heijn's words:

> The manufacturer could work upon the final consumer over the heads of retailers. The retailer was faced with ready-to-sell propositions; he was a distributor in the literal sense of the world. Nowadays, the retailer is in a position to act as a filter of the manufacturer's marketing policy, and either weaken it or concentrate it depending on how well or badly the manufacturer's proposition fits in to the retailer's store concept.

In effect the retailer is saying to the manufacturer: 'You can stop worrying about what the public wants. We are closer to the public than you are, and *we* will worry about what the public wants. Then you need only worry about what *we* want.' It is understandable that retailers should wish to swing the pendulum the other way, from total dominance by manufacturers, but it is now up to manufacturers to ensure that it does not swing too far. If they were to acquiesce in the assumption by retailers of the marketing role to the public they would rapidly find themselves cut off from direct appeal to their own consumers and entirely dependent upon whatever supply commissions the distributive trade should see fit to pass on. This would put the manufacturer in a position little better than the producer of 'own brand' merchandise for a retailer with no direct consumer franchise of his own at all.

The twin strategies

What the manufacturer must do therefore is to cultivate the development of his marketing policy *through* the trade by equal attention both to the needs of the consumer and the needs of the distributive trade. This requires the development of double, complementary strategies: (a) for the marketing of the product by means of effective *appeal to the consumer*, and (b) while achieving distribution by means of effective *appeal to the distributive trade.*

To achieve this will entail a new emphasis on *joint planning* between the traditional company functions of product marketing and selling to the trade. For this joint process – vital to a successful business strategy – it seems appropriate to coin a new title and call it 'marketing through the trade'; or even more simply 'trade marketing'. The concept brings many and far reaching implications which deserve consideration in detail.

Figure 2.1 shows in diagrammatic form how the two complementary strategies interlink and are dependent on each other. Every successful business, or business which intends to be successful, must have a very clear idea of what its overall business strategy or business mission is going to be. This is the definition of the broad area of production, or provision of service, in which the company proposes to generate profit and achieve growth, based on a realistic assessment of its assets and its know-how. Failing such a clear understanding of its mission, a company is in a perpetual dilemma of choice over what to do next, whether to undertake or decline each new proposition that comes up; whereas with a clear identity of mission, such offerings either quickly prove or eliminate themselves. In the new view which we are trying to express here, the business mission subdivides itself into the two complementary strategies, one for the marketing of the product range to its consumers, and simultaneously one for achieving this marketing through the distributive trade.

Product marketing strategy

The product marketing strategy should start with a statement in the broadest terms of the three principal objectives of product policy:

1. The type(s) of consumer aimed at
2. The kinds and range of product or service to be promoted
3. The market share and therefore the sales volume thought feasible, for each product.

As appropriate, the product marketing strategy will also define the resources which will be required for the achievement of these objectives, for example the production facilities and capacity, the manpower and staffing requirements, and the expenditure on advertising and promotion.

Within the overall product strategy there must be worked out for each particular product line the definition of exactly how its appeal to its users is going to be made; in other words its marketing platform. Where necessary, this will again specify the particular consumer group aimed at, and define:

1. The physical properties of the item; that is to say, what and how it will perform in use, and what is its formulation for achieving this. This kind of practical definition is applicable to any kind of product, from a motor car or a toilet soap to an animal feeding stuff or an industrial raw material.
2. Its 'emotional qualities'; that is the associations and impressions it is hoped to evoke in the user from the product's appearance or from its method of presentation or from its advertising message. It should not be thought that this aspect of marketing is limited to items aimed at the impressionable public. Hitting the right note to the industrial user is in the highest degree effective as well; often in the sense of conveying 'quality' or 'reliability' or 'reassurance of using the best'.
3. The price bracket to the consumer.
4. The form of presentation or promotion or advertising which will be used. This may cover everything from the type of display pack to the advertising slogan, and will define the expenditure budget.

Dependence on the trade

It is important to note that of all the multiple facets of the marketing platform designed to

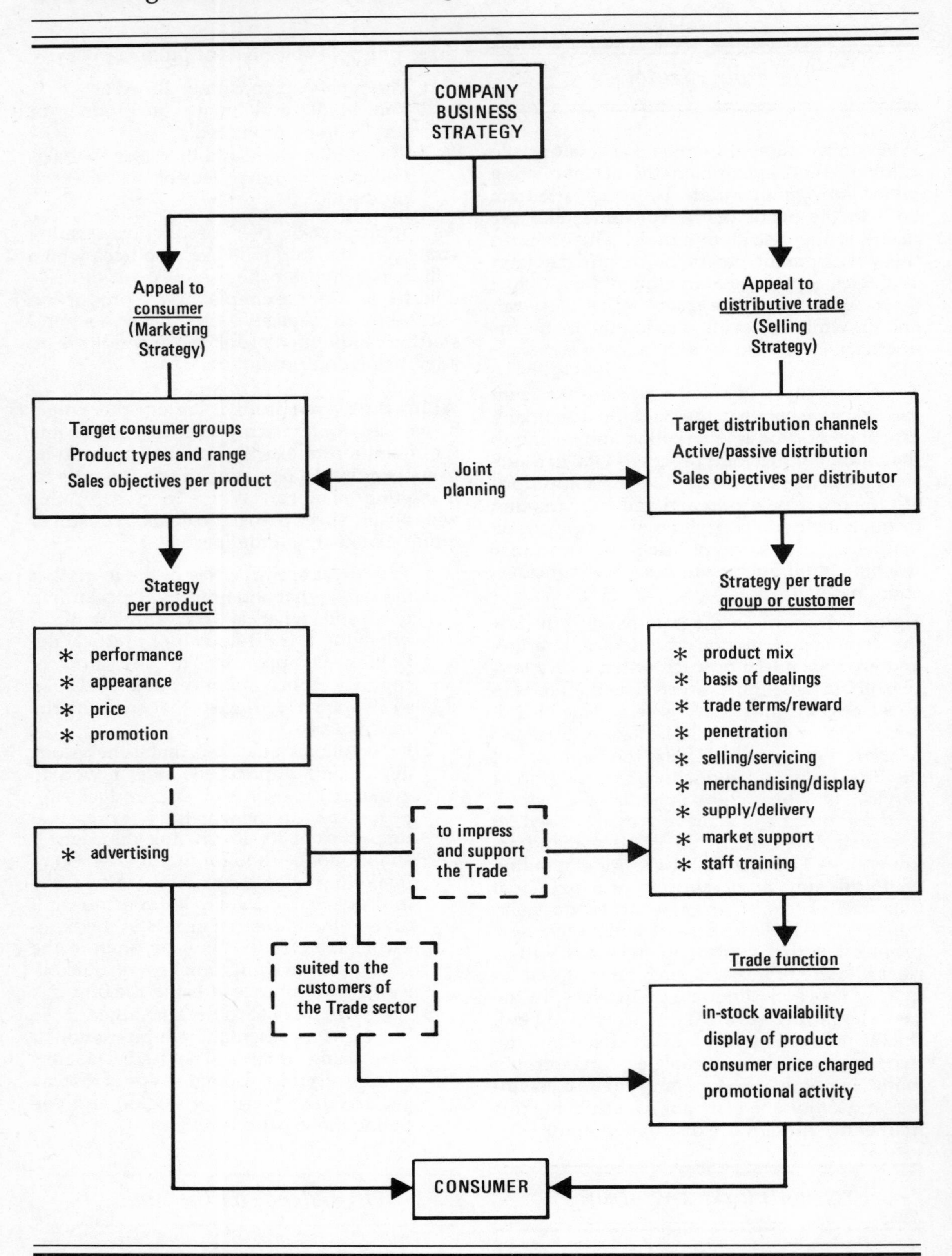

Figure 2.1 The twin marketing strategies

appeal to the consumer, only the single factor of media advertising is capable of reaching the consumer directly, independently of the intervention of the trade. All the other features which have been so ingeniously planned are totally dependent on the distributive trade performing the functions assumed of it, if they are ever going to influence the consumer. For a start, if the trade does not choose to invest in the product and make it available in distribution, the user will never have the chance to find out how the product performs. (Unless the manufacturer goes in for widespread free sampling – but that is another story.) The special effect the product's appearance is intended to produce will be nullified if the trade does not give it the intended prominence of display. Perhaps most important of all, the price actually charged to the user is very largely in the control of the distributive trade. The manufacturer controls only the price at which the trade buys; and it may be that his ideas of the profit margin which the trade should take do not correspond with the ideas of the trade itself. We shall have a great deal more to say about this subject later as it is central to the success of market distribution. For the moment, it is enough to note that the price the user will pay is a matter for the trade to decide, not as a rule the manufacturer.

Promotion of a product is usually also very dependent on the co-operation of the trade, in passing on whatever kind of special offers are intended for the consumer, and in putting on any special activities. For the manufacturer to attempt to mount these directly to the consumer without trade participation is likely to be as expensive as selling directly to the consumer would have been in the first place.

Impressing the trade

While media advertising is aimed principally at influencing the ultimate consumer, it must not be overlooked that it also has a highly important indirect effect – that of making an impression on the distributive trade. The trade has to be convinced of the seriousness of the marketing intention to make an effective appeal to the consumer, and that it will not be left alone and unsupported in its own efforts to make sales to those consumers. This therefore becomes a substantial part of media advertising objectives. A campaign must not only be effective in actually persuading consumers; it must convince distributors that it will be so effective. Multi-million pound advertising budgets therefore in large part have trade as well as consumer objectives, and are supportive of both halves of the joint marketing strategy. Ensuring that the trade is fully aware of plans for the media, and enthusiastic in its approval of them, must be an essential part of advertising policy.

Trade marketing strategy

Turning now to the second leg of the diagram in Figure 2.1, the strategy for marketing through the distributive trade is the definition of how resources in manpower, staff, supply services and financial reward to chosen trade sectors will be used to move the product profitably through to the consumer. This strategy outlines the broad decisions on:

1. Which sectors and channels of the distributive market will be made use of. For example, is the product range to be supplied directly to retailers; if so, to which classes of trade; or to wholesalers for resale to retailers; or to some group of specialised merchants and stockholders.
2. Whether supply to the chosen sectors is to be wholly unrestricted, depending on free market forces to move the product to its destination; or whether active distributors will be recruited on a selective basis, tied to the manufacturer with a franchise agreement, in order to promote the product's sale positively.
3. What volume of sales is anticipated through each of these channels and sectors. If individual distributors are going to be large, this breakdown of sales may have to be made for each individual.

Joint planning

It is at this stage that the first aspect of joint planning arises between product marketing management and sales management (or trade marketing management, as we can now call it). The sales estimates for each product and product group must reconcile in total with the sales estimates for each distribution channel and even for each individual distributor. Whatever sales target product management has in mind for a given product, and however enthusiastic they are about its reception by its consuming public, it must be possible for trade management to concur that this volume of throughput is feasible through selected distributors and trade channels. This is not to say that trade management or sales management should only be concerned to pour cold water on the plans for products. On the contrary, they should be equally positive in pointing out that their trade channels are able and eager to handle a particular volume of business, and enquiring if there are sufficient products available to satisfy this. When the volume of any one product is confirmed to be perfectly feasible for the trade to handle, the position must be checked again for all products in total. It may well be that all the product plans individually are perfectly acceptable, but that the total volume proposed is unfortunately too much for the distribution chain to handle in its present state of development; or, the ability of the distribution chain to handle products may be more than the total production capacity of one business could provide. Joint planning of products and trade is an iterative process in which initial ideas on each side are compared one with the other and gradually brought into alignment. If there is a shortfall on one side or the other, action can be started to rectify this.

The essential thing is that the joint planning process for products and trade should be conducted simultaneously and co-operatively by both groups of management – not pre-empted by one group and then 'agreed' by the other. If two planning exercises are carried out independently it is inevitable that one will tend to dominate the other and the weaker one will then be subject to a 'reconciliation' which defeats the purpose of joint planning. At every stage a working consensus must be reached that on the one hand the product plans are realistic when projected across the proposed distributive channels, and on the other hand the market potential in each channel is adequately filled by the available products.

Figure 2.2 shows a format in which the results of such a planning exercise can be summarised. The sales volume for each of the range of products is broken down over the range of distributive channels, and vice versa. First of all, this format brings home the need to keep the planning exercise within bounds – a range of ten products across ten distributors or trade sectors will already mean no fewer than 100 separate planning elements. Excessive detail will negate the whole exercise. At the same time, the format is intended to show only the likeliest probability in each case, and the sum of the probabilities. There is as much scope for permutation as in any football pool coupon. Any one line or any one column could consist of a different set of figures and still come to the same acceptable total, as long as other totals remain acceptable as well. One distributor might sell more and another less, without affecting the product total; or one product might sell more and another less without affecting the distributor total. The purpose of setting plan figures out in this way is so that both parties to the strategy can see clearly the implications of what it is that they have agreed to; and also what would have to happen to other parts of the plan if any one part falls behind. In companies which have not practised joint planning before, the effect of looking at all these interactions simultaneously gives a revolutionary new insight into problems and opportunities.

Trade penetration

In Figure 2.1, the broad distribution plan, as agreed with the product plans, has next to be broken down into the detailed strategies of how this will be implemented in each trade sector, trade channel or single important distributor. If only one trade sector is to be used, there will be only one trade strategy. From the earlier part of the planning process, the envisaged mix of products to be handled by each sector is already known, as is the planned sales volume. It remains to specify what degree of *penetration* and *distribution* within the sector is necessary in order to achieve this volume. By penetration we mean the percentage of outlets within the sector which will adopt the product as a normal stock line; and by distribution is meant the percentage of outlets which actually have the product available in stock at any given moment. Even if the trade sector in question consists of only one distributor business, these factors have still to be considered. Major distributors usually have many branches, and one of their first concerns is to decide which of their branches will stock

Estimated sales per product
and per trade channel

	Product group X	Product group Y	Product group Z	etc.	Totals per trade channel
Distributor A					
Distributor B					
Distributor C					
All other Wholesale Sector					
Retail Multiple D					
Retail Multiple E					
All other Multiples					
etc.					
Totals per product					

Grand total

Figure 2.2 Format for joint planning

which products. Indeed, in a market dominated by large distributors, the extent to which a product *can* be given geographic distribution becomes another of the issues which passes out of the control of the producer, and into the discretion of the distributor. If all the outlets in an area belong to one or two distributors, and those distributors do not believe it worthwhile to stock a product in that area, there may be little more the producer can do to get coverage. So the extent to which a product will be adopted *within* a multiple distributor has to be made the subject of persuasion.

Distribution availability

Availability in stock (itself confusingly referred to as 'distribution') is another matter. There will be an inevitable shortfall between a distributor intending in principle to keep a given item in stock, and that distributor actually having it in stock and available at all times. This will be the consequence of any failings on the distributor's part to foresee demand and order correctly, and also of any failings on the part of the manufacturer in being able to supply when required. The two must be assessed with some degree of realism.

When asked what level of distribution in the trade is required for the product they are about to launch, product marketing management will almost inevitably say 100 per cent. One hundred per cent of anything is rarely attainable and no more so in this case. Allowance must first be made for the percentage, however small, of distributive outlets which will not stock the product at all, for one reason or another. Do not forget that this may have to include those who cannot be allowed supplies for reasons of credit worthiness. After this comes the difficulty of maintaining stock availability at all times in all other distributors. No distributor is going to exercise the degree of vigilance of all his stocks in all his branches necessary to avoid occasional stock-out errors in some items; nor for that matter is he going to invest capital in the very high stock levels which would be required to meet every possible demand in full. Ensuring that a good level of stock cover is maintained is one of the principal functions of a supplier's field sales force, reminding the distributor when a re-order is due. Trying to obtain a very high percentage level of in-stock availability would therefore call for very frequent supervisory visits by the sales force on all outlets, at a correspondingly high cost. A high in-stock percentage is yet another of those desirables the cost of which rises disproportionately to the result achieved, the higher you try to go.

Making a distribution survey

The level of distribution availability which it is reasonable to expect for a given type of product in a particular trade environment is something which can only be discovered by experience. A start can be made by finding out exactly what level is being attained at present from the current level of effort. Market research firms are of course available to provide this kind of information either as part of their regular surveys of the market in general, for certain classes of consumer goods, or, more expensively, by means of a special one-off study of a particular trade. But equally well this can be done by the manufacturer's own sales force, if he has one. The presumption is that the sales force will be calling in any case on all those distributors to whom the product is being sold directly from the manufacturer. What proportion this is of all distributors in that class of trade will presumably be known; or at any rate should be known as part of a planned approach to market distribution. This gives a measure of the degree of market penetration of the product. Thereafter all that is required is for the sales force to make a record in the course of their routine visits of whether or not the given product was in stock when they called at each outlet. The quantity of product in stock is immaterial for this purpose – as long as there was at least one unit, the product was available.

Figure 2.3 shows a simple layout of a form which can be used for this task. Several products can be included at any one time, and possibly also some competitors' products, as long as it will not require more than a minute or two of the salesman's time to complete the record in any one outlet. The record is made long enough to accommodate all the calls a salesman is likely to make in any one day. Details of the customer are not required; all the salesman has to do is to place a tick against each product found in stock in each successive

DISTRIBUTION SURVEY

Class of Trade WHOLESALERS Date 5 June

Salesman JBC Territory A12

Call No.	Product A	Product B	Product C	etc.
(1)	✓		✓	
(2)				
(3)			✓	
(4)	✓	✓	✓	
(5)	✓	✓		
6				
7				
8				
etc.				
Availability	3/5	2/5	3/5	

Note to Salesman : Circle call numbers in sequence for each call made.
Insert tick in product column only when stock was available at time of call.
Send in to head office daily.

Figure 2.3 Salesman's distribution check

call. If more than one class of trade is being visited, a separate, distinctive, form should be used for each – say, pharmacies, or wholesalers, or builders' merchants, or whatever it may be – so that each type of form represents one class of trade. Daily or weekly the salesmen will send in their records to the head office, where the number of ticks per product is added up against the total number of calls made, to give the percentage distribution availability for that product in the outlets called on. This kind of survey need not be made continuously, but only when an update of current performance is required. Making a survey of distribution in outlets which are not normally called on by the sales force – such as retailers buying from wholesalers – must either be done through special visits or by commissioning an independent survey.

The selling function

Thinking in terms of market penetration and distribution availability is of the utmost importance to a trade marketing strategy, since in the end it is the truest measure of what the sales management, or trade marketing management side of the business should be trying to achieve. At the extreme, if a product ever could attain 100 per cent distribution in the appropriate trade sector – in stock, available and on display everywhere – it could be said that there was then no more the sales force could do to increase sales. Any further increase would have to come from additional response by the consumer to the appeal being made to him by media advertising, and by the presentation of the product itself – in other words, increase would have to be the responsibility of product marketing management. Sales management would have done all that is in their power to do to *sell in* the product to the trade. Of course, as any such highly satisfactory level of trade distribution is approached, a sales force would not simply take a holiday – it would instead redouble its efforts to assist the trade in *selling out* to the target consumers; by means of still further improving displays, or putting on demonstrations, or assisting the distributors' own sales people. Vice versa, where full trade coverage is far from being achieved, the appeal of the product to the consumer is effectively being thwarted, and it is sales management's responsibility then to increase sales by making a more effective appeal to the trade to stock it.

It is very salutary for both product and trade management to learn to see matters in this light. Product management should begin to develop a feeling for the level of trade distribution which would be required for the proposed sales volume of a product, and to discuss their forthcoming plans with trade management in those terms; while trade management should be able to say what levels of trade distribution are realistically possible, and what would be the cost of achieving them.

Strategies for all sectors

Returning again to the strategy diagram in Figure 2.1, the detailed strategy for each trade sector or distribution channel should go on to specify the basis of dealings with the sector, for example, whether as free market stockists, or as tied or franchised distributors under contract, or even as second or third tier distributors who do not purchase directly from the manufacturer at all. This is an extremely important point. If the market distribution policy is one where more than one level of distributor is going to be used to reach the ultimate consumer – for example selling to wholesalers who will in turn supply retailers – it is still vitally important to develop a strategy for this second, retail sector, even if as manufacturer you never have direct dealings with them and do not actually know who they are. The fact that they are not sold to directly is immaterial; their participation is being counted on to move the product and their anonymity merely makes it the more essential to plan effectively for their motivation. For instance, how much profit are they supposed to make out of the product? This and other matters must be part of the strategy. In developing countries where products pass through many hands in the market, the final link in the distribution chain may well be a petty trader with a tray of goods at the roadside. He still has a vital part to play in the scheme of things, and should duly figure as a trade sector in the strategy.

Products suited to the trade

The trade strategy taken as a whole will be the

means whereby the trade is induced to perform the functions on which product marketing management will rely to consummate their appeal to the target consumer; that is, to have it available in stock, to display it to best advantage, to charge the right price for it, and to promote it in the ways intended. To consolidate finally the comparison and synchronisation of plans between product and trade management it is necessary to check again that the trade sectors chosen are the ones which can best address the consumers at whom the product is aimed. Vice versa, products can be developed or modified to be better suited to the consumers who make use of the trade channels into which an entry can be obtained. This can involve developing a whole new range of products aimed at an entirely new market, or merely modifying something as simple as the packaging to make the product suitable for, say, self-service selection by customers. An example of this can be found in the building supplies industry where a significant part of output, instead of being sold through traditional builders' merchants to tradesmen users, is now sold through self-service retailers to do-it-yourself householders. Everything from pre-cut timber to nails, screws and accessories now has to be packaged and presented suitably for self-service display.

Strategy documents

In many marketing oriented companies it is already standard practice for product marketing plans to be set down on paper along the lines indicated, and to be updated at regular intervals. A typical planning sequence would be to produce a relatively long term plan, for a time span of three years or five years, in which the broad product strategy forms a basis for the entire forward planning of the company, its growth targets, its manufacturing strategy, its manpower and management requirements, and its financial planning. Within this framework would be produced each year its detailed annual operating plans and budgets, in which the product marketing plans are expanded to the level of individual product lines and items, with their advertising campaigns mapped out, their sales for the year estimated, and their costs and revenues budgeted for. From this, all other operating expenses of the business can be estimated, and detailed budgets set against which to control performance for the rest of the year.

What may be new to companies and their managements is the concept, outlined in this chapter and central to the theme of this book, that a sales strategy, or trade marketing strategy, should similarly be worked out and committed to paper, both at the long term plan stage and in annual operating plans. Until this is done, the product marketing plans by themselves have no validity, as they do nothing to demonstrate how, or if at all, trade channels can be used to bring the product plans to fruition. Similarly the costs, revenues and profits which figure in the detailed budgets can only be arrived at by making assumptions about what level of reward will be due to the distributive trade and what resources will be required to service it; none of which can be accepted with assurance until a trade strategy has been worked through in detail.

If a trade strategy or sales strategy document does not already exist in a business, the purpose of this book is to persuade the reader to set about the task of writing one. The points that will have to be covered have already been outlined, and the remaining chapters of the book discuss these in detail, one by one. Not all of them will apply to every market distribution situation, but every market distribution situation will require consideration of some of them. The checklists at the end of each chapter will give guidance on appraising a business in regard to each topic, and at the end of the last chapter will be found a suggested format for a complete trade strategy document. If there is any uncertainty about any of these issues, some gap in strategic thinking will have been exposed, and the company's attitude to it will have to be re-appraised very thoroughly.

The checklist for the present chapter concentrates on existing product marketing plans, and the existing level of trade distribution.

Checklist 2

Trade marketing

2.1 Marketing plans

(a) What is the complete list of company products, types, styles, pack sizes, etc., subdivided by group?
(b) Do written marketing strategies or plans exist covering all of these, individually or by group?
(c) What are the current sales targets for each of these? Are they being met?
(d) Do the marketing plans stipulate or imply the levels of distribution availability required in each class of trade?
(e) What if any other kind of support from the trade is required?

2.2 Distribution

(a) Can previous sales figures be obtained, if required, broken down by customer type, period, product, region? Against numbers of customers, numbers of transactions? And in what other ways?
(b) What proportion of outlets in each trade sector normally purchase which products?
(c) How does this compare for competitors' products?
(d) If some trade sectors do not buy direct, e.g. buy through wholesalers, what if anything is known about the proportion which normally buys?
(e) Are any figures available from market research or otherwise on levels of distribution availability of products per trade sector?
(f) Could the sales force collect information on stock availability in outlets visited?
(g) Does the sales force visit all outlets? or all outlets which buy direct? at what frequency?
(h) How many products could be checked at each visit?
(i) What therefore would be a suitable questionnaire for a stock availability survey by salesmen?

3

Choice of distribution channel

The initial stage of a trade marketing strategy is to decide which distribution channel or channels to adopt. In the great majority of businesses which are already in existence this may not seem to be a matter leaving a great deal of room for choice. The company's products are already achieving their market distribution by one means or another; there may appear to be no alternative trade sectors for the handling of that class of product; and the prospect of making any kind of a change may be quite unthinkable. Nevertheless it is still a very worthwhile exercise to survey the market distribution system from first principles and rationalise what is being done. After all, if the present choice of distribution method is the only possible one, it will not take long to marshal the arguments and the costings which will prove it.

In many cases, however, it will be found that some scope for using alternative distribution channels does exist, and that the advantages of each method are by no means obvious. Or it may be possible to use more than one channel, with better results in total. Markets are always changing; the urgent need to find a different method of distribution may arise quite suddenly, or else a possibility of an alternative may come about where none existed before. As already mentioned, there is always the basic choice of whether to ignore the distributive market altogether and try to sell to consumers direct. However absurd this may seem at first sight, it is worth investigating – methods and possibilities of selling direct to the consumer may be changing, or there may be some part of the product range which could be handled in this way to some particular group of consumers. Within the distributive trade itself, choice is likely to lie along the lines of:

1 How many different but parallel classes of trade are there for the sale of the same product to consumers? For example, books can be sold through specialist bookshops, through newspaper shops, through department stores and, increasingly, through self-service supermarkets.
2 For each class of trade, is there more than one level of distributor? For example, are there wholesalers supplying to retailers; and if so should they be used?
3 Are sales to be unrestricted to all distributors or are agency agreements to be made with a selected few?

The basis for choice

Fundamentally, it is not difficult to see the basis on which the choice of distribution channel must be made: it will be that channel or combination of channels which will produce the maximum profit yield in total, that is to say, the total volume of sales multiplied by the net profit margin in each case. If the distribution channel is effective, it will produce the volume of sales; if it is economic, it will produce the profit margin. The optimum combination of both is what we must seek. Some of our alternative methods are likely to be mutually exclusive, in whole or in part. If we insist on selling to retailers ourselves we shall find that wholesalers are not very enthusiastic in stocking our product. What we have to predict is what the actual volume of sales through either or both is going to be.

Even if the volume of sales by different methods is problematic, at least it should be possible to work out the costs and profits quite accurately. To do this, it is necessary to take a view on two separate but complementary issues:

1 What level of financial reward will be required by the trade channel chosen, and therefore what will be the net revenue remaining to the manufacturer after allowing for special prices and discounts to this sector of the trade?
2 What kind of supervisory and support services will have to be provided for that trade channel? For example, salesmen's visits, merchandising assistance, depot and delivery services; and therefore what level of operating costs will be incurred?

Each of these issues is sufficiently complex to be given a chapter to itself in due course, but let us assume for the moment that both assessments have been made, so that we know what our pricing and discount structure will be, and also what size of sales force and delivery services will be required, for all alternative distribution methods. Note merely at this stage that financial reward to the trade is a *variable cost;* that is, it arises only when sales are actually made, and therefore *varies* with the rate of sale; whereas a sales force is largely a *fixed cost,* in the sense that it is there and has to be paid for whether sales are made or not. Delivery services may be partly fixed and partly variable. If an outside transport contractor is used for the purpose, the cost should remain entirely variable, as the transporter has to be paid only when a sale has been made.

Calculating the outcome

Assuming then that all these costings are available, the kind of calculation that has to be made is shown in basic form in Tables 3.1 and 3.2. The figures chosen are for illustration only, and have been deliberately kept simple, but nevertheless they are derived from a real life situation and show the kind of options which actually arise in practice.

Option 1 shows the projected consequences of selling the 'product' directly to 6,000 retail out-

Table 3.1
Alternative distribution costs

Option 1

All sales made directly to 6,000 retailers

		£000s
a) Estimated annual sales volume:		
1 million units @ trade list price		20,000
Average discount 5%	1,000	
b) Direct supply to 6,000 outlets:		
Transporter's quotation 50p./unit		
1 million units @ 50p.	500	
c) Direct selling contact with 6,000 outlets at average 2 weekly frequency:		
No. of salesmen required: 60		
Average cost per man, including travel, supervision, etc: £15,000		
60 men @ £15,000	900	
Total expenses		2,400
Total net contribution from sales		£17,600

lets, which in this case is the largest practicable number which can be contacted economically. It is estimated that 1 million units will be sold annually by this means. At the normal trade prices this will bring in £20 million; but, on average, it is calculated that retailers will get a further 5 per cent discount on these prices by way of special terms and inducements.

For simplicity, we assume that we are going to use a transport contractor who quotes a flat rate of 50 pence per unit for deliveries made direct to all 6,000 outlets, irrespective of distance.

Our sales force will also have to make calls on these 6,000 outlets at, say, an average of one call every two weeks. On the basis of each salesman making 10 calls a day (quite a high average) he can visit 100 customers in total every two weeks, each of 5 working days. Therefore for 6,000 customers we are going to need 60 salesmen. Allowing for travelling costs, supervision, and all other incidentals, this is reckoned to cost £900,000 a year. Remember, this is a fixed cost, whether or not the 1 million units are actually sold. If they are, the total 'contribution' from their sale is £17.6 million towards the rest of the costs of the business.

Turning to option 2, the proposal now is that sales should be made directly only to the top 500 retail outlets. All other sales would be made to 100 wholesalers, who can be expected to resell to a rather larger number of retailers than were previously able to be reached when selling direct. Sales to each of these top retailers will of course be higher than the previous

Table 3.2
Alternative distribution costs

Option 2

Sales made directly to 500 top retailers
All other sales through 100 wholesalers

		£000s
a) i) Estimated annual sales volume to retailers: 250,000 units		
Sales value @ trade list price		5,000
Average discount 5%	250	
ii) Estimated annual sales volume to wholesalers: 800,000 units		
Sales value @ trade list price		16,000
Average discount 15%	2,400	
		21,000
b) Direct supply to 600 outlets		
Transporter's quotation 25p./unit		
1.05 million units @ 25p.	262	
c) Direct selling contact with 600 outlets at average weekly frequency:		
No. of salesmen required: 12		
12 men @ £15,000	180	
Total expenses		3,092
Total net contribution from sales		£17,908

average, but will bring in only £5 million in total, less 5 per cent discount as before.

With sales to wholesalers at 800,000 units, the total sales volume is estimated to be slightly higher in total than under option 1. This is a perfectly reasonable assumption to make, if it is correct that wholesalers will be able to reach a larger number of retailers in total. But, being wholesalers, they require a higher level of discount – possibly 15 per cent.

The transporter's quotation has now gone down to only 25 pence per unit delivered, on the basis that now only 600 outlets have to be supplied, and the average amount delivered to each will be very much larger.

The sales force also need now only call on 600 outlets instead of 6,000, but we assume that, the outlets being more important, the salesmen will have to call more often – perhaps weekly. By the same calculation as before, this will require 12 men instead of 60.

The total net contribution from option 2 then comes out at £17.9 million, just marginally higher than under option 1. Since this is only a worked example, we need not worry about arriving at any conclusion except to note what effects the different factors have upon the outcome. Under option 2, the proportion of variable expenses in respect of discounts is higher, while the fixed cost of the sales force is less. If sales volume were to increase for the same amount of selling effort in both cases, then option 1 would overtake option 2 and yield a greater net revenue for an equivalent sales volume. Of course, beyond a certain level, the size of the sales force would probably also have to be increased to cope. To facilitate strategic planning, the relationship between all these variables can be arranged into a realistic 'model' of how the two optional approaches would operate, and made the basis of a simple computer program to provide the answers under all different circumstances.

In a real business situation, the detail of the calculation is likely to be still more complex, but the principles are the same in every case:

1. Estimate the sales volume to be achieved by each distribution method.
2. Calculate the sales revenue, less discounts, to be obtained.
3. Deduct the costs of supply and delivery using a realistic model for the method proposed.
4. Deduct the costs of selling in to, servicing and supporting the trade in these circumstances.

Wherever a conceivable alternative distribution strategy exists, this calculation should be made conscientiously, whatever one's preconceived views about the practicability of any particular method; and the figures updated at perhaps annual intervals with each annual plan. The crux of the calculation in each case is of course the level of sales which it is believed will result. It is management's judgement of the overall *effectiveness* of any proposed method which determines the estimate of sales volume, and therefore the final profit contribution by that method. Thus the comparison of the figures does in fact give full consideration to the subjective or even instinctive judgements of the experienced managers who have taken part in the planning exercise. Note however how much more satisfactory it is to have these judgements quantified on a comparative basis, rather than simply expressed emotionally. Dismissing a suggested method simply by saying: 'That would never work', or: 'You would never be able to sell through those people' is to over-simplify. What we really mean in such circumstances is that the proposed method would not work as well as another; and what we ought to do is to clarify in our own minds and for the benefit of others exactly how much less effective we think it would be.

Other factors

There are nevertheless certain other factors to be taken into consideration which may not directly emerge in the financial projections, at least not in the short term. The first of these is risk. Selecting any trade channel of distribution is necessarily to make something of an investment in the stability of that particular sector of the trade, and it is essential to consider carefully what the prospects are in that sector for some time to come. For instance, it would be imprudent to relinquish direct contacts with retailers, and put all one's business through wholesalers, if there were signs that wholesalers as a group were declining and liable to go out of business in a few years time. This might be because other manufacturers were pursuing the opposite policy, taking their business away from wholesalers, and selling direct to retail.

What the competitors are doing is relevant in more ways than one. Not that the competitors are necessarily right in what they are doing; and it may very well be that the correct thing is to choose a deliberately different approach to trade distribution, so as to avoid a direct conflict in the sector the competitors use, while getting undiminished support in some other sector. As an example, if your main competitor sells direct to retailers, you can make yourself the wholesalers' friend by putting all your business through them. On the other hand, it may not be wise to be too unorthodox. If a particular way of trading has become the custom and practice in some type of commodity, users may be uneasy with a supplier who operates differently from all the others. Even if the normal channel seems illogical, it may be necessary to go along with it for the sake of conventionality. Whatever method of distribution a manufacturer chooses, it must always be with the objective of performing better than the competition, whether using the same methods or different ones.

It has to be remembered that often a third party distributor or wholesaler can, if he wants to, provide the same selling and distribution services more cheaply than a large manufacturing company can. It is a fact of life that the smaller, freelance operator can and does employ lower paid staff, occupy cheaper premises, run his transport more cheaply, maybe even to the extent of disregarding regulations, and generally cut corners in ways which the large company cannot. This is perhaps especially true of the situation in developing countries. It is therefore genuinely possible for a distributor to provide services *and* make a profit out of a margin which is less than the cost to a company of providing the same services itself. Against this must be offset the risk of unreliability and the fact that the distributor may at any moment stop providing all the services he should. Costs of extra supervision and direct intervention by the company then have to be taken into account.

Use of parallel channels

The optimum solution in any given case is often to use *more than one* channel of distribution at the same time, in order to get the advantages of both while trying to avoid any of the disadvantages. Clearly, this may call for careful management.

A good guiding principle is to examine first the most direct method of moving the product to the user, and then, for the cases where this will not work, consider the second most direct method. Starting with the whole spectrum of users, are there any to whom it would be advantageous to sell direct? Then look at the whole population of first-line distributors. Is it possible to sell to all of *them* direct? If not, are there any higher level distributors through whom they can be reached? The ideal is to be able to go on supplying directly to the larger customers at each level, where it is advantageous, profitable or even essential to do so; and to use higher level distributors only in order to reach the remainder in each case. This could be thought of as quite blatantly creaming off the best customers for oneself and leaving only the second best for the distributive trade. Distributors are indeed very likely to think of it in just that way. The objective then is to persuade them to co-operate anyway.

Selling to retailers

In exactly the same way, a manufacturer of consumer goods should first examine all possibilities of selling directly in the first instance to retailers; and then consider what use will have to be made of wholesalers. Few manufacturers can hope to be able to sell directly to all those retailers who *ought* to have their product in stock. The numbers are against it. In Britain in the late 1970s the total number of retail outlets of all kinds was around 350,000. In any one type of trade the numbers are still vast: over 50,000 grocery and general outlets for instance, and another 50,000 confectionery, tobacco and newspaper shops. To visit 50,000 retail customers regularly would require an army of several hundred salesmen.

In other countries, the numbers are similar, and in developing countries as we have seen the ultimate retailer may be a petty trader or market seller without any permanent premises or address of his own. Most of these situations will come close to displaying the type of distribution in which 80 per cent of the business is done by 20 per cent of the outlets. This state of affairs is known as a Pareto distribution after the economist who first identified this as a natural probability of things. In any collection of businesses of the same type, the range from the very large to the very small will tend to spread in these proportions, forming a large head and a very long thin tail. It follows that in any line of business, there are likely to be at least *some* retailers to whom a manufacturer must consider selling direct. These retailers are likely to be:

1 Firstly the largest; at least the top 20 per cent which does 80 per cent of the business, if these figures apply. These are likely to include the large multiple retailers, department stores, superstores, hypermarkets, supermarkets and so on in the urban centres or the out of town shopping sites, which are easy to identify, contact and supply direct.
2 Possibly certain specialised types of retailers, say pharmacies, which are suitable outlets for the product but which would not normally deal with the wholesalers who would stock it, and can therefore only be reached through direct sale.
3 Any other retailers to whom it is more profitable to sell direct than through wholesalers, according to the type of calculation shown in Tables 3.1 and 3.2.

A case study

Experience suggests that it is distinctly better and easier to make it clear to the trade in the first place that some larger customers will be withheld from them; rather than letting them think they will have the whole of the trade, and then having to negotiate to get some of the larger customers back. A case in point was in the animal feeds business mentioned in chapter 1. A manufacturer who specialised in selling feeding stuffs direct to all farmers was eventually merged into a larger group. This group decided that its policy would be the opposite and that all its sales would be channelled through agricultural merchants, with no direct sales to farmers. To secure the co-operation of the merchant community, a public undertaking was given to this effect.

Before long, it became apparent that a significant number of users were simply too large to be handled through the merchants. One of the consequences of factory farming is that units for the rearing of pigs and poultry can be huge; factories in fact. Such operators for a start decline to discuss their requirements with an insignificant merchant, but will do so, if at all, only with the manufacturer. Naturally, they then require special prices which would make it very difficult to leave any profit margin for a merchant at all. Orders when they materialise are so large that the average merchant would be quite unable to finance them unaided. It would be invidious to channel this huge amount of business through one favoured merchant out of the many, while the user would certainly refuse to split his requirements between several merchants.

In consequence, the new manufacturing group had to go back on its promise to its distributors, and start supplying to the very large users direct, causing a certain amount of ill-feeling by doing so. This case study illustrates not only the kind of reasons which make it essential to deal direct on some occasions, but also the fact that it would have been better to identify these direct customers in the first place. The proposition to potential distributors could then have emphasised the positive aspects rather than the negative. Instead of telling them that they were being deprived of certain customers, the negotiations could have concentrated on the other customers which were being offered to them. It can be made plain to distributors that they are not losing any business which they ever had any realistic prospects of obtaining. If you as a manufacturer do not supply such large users directly, one of your competitors will, and distributors will not get the business in any case.

The need to intervene

There may also be special circumstances which justify direct selling to retailers some of the time, even when such retailers are normally supplied through wholesalers. For example, this could be the case for a particular item in the product range which requires direct personal selling to retailers in order to achieve market penetration, and where the margin is high enough to cover the cost; while the remainder of the range is not in this category. Or it could apply to the launch of a new product where the exceptional costs of introducing it directly to the retail trade can be justifed as an investment for future success in the market. Note that there is no reason why some items should not be sold directly to retailers, even when they are already buying other items indirectly through wholesalers. It can be made quite clear in advance both to the retailer and the wholesaler that the company is only trying to ensure the distribution of certain particular products direct, without wishing to disturb existing regular business between the wholesaler and the retailer. To ease the arrangement, it can even be worthwhile to pay a small overriding commission to the wholesaler; or else actually to route the supply through him at a nominal profit, once the sale has been concluded directly with his customer.

Passive distribution

Independent distributors whether retailers, wholesalers, cash and carry warehouses, or specialist merchants, are in the main wholly passive distributors in response to market forces and their own customers' desires. The kind of arrangement a manufacturer makes for the distribution of his products through the trade must therefore depend on:

1 How far the company can rely on free market forces in moving the product through to the consumer.
2 How far the company must itself encourage, guide, support, direct and control this distribution process.

Releasing a product on to the market through a comparatively small number of independent wholesale distributors, and relying on them to make the product filter down through all levels of trade to all classes of user, can be an apparently very economical way of doing business. Output of effort by the company itself is at a minimum, while a large sales volume can still sometimes be achieved, especially in developing countries. The economy is only apparent since the costs do not appear in the company's books. The company makes all its sales at a price to the trade but the actual cost of the market distribution process is passed on in the price to the ultimate consumer. When market forces turn against it, when dealers lose interest, or spoil the trade amongst themselves, the company is not in control of market stocks or prices, and lacks any points of contact where intervention could stimulate sales.

In some cases independent wholesalers and distributors maintain sales forces of their own, and pursue a policy of active canvassing and selling among their own customers, but their salesmen will have literally hundreds or even thousands of items on their lists and cannot be expected to give prominence to any one item – unless encouraged. In particular, very little support is likely to be given to the launching of a new product. Competitors' products will happily be substituted when the company product is out of stock. Conditions of storage and stock rotation may be poor. The most that can be expected from independent distributors of this type is to get a fair share of their total ability to make sales, whatever that may be, for as long as market conditions are favourable, and where at least the costs of selling, shared with hundreds of other items, will be low and can be covered by a modest level of margin to the distributor.

Even if some manufacturers are in the happy position of being able to dispose of all they can produce on the open market, they should still give some thought to what may happen if market conditions change in future and their products have to be actively sold. Action to encourage the distribution process can broadly take two forms:

1 The manufacturer can make his own approaches to distributors' customers, pushing sales on behalf of the distributors.
2 The manufacturer can make special arrangements with distributors and inter-

mediate traders to gain their loyalty and support in actively selling the product.

Very often these two approaches would be combined although with varying emphasis on one or the other. Making sales in the market on behalf of one's own distributors is known as *support selling*. Securing positive support from the trade would normally be done by means of *distributor agreements*.

Support selling

The selling function of distributors can be assisted in a great variety of ways, depending on what the distributor's selling method is in the first place.

1 If the distributor operates as a cash and carry wholesaler, for instance, and does not make any sales visits of his own to customers, the best thing the manufacturer can do in support of this form of distribution is to employ some part of the time of his own sales force to visit those customers himself. In the course of these visits the manufacturer's salesmen build displays, give demonstrations, supply publicity material, check stocks and generally supervise the effectiveness of the redistribution process.

2 The manufacturer's sales force can go further and actually take 'transfer' orders for transmission to the main distributor or wholesaler. This sets an example to the distributor of what can be done both in finding new customers in the market and in increasing sales to existing customers. It keeps the manufacturer himself in touch with the realities of the market place and strengthens his hand in negotiations with distributors. However, there are two areas of difficulty:

   (a) Orders have to be transferred to the correct distributor in each case. If the customer has a regular supplier this is no problem, but it may be invidious to choose which distributor to favour with business from a new customer.

   (b) Very close co-ordination is required with all distributors to ensure that transfer orders are booked at prices acceptable to them, and that customers are credit worthy.

3 As a variation on taking transfer orders, it may be possible in some trades for the manufacturer to operate a van-selling service directly to small stockists, making cash sales of stocks which have been drawn from the main distributors.

4 In the other cases where the main distributor or wholesaler does employ a sales force of his own, obviously the manufacturer's support should be directed to assisting the work of that sales force rather than in making independent, and perhaps conflicting, approaches to the market himself. The manufacturer's salesmen can either accompany the distributor's salesmen, giving on-the-job training and encouraging systematic selling; or else they can co-ordinate a schedule of visits of their own which will supplement the distributor's calls.

5 Again, as an alternative, the manufacturer can provide a salesman to go round with the distributor's vehicle, selling stock for cash, setting up a regular and systematic coverage of the market, an training and employee of the distributor at the same time. In some developing countries, this works extremely well. The vehicle used may be a bullock cart or a hand cart; the principle is the same.

All these forms of support selling of course raise the question of whether the manufacturer is not going too far in doing the distributor's job for him. If the manufacturer is sending his own sales force direct to the market, why not make the sales directly for himself, and avoid using a distributor altogether? This is a very fair point, and indeed the cost of support selling requires careful justification. As long as the distributor is still performing a useful function – even if it is only providing a stockholding service – and his reward is modest in proportion, then support selling may be a very effective way of combining tasks and functions between manufacturer and distributor, to the advantage of both.

One last word of warning – a sales force employed on support selling requires very close supervision. Since it is not taking direct orders, there is no immediate measure of what it is achieving, and if its work schedule is tied to the distributor's activity, there may be no control of how it spends its time either. It is unfair to the salesmen to let them get the impression that they can occupy themselves as they like – activity and performance must be tightly controlled.

Distributor agreements

The best motivation for a distributor is the profit he makes: this will not be discussed here as the whole of chapter 5 is devoted to it. The second most powerful motivation comes from giving him a more or less privileged, exclusive or protected position in the distribution network. In exchange for privileges of this kind the distributor is tied to the manufacturer so as to become, to a greater or lesser degree, his active agent in achieving sales. His livelihood becomes increasingly bound up in the manufacturer's product and instead of being an independent distributor of what he judges the market requires, he becomes an appointed distributor in the interests of the manufacturer.

The arrangements covered by a distributor agreement must be a balance between what the distributor undertakes to do, and what the manufacturer gives him in return. The agreement itself should be a document in legal terms, not so much because either party is likely to go to law over it, but to prevent any ambiguity in the wording. What is important however is the intention on both sides. The following are examples of the kind of terms that might apply, and a particular agreement might be a combination of some or all of these things on each side.

Undertakings by the distributor

1. To provide sales and supply coverage for the manufacturer's products in a specified area, or to specified customers.
2. To employ a specified number of salesmen wholly or partly for the manufacturer's products.
3. To carry specified stocks of a specified range of the manufacturer's products.
4. To provide specified storage, warehousing and/or servicing facilities.
5. To provide specified delivery services.
6. Not to sell any competitors' products.
7. To achieve a specified sales target.
8. To supply information on customers and sales statistics.
9. etc, etc.

Undertakings by the manufacturer

1. To give the distributor sole selling rights in a specified area.
2. Alternatively, shared selling rights with a specified number of other distributors.
3. To allow a specified level of profit margin on sales.
4. To provide a specified level of support selling or other assistance.
5. To provide specified credit facilities.
6. To provide training programmes and product education.
7. etc, etc.

From the manufacturer's point of view, the object of appointing distributors is above all to secure active participation by the trade in achieving sales. There can be a number of subsidiary benefits as well:

1. The elimination of competition and mutual price cutting between rival stockists.
2. The denial of good distribution channels to competitors.
3. A substitute for own depots and warehouses.

In granting exclusivities to distributors in return for this co-operation, the manufacturer must be careful that he is not at the same time restricting his distribution. The customer's choice of supplier now becomes limited. In his own area there is only one distributor he can get the product from, and he may prefer the distributor of a competitor, or the sole distributor may be too remote for convenience. Often it may be necessary to refuse to grant absolute exclusivity in a territory, but instead to have two or three equally sharing distribution in one area, so that customers have some freedom of choice, and monopoly abuse is prevented. Similarly, territories must be limited to what distributors can cover effectively, which does not always match their claims.

From the distributor's point of view, the more he is required to do in support of the manufacturer's products to the exclusion of other business interests, the more he has to depend on the profits from these products and therefore the higher will be the cost of the arrangement to the manufacturer. At the extreme, when the distributor is working solely for the manufacturer, his costs and profit can be directly compared to the cost to the manufacturer doing the job himself. Assurance is required that the distributor will not lack the finance to run the distributorship properly and grow with it; or that he will not divert cash flow away from a successful distributorship and invest it in some other interest. It will always be a problem to find satisfactory distributors who are not already tied to a competitor, and who can provide exactly the required geographical coverage.

Agreements must always make provision for their termination after stated periods or with a stated period of notice, and also stipulate very clearly whatever rights the manufacturer intends to retain in appointing other distributors in future, or in selling directly to large users and so on. Such reservations should be made at the beginning of the arrangement, and not left to be negotiated afterwards.

A case study

The XYZ tobacco company is an independent manufacturer producing a brand of cigarettes appealing to the upper end of the market, and heavily supported by national advertising. Market research figures show that it commands a reasonable market share in the south east of England, but that this declines to almost zero in the north and the west. The public buys cigarettes mainly from small tobacco and general shops, of which there are around 50,000, although increasing quantities are sold through supermarkets. The major competitive brands, each with 20 per cent or more market share, are sold by their manufacturers directly to the retail shops, since the quantities involved can easily support the costs of direct selling and delivery throughout the country. The XYZ company on the other hand believes this would be too expensive for its limited volume and instead makes all its sales in bulk at slightly lower trade prices to wholesale stockists, of whom there are around 1,000, for redistribution to retailers. At the same time it employs a force of travelling representatives who visit as many as possible of the small shops throughout the country, but only to help with displays and advertising material and generally to encourage the purchase of stock from the wholesalers. This field force is well supervised and achieves a remarkably high number of shop visits.

Unfortunately, the XYZ company is not improving its market share and is not getting the response it should from its expensive advertising campaigns. It appears that the wholesaler stockists are not pushing the brand, and retailers are not bothering to stock it.

While the company's own field force can stimulate sales when they concentrate on a particular area, sales fall again when they move elsewhere. Can a more effective method of distribution be found?

The XYZ company is of course fictitious, but the situation described contains real-life elements from a number of sources. On the figures used, calculations would show that the higher prices obtainable when selling to retailers rather than to wholesalers would just about cover the cost of the extra salesmen required to make the contact, but would not cover the cost of the supply depots that would have to be set up for small deliveries nationwide. It was therefore decided that no one method of distribution would be satisfactory for the whole market. Instead, the following plan for a multiple attack on the distribution problem was worked out and is now being adopted.

> While depots throughout the country would be too expensive, only a small outlay is required for extra storage at the factory in the south, permitting the preparation of small to medium size orders for direct despatch to retailers within a given radius of the factory. This is a very substantial part of the total market. Within this area, the field force is to be converted to a direct selling force calling on at least the larger retailers whose requirements will then be despatched directly from the factory. It is being explained to the wholesalers who may thereby lose business that the object is to increase sales in total through harder direct selling, and that in the end they may well get the same total amount of business back again through increased demand from their remaining customers.
>
> One of the major wholesalers is anxious to increase his own share of business in the north. He is therefore being given sole

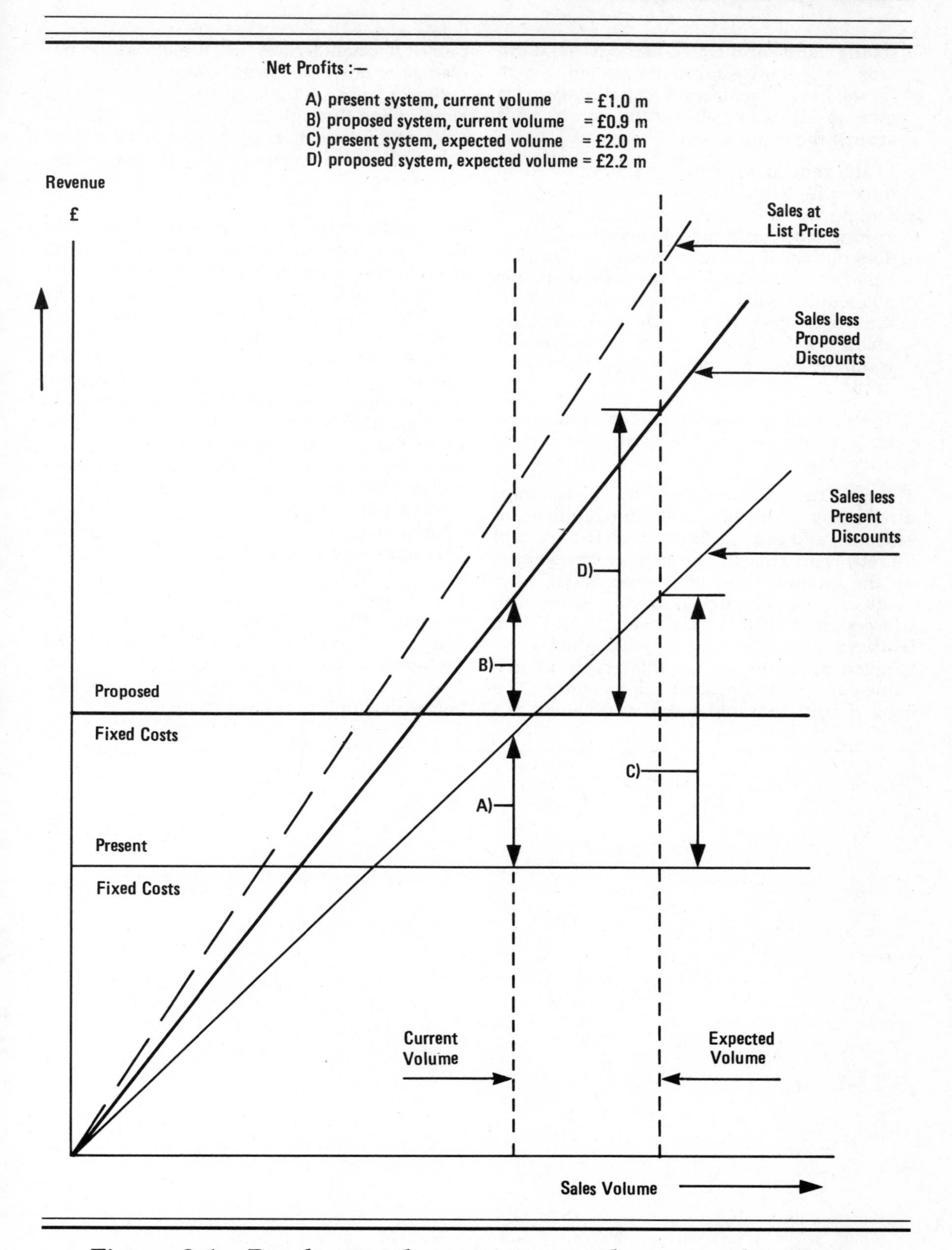

Figure 3.1 Breakeven chart present and proposed systems

selling rights for the XYZ brand in the north only, at a slightly improved margin, where he will have every interest in building up his own position by selling the brand hard against the competition.

In the remainder of the country, the field force will work closely with wholesalers, finding out who their customers are, and visiting those customers to book transfer orders on behalf of the wholesalers. On new business introduced by the salesmen, the wholesalers will take less margin. In effect, the wholesalers will provide the local stock-holding and delivery service, while the XYZ company itself provides most of the selling impetus.

The present routine visiting of small shops for purposes of trade relations only will be discontinued.

The *fixed costs* of the selling and distribution arrangements, in terms of extra numbers of salesmen and extra facilities at the factory, will thereby be increased. The average *variable costs* on the quantity sold will come down, as a result of less discount paid to wholesalers. The consequences of this have been plotted on a *breakeven chart* of which a suitably edited copy is given in Figure 3.1. On this graph, money values are plotted against sales volume. The level of fixed costs, old and new, is shown as a pair of horizontal lines, i.e. these costs do not change relative to sales volume. The total value of sales at trade prices is shown as a sloping line through the origin. The values of sales after deduction of discounts to wholesalers therefore appear as lines sloping at lesser angles.

The existing situation is shown by the set of thin lines. After deducting current fixed costs from sales revenue after wholesalers' discount, there is a margin of approximately £1 million. Under the new scheme, shown by heavy lines, both fixed costs and net revenue will be higher, and the margin will be slightly less at approximately £0.9 million. Thus the new scheme is less profitable, at present rates of sale. But the XYZ company is confident that under the new scheme, sales will increase substantially. It will be seen that in this case there will be a *greater* margin than with the same volume of sales under the old system. The new system of distribution should therefore be not only more effective but also more profitable.

It will remain to be seen whether the XYZ company has predicted correctly. It has at least carried out a conscientious review of all the possibilities for its distribution, and evaluated the results to the best of its ability before deciding to make a change.

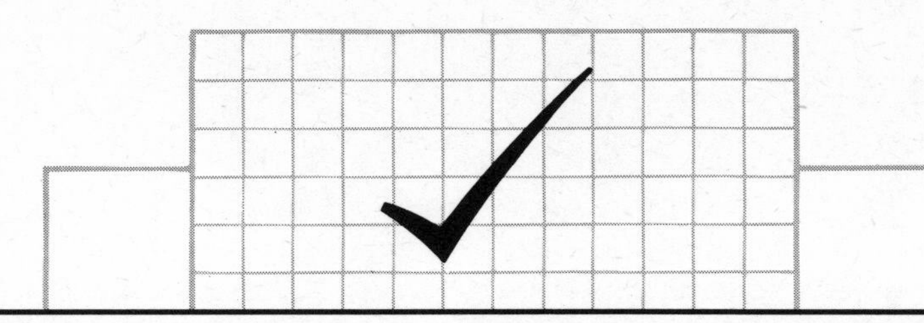

Checklist 3

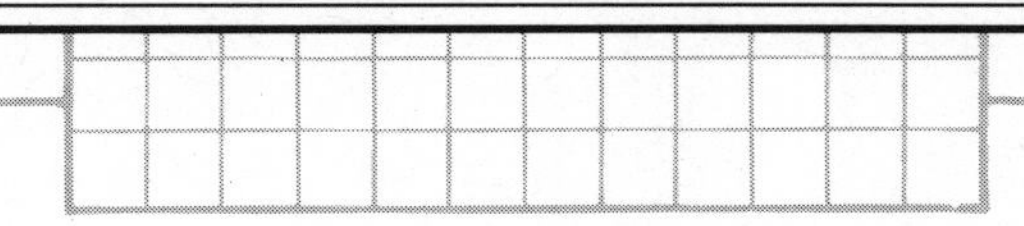

Distribution channels

3.1 Options

(a) Are there any alternative channels of distribution which could conceivably be used instead of, or in addition to, the present arrangements?
(b) If so, what would be the best estimates of sales volume through the new channels?
(c) If the existing channels are still to be used as well, would present sales through these channels be affected? By how much?
(d) Can any specific risks be identified in connection with the alternative channels?
(e) How far are the alternative channels used by competition?

3.2 Levels

(a) If the arrangements would involve selling directly to more than one level of distributor, what would be the basis for getting the agreement of all the parties?
(b) What would be the criteria for selecting the customers at the lower level?

3.3 Support

(a) Would all distributors be treated as free market customers, or would distributor agreements be necessary?
(b) If so, what would be the main conditions on either side?
(c) What forms of field support, selling and servicing would it be necessary to give to the direct buying distributors?
(d) Would any support services be necessary in assisting sales to their customers?

4

The major account

Whatever channels of distribution are used, it is likely that they will include one or more very large customer. By a very large customer we mean one who alone accounts for at least 5 per cent of total sales. Five per cent may not sound a very great deal, but if all customers each represented 5 per cent of sales there would only be room for 20 customers altogether. To have all one's business limited to such a small number of buyers would be a very vulnerable state of affairs.

Multiple accounts

If, as we have seen from the previous chapter, there is a natural tendency for large and small customers to spread themselves out in such a way that 20 per cent of the customers come close to doing 80 per cent of the business, then clearly there is an excellent chance that the top one or two customers will each do more than five per cent. Of course there is nothing immutable about these figures, merely an indication of natural probability; and there is no reason why in practice the disparity between the largest individuals and the straggling 'tail' should not be even steeper. The causation behind this concentration of buying power is likely to be the simple fact that nothing succeeds like success. The distributor who develops some kind of an edge over his competitors begins to use his advantage in purchasing power to get better terms, and his advantage in cash accumulation to invest in a still bigger business. Thus, there is a strong tendency for the trader with a slight advantage in the race to go on pulling away from the rest of the pack by a kind of multiplier effect. Growth occurs as much by mergers and the absorption of competitors as by the increase of the original business itself. The result is that the largest customers, as well as being powerful, tend also to be widely spread geographically, with many branches and subsidiary operations, organised as a 'multiple' or a 'chain' operation. It is for this reason that we refer to such organisations as 'major accounts' rather than as major customers. In operating terms they may well require attention at a large number of different locations as if each were a separate customer. But the important thing is that they are all co-ordinated into one 'account' which pays the bills, combines the buying power, and conducts the negotiations.

Trade concentration

In recent years, the tendency has been for the concentration of distributors to increase. Throughout Europe, food and general retailing has been dominated by the growth first of the self-service shop, then the full size supermarket, and eventually the hypermarket or superstore. Correspondingly the number of small independent shops has declined. The number of grocery type outlets has therefore reduced in total: in Britain from 70,000 in 1976 to 52,000 in 1979; in Holland from 21,500 in 1965 to 12,700 in 1975. Along with the increase in the size of the retailing unit has gone an even greater concentration of *ownership*. In Britain now, the top five chains command around 50 per cent of the market, with the leaders jockeying for 12-14 per cent each. The days when the manufacturer could divide and rule among vast numbers of small independent distributors, not acting in concert with one another, have disappeared with the advent of the large multiple operation.

Making use of 'major account' distributors as a means of reaching the market may therefore not be a matter which is left to the free choice of the manufacturer. If the major accounts between them control an important part of the total trade, there may be nothing for the manufacturer to do but to try to win their co-operation if there is to be any hope of reaching a sufficient number of consumers. Before winning over the actual users of the product, it is first necessary to win over the distributors who control access to those users. On the other hand, it could be that the choice of the major distributor is intentional. Even where a sufficient number of smaller distributors exists, enough to make the product available to all the consumers it is aimed at, it may still seem preferable to use the large, well-known distributor as the most effective channel through which to concentrate sales effort. The greater efficiency of the large operation in providing keener prices and all round service to customers might be seen to outweigh the disadvantage of its concentrated negotiating power.

Vulnerability

Either way, from a manufacturer's point of view, having even one major account responsible for at least 5 per cent of sales may very well hold the balance between profit and loss. Few manufacturers could accept with equanimity the sudden total loss of 5 per cent of their turnover, let alone 10 per cent or 15 per cent, and this is precisely what is at risk if the one major account should for any reason, good or bad, choose to switch its business to a competitor. Where the concentration is still greater, the results can be catastrophic. A very good measure of the vulnerability of a business is to check how many accounts, in descending order of magnitude, represent the first 50 per cent of sales. This could almost be thought of as the 'half-life' of the business, in the same way as the half-life of a radioactive substance is the number of years it will take for 50 per cent of its activity to decay. If there are fewer than about 25 accounts in this top 50 per cent an uncomfortably high proportion of the business is likely to be in single hands. Many manufacturers of course have to exist with far fewer accounts in the top 50 per cent: 20, 10, 5 or even less. The most notorious situation is in Sweden, where well over 90 per cent of grocery and general retailing is controlled by no more than three major groupings. Such conditions have all the qualities of a nightmare for the manufacturer seeking distribution.

Accounts and products

The immediate consequence is that each major account assumes an importance to the supplier, in terms of contribution to total sales volume and to profit, probably equal to or even greater than any one of his product lines. Obviously the large account therefore merits the same degree of planning, nurturing and monitoring as any product – in other words the same degree of marketing attention. In chapter 2 we emphasised the need to devote as much attention to marketing through the trade in total as to the product range in total; where major accounts are concerned, the individual account rates a marketing strategy of its own, the same as any single major product. The major account cannot for the purposes of planning be grouped together with all others large and small and all treated as part of the same trade sector. A trade sector, to be treated as an entity for planning purposes, should at least be homogeneous; and it cannot be homogeneous if it has one or more very large 'lumps' in it, i.e. the major accounts, each of which is liable to behave in an highly individualistic fashion. For another thing, as we shall see later, the major account is almost inevitably going to receive rather special prices, terms and concessions for one reason or another, so that the costs and revenues arising from dealing with major accounts are likely to be rather different from the rest of the trade sector. When it comes to estimating financial results, each major account simply has to be computed as a special case.

In the planning format recommended in Figure 2.2 in chapter 2, where sales per product are reconciled against sales per distribution channel, these distribution channels should certainly show separately the top few major accounts which are of equal importance as products. Then the *remainder* of the trade sector after excluding these major accounts would be another planning category on its own. For example, if planning grocery distribution in Britain, one might have separate lines for: (a) Tesco, (b) Sainsbury and (c) all other multiple supermarkets, and similarly in other classes of trade and other markets.

Account management

Planning is one thing: implementing the plan is another. Many marketing oriented companies concentrate the responsibility for the marketing strategies of their products by appointing *product managers* or *brand managers* to undertake this. The brand manager becomes what has often been referred to as the 'managing director' of the brand. That one item becomes, as it were, the brand manager's private business, to which he devotes the whole of his energies, working out the optimum plans for its advancement, supervising every aspect of its progress, and ensuring that every profit advantage is obtained from it. In exactly the same way, a marketing company whose fortunes are bound up in a few individual large accounts should consider the advantages of appointing *account managers* to undertake the responsibility of looking after them.

The function of the account manager is to ensure that all dealings with the major account are co-ordinated into furtherance of the strategic plan for profit from that account, which he will also have had a large part in producing in the first place. In detail this means that he will collect the information, prepare the plan, conduct negotiations with the customer, secure the best agreements and understandings he can, and then ensure that all concerned are fully informed of the arrangements that have been made, and implement them correctly. The account manager must cultivate the closest acquaintance with all the decision takers in the organisation of the major account customer, earn their respect and understanding, and be ready to intervene and sort matters out if ever any error should occur in the smooth handling of their business. The account manager's role is, if anything, more exacting than that of the product manager, since he has to achieve his objectives through the management and persuasion of trade partners, rather than through the simple commissioning of agencies to carry out his intentions for a fee. The account manager has to be something of a diplomat and a skilled negotiator, as well as a first class administrator who is fully conversant with the workings of his own organisation and capable of ensuring that all parts of the system function properly.

Without such an account manager, dealings with the major account are liable to be divided between far too many people, with no proper co-ordination between them. The organisation of a marketing company is likely to be on territorial lines, with responsibilities subdivided according to areas and regions. Major accounts tend to be multiple organisations with many branches, so that dealings with all the different parts of the operation will tend to cross the regional boundaries of the supplier's organisation. Unless there is a strong central co-ordination, it will not be easy to ensure that agreements made with a major account are interpreted identically in all regions, or implemented everywhere with the same thoroughness.

Three different considerations arise in the handling of major accounts, which can be summarised as follows:

1 The level of seniority and authority required to conduct negotiations.
2 The amount of time and attention required to supervise the account properly.
3 The geographic spread of dealings with the account.

The seniority of whoever is made responsible for handling the major account reflects the degree of importance which the supplier attaches to the business and has to be judged correctly. Clearly it would not do just to send along an ordinary salesman for a major negotiation, just because the customer's head office happens to be in the salesman's territory. At the other extreme, no major customer, however important, is going to be so unreasonable as to insist on seeing the chairman or the managing director every time. They may well feel that at least the head of the sales organisation ought to come to see them – that is, the sales director or the general sales manager. Very often, it will be entirely appropriate that he should.

But then a second consideration comes in. The head of the sales organisation with all his other duties is not likely personally to have the time to ensure that the major account's affairs run smoothly. If there are only one or two such accounts, it may in fact be possible for the head of sales to take them on; otherwise, the responsibility must be delegated to an account executive who will be seen to have authority of his own, with his superior always being available, in the background, in case of necessity. The ideal incumbent is often a younger man, seen to be intelligent and competent, not yet as senior as the buyer with whom he is negotiating, but who can nevertheless establish sufficient respect for himself in dealings with the other side.

The geographic spread of the major account's business affects the issue according to whether it covers more than one of the supplier's organisational regions. If it does, then clearly dealings with that account have to be co-ordinated centrally, in liaison with the several regional managers and regional sales forces which will have the job of implementing the arrangements made. The account executive in charge of such an account would therefore have to be a *national accounts manager*, based at the supplier's head office.

However, some quite large customers' operations are confined to only one region, and thus fall entirely within the purview of one part of the supplier's organisation. In such a case, all the necessary negotiation and co-ordination of activity for the account can be carried out entirely within the one sales region, and the account executive can therefore be a *regional accounts manager*, based in the region itself rather than at company headquarters. Again if there were, say, only one or two such major accounts in the region, it might be quite possible for the account executive function to be undertaken by the manager of the regional organisation himself, in addition to his other duties.

Negotiating, not selling

Dealing with major accounts demands the skills of negotiation rather than selling. Selling as a skill is concerned mainly with convincing the prospective buyer of the merits of the product being sold, whether as an article for his own use, or as an item which will be in demand from his own customers; and also with the techniques of appraising the prospective buyer's needs, closing the sale and clinching an order. None of these elements is totally absent when dealing with a major distributor, but emphasis is very much more on negotiating the exact terms and conditions on which sales can be made and maintained. To a large extent the major distributor will already have made up his own mind about whether a given product is a likely candidate for adoption as a stock line. If the result had not been favourable the negotiation interview would never have progressed this far. The question to be settled is not so much whether to buy, as on what terms. The decision when given will affect not just one particular delivery of the product but (probably) whether the product will be given distribution by being stocked throughout the whole of the distributor's organisation, until further notice. If the person conducting negotiations on behalf of the supplier is too sales oriented, there is a distinct danger of his being over-influenced by the volume of the business in prospect and failing to keep a strict enough control over what it is he is agreeing to.

Negotiating techniques

In business as in any other negotiations, the first consideration is the substance of the proposition being made and the counter proposition from the other side. Each party has to make his own value analysis of the consequences of accepting versus rejecting what is on offer. The buyer who has a need for the goods has to evaluate whether he will be better off accepting them at the price offered, or doing without them. The seller must assess the benefit of taking a lower offer, versus not making the sale. If these issues were totally quantifiable and objective, negotiations could perhaps best be carried out by computers on either side, each comparing the opposing offer to a meticulous calculation of its own advantage. But this is not the case.

It is essential in the first instance for a negotiator to make such a calculation and to be quite clear about what his final position is. For a seller, this is the price and terms below which he would make a loss, or could sell the same amount of goods better elsewhere – a point at which he has no hesitation whatever in saying no. Similarly for the buyer, there is a price above which he would lose by buying, or could buy better elsewhere. If there is a gap between these two positions, no amount of negotiation is likely to close it, as long as both parties know what they are doing. The first stage of preparing for a negotiation should therefore be the entirely rational one of working out not only one's own final position, but also what this calculation ought to be on the other side. If the two do not meet, there are really no grounds for hoping that pure skill in negotiation will hypnotise the other party into agreeing against his better judgement. Before starting, the proposition should at least be one which it would be reasonable for the other party to accept. If he does not seem to think that it is, he will have to be rationally persuaded and convinced that he has not been evaluating it correctly. This re-selling of the merits of the proposition will often have to be a preliminary to the negotiation, but it is not the crux of the negotiation itself.

What negotiation is really about is when there is in fact some overlap between the final positions on both sides. Between the offer and the counter-bid both parties would still benefit more from accepting rather than rejecting outright; the issue is how far can the final terms be moved to the greater advantage of one side or the other. The situation is illustrated in Figure 4.1. For as long as there is a gap between the final positions, it is easy for both sides to say no, and proceed no further. Where the basis for an agreement does in fact exist it is quite difficult for either side to know at what point to say yes.

At this point in a negotiation, the process ceases to be one of purely rational calculation of benefit, and becomes one of inter-personal skills instead. Psychologists may analyse the process, but insights do not necessarily help to improve performance. Without going too deeply into such matters, the following guidelines have been found useful in practice, and may be worth remembering. The negotiator has at his disposal three basic techniques: (a) outsmarting, (b) bluffing and (c) intimidating. Faced with some or all of these approaches, the selling negotiator must learn to recognise them, counter them, and use them himself. The only answer to outsmarting is to be smarter still. The opponent is continually trying to slip something in; to ask for a concession which sounds innocuous until it is evaluated. It is vital to be prepared with all the facts, costs and prices memorised, and to have rehearsed every conceivable combination of terms and benefits that the other side may ask for. Even so, one should not be intimidated from asking for time to work out the consequences of any proposal. These should not omit any indirect consequences, in terms of risks, or setting of precedents, or reaction from other customers. If a discount is given to this customer, will every other customer want the same? If a price concession is given this year, will this set a precedent for another concession next year?

When the buyers have made a counter-offer which is already above one's lower limit, one can do worse than use the classic bargaining ploy of offering to split the difference between offer and counter-offer. Lengthy negotiation may produce nothing better. Otherwise, it may be useful to plan in advance a point at which to play one's own bluff, by refusing to concede anything further and risking what one hopes will be only a temporary breaking-off of the negotiation. In a wage negotiation this would be where one lets a strike take place, knowing that there will be further talks. In selling terms, one risks delisting as a supplier to this customer. The door must be kept open for a resumption, when having as it were given notice of nearing the limit, one more concession may be sufficient to reach agreement.

Finally, when faced with intimidation, the only thing to do is to keep cool, recognise it for the play acting which it is, and remember that the person using it is probably a nice chap really. The other side of the coin is also to recognise how strong is the human desire to be liked, and to appreciate that this is a luxury which the negotiator cannot afford. It is necessary to be completely impersonal and unworried about appearing disagreeable to the other side in not making concessions. In fact such worries are quite unfounded, as the other side has nothing but respect for a competent negotiator.

Buying managers in distributive organisations are often more strongly motivated to obtain advantages in prices and terms on the goods they buy, than sales managers are to resist them. Apart from actual money commissions, buyers may be given professional credit for the size of any special bonuses, overriders and the like which they are able to obtain from

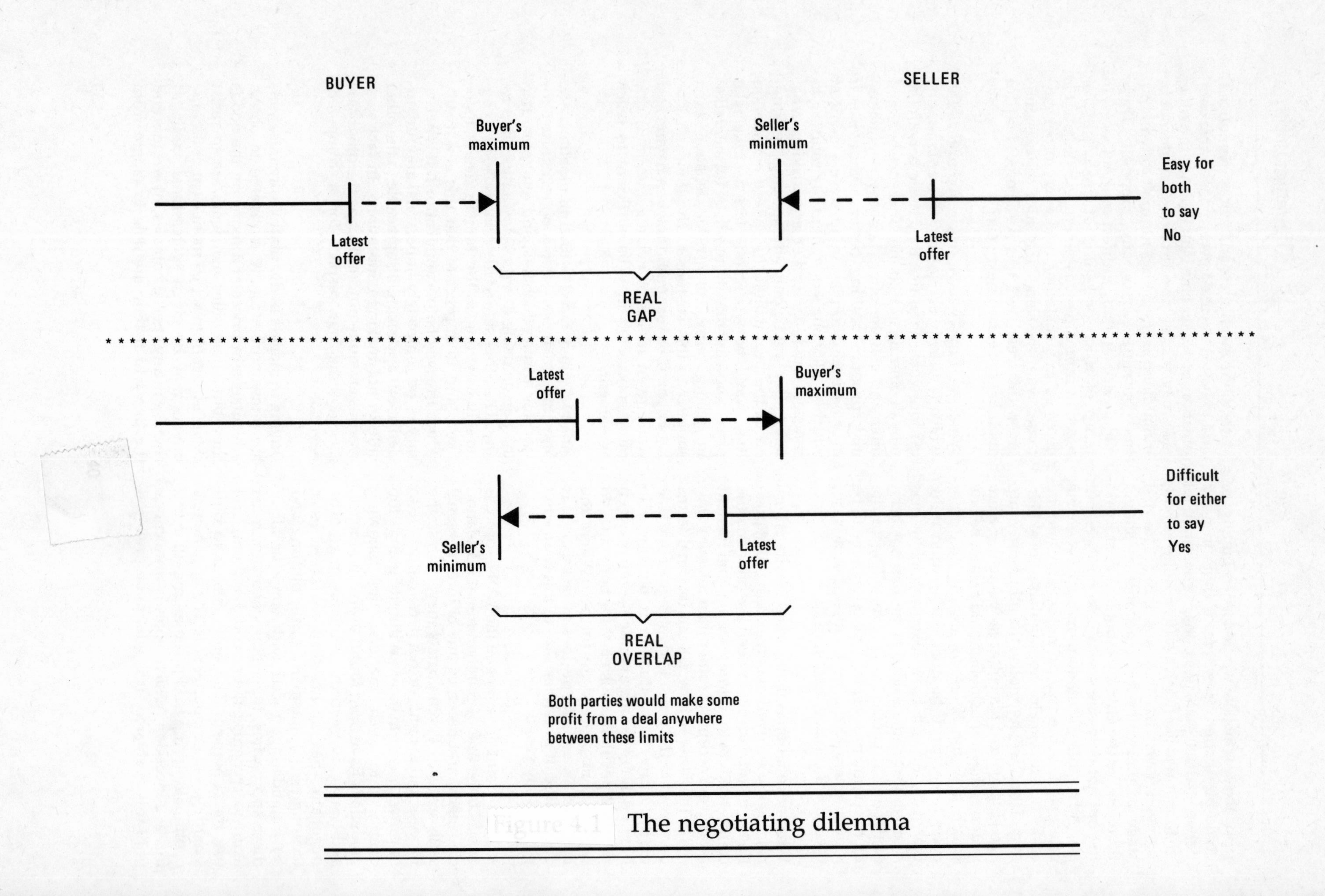

Figure 4.1 The negotiating dilemma

suppliers. It is very worthwhile to find out whether anything like this applies, and turn it to advantage by offering as concessions those things which will mean most to the other person.

Profiles

An essential part of planning for the major account distributor is the preparation of a detailed profile of the customer, to assist in the identification of problems and opportunities, and in the development of a successful strategy. A customer profile falls conveniently into two parts: information on the customer's business and its operations; and information on all current dealings from the supplier's point of view. Both of these will require regular updating. Typical headings for information would be:

Customer operations

1. Type of business, trade category etc.
2. Size of operations, overall sales turnover and market shares, as far as known.
3. Sales (estimated) and market shares in the supplier's type of product.
4. Profitability, capital structure, liquidity, credit-worthiness.
5. Marketing policy, target customers, pricing policy, perceived image, advertising practices.
6. Organisation structure, numbers of branches and locations, levels of authority and responsibility, buying methods, buyer personalities, methods of profit calculation, incentive systems if any.

Current dealings

1. Sales history, share of business obtained, levels of branch penetration and distribution availability.
2. Pricing arrangements, discounts, concessions, terms, contracts.
3. Calculated profit contribution, if available (See chapter 10).
4. Strategic plan objectives and comparison with current progress.
5. Persons with whom currently dealing.
6. Levels of service provided, e.g. delivery arrangements, sales force visits, support selling, locations served, costs.

Using this information as his background, the account manager will constantly be seeking ways of exploiting opportunity, ensuring that the current strategic plan for the customer is being met, and devising means of improving on it for the future. There are four main questions that he will be asking himself:

1. *Volume:* is the level of sales commensurate with the supplier's overall market shares and with the customer's total business in products of those types?
2. *Product mix:* is the mix of products sold giving fair prominence to higher margin items?
3. *Pricing:* are prices, discounts, terms and overall profitability in line for this class of customer?
4. *Costs:* are costs of selling and servicing no more than the minimum essential for the business done?

Mutual need

The major account distributor can be the manufacturer's greatest ally in the marketing of his products, but also one of the greatest threats to the security of his position. If his support and co-operation can be gained, a wide and strong channel of distribution to the consumer opens up. The account manager returning after a successful negotiation of an annual supply agreement, has the satisfaction of knowing that perhaps 5 per cent or 10 per cent of next year's sales has been assured before the year begins. On the other hand there arises a grave risk of imbalance of mutual need between the supplier and the distributor. Put at its crudest, this is the point where the distributor can afford to do without the supplier; but the supplier cannot afford to do without the distributor. However popular and merchantable the supplier's product, he is unlikely to have a monopoly in the line, and the distributor probably can, without too much loss of business, substitute a product from another supplier. For the supplier, it may be literally impossible to replace the same amount of distribution elsewhere.

The major distributor has to be convinced that in fact the manufacturer does provide something irreplaceable: and that is the franchise that the product holds over the consumer. The distributor's objective is often to take over the consumer allegiance himself, and transfer the

A case study

In Western Europe, the market for toilet preparations is both large and extremely diverse. At the top end of the trade these items are almost indistinguishable from the world of high fashion cosmetics, while at the other end the typical item is a litre-size plastic bottle of inexpensive shampoo for use by all the family. There is an equal lack of identity in the distributor concept – beauty salons, perfumery departments in stores, pharmacies, and the cheapest discount supermarkets all compete for an undemarcated share of the trade. Supermarkets in particular have tended to treat the market as a commodity one, and to disregard any consumer preferences for brands as long as an article of more or less the right specification was available at a low enough price. Distributors' own brands and unheard-of brands from unknown suppliers proliferated. The result, understandably, was that consumer confidence was lost and the supermarket share of this growing trade failed to pick up.

In Germany, the AB toiletries company wanted to find some way of encouraging the supermarkets' share of the business, and winning a large part of it for themselves, without becoming a mere producer of unbranded formulations. They put the proposition to a number of large scale supermarkets and popular department stores that the manufacturer of long experience was probably better qualified to gauge consumer preferences and reactions than they were. The distributor has a large enough function to perform in meeting the public's desires for specific merchandise, without having to create the merchandise as well. A basis for partnership was struck in a number of cases, whereby the distributor attempted to define the type of customer seeking merchandise in his store, while AB toiletries undertook to formulate, advertise and launch a range of merchandise aimed specifically at that group. While the merchandise would be branded and trade marked by AB toiletries, it would not be put on sale indiscriminately, but would be reserved for the distributors who first commissioned it and for a few others of the same class. The process could be likened to an author writing a book commissioned by a publisher for a specific public, where the author has to produce what the public wants and takes the credit for it, but the publisher has the distribution rights.

It would be agreeable to be able to record that this experiment in marketing by the AB toiletries company has been an unqualified success. Business arrangements are rarely so simple, and all that can be said is that AB toiletries' sales with supermarkets have increased, and product margins are higher, but costs have been equally high. In this particular case, it may be that the market for the type of product is not quite large enough, and not sufficiently well demarcated, to support all the costs of product development and launching in a single sector of the trade. A wider distribution has to be found for each newly launched branded range without destroying the original concept of exclusivity to a particular class of retailer.

The technique of second brands as a means of getting wider distribution is not at all new. Manufacturers of electrical and radio equipment often put out their 'main' brand through one set of distributors, while marketing a cheaper range under another brand name through another chain of distributors. So do motor manufacturers. What is new is the concept that the second brand should be created to fit the business of the distributor, rather than distributors found to suit the brand.

---

loyalty of the consumer from the product to the distribution service. At its extreme, in the retail world, this is where the large distributor adopts 'own brand' merchandise and picks a manufacturer to put together the product to a specification and at a price. As long as the distributor has sufficient volume of business to justify the larger investment in time and money which this entails, he has no difficulty in getting supplies from one source or another. The only response the manufacturer has is to demonstrate that he is in fact much better at knowing what the consumer wants, and is willing to pay for. This is the justification for the division of function between manufacturer and distributor whereby the former appeals to the user population as consumers, while the trade appeals to them as buyers. It may become more and more necessary to do this with specific reference to the consumers who normally buy from that particular distributor; in other words by joint planning of product and trade strategies so that the product is made suitable for that distributor's customers.

Checklist 4

Major accounts

4.1 Concentration of customers

(a) How many active buying accounts are there in total? Have they been ranked in descending order of annual sales?
(b) In descending order, how many accounts represent the top 50 per cent of sales? The top 80 per cent? Does the Pareto distribution apply?
(c) How many accounts each represent more than 5 per cent of sales? How much does the largest account represent?

4.2 Account management

(a) Who is responsible for the supervision of business with major accounts? How does his authority and standing compare with that of the buyer? For how many such accounts is he responsible?
(b) What is the spread of operations of these accounts? What arrangements are there for co-ordinating dealings across all regions concerned?
(c) Are negotiations prepared in advance?

4.3 Profiles

(a) Are major accounts planned for on an individual basis?
(b) Does profile information exist, and under what headings?
(c) Do the profiles suggest any opportunities for new business?

4.4 Trade partnership

(a) Do dealings with major accounts reflect co-operation or antagonism? If the latter, is there no scope for working to mutual advantage?

5

Motivating and rewarding distributors

Whatever channels of trade the manufacturer chooses for the distribution of his product in the market, they have to be allowed to make sufficient profit from handling the product to motivate them to provide this service. In the main, distributors do not perform their services in return for a set fee. They are in business for their own account and to make a trading profit from what they buy and sell. The manufacturer's concern therefore must be that distributors make their profit on his products by selling the products to the ultimate users at the prices which he, the manufacturer, had in mind for them.

Consumer prices

The price which the ultimate user has to pay for the product must be of the very greatest concern to the manufacturer. In determining the marketing platform which the product is going to occupy in presenting itself to consumers, the question of its price may well be the most important factor of all. Yet the actual price charged to the user is likely to be the one aspect of the product profile which the manufacturer cannot absolutely control.

Concern for the consumer price works both ways. The manufacturer does not wish the price to be higher than planned, so as to maintain the competitiveness of his product to the user. This may be difficult to ensure if distributors choose to take more profit than was intended or if the product has to pass through many hands, each making a profit. On the other hand the manufacturer may be equally concerned that the consumer price is not *less* than intended either; possibly so as to prevent the value of the product from being depreciated to users; or more likely so as to prevent distributors from competing on price between themselves and so spoiling the market altogether. As the markets of Europe became more highly organised, the practice grew up of manufacturers of consumer goods requiring retailers to adhere to the retail prices set by the manufacturers. Retail prices were usually printed prominently on the packs of consumer items. Observance of these prices was made a condition of the contract of supply, and the manufacturer was able in law to withhold any further supplies from a distributor who broke the agreement. He was even able to sue for damages. In Britain, this practice went under the name of 'resale price maintenance' or 'RPM' and similar practices existed in other countries.

While this lasted, the effect was a stability of pricing throughout a market which is hard to imagine nowadays. Competition on price between retailers for branded goods was unheard of, and the buying public was conditioned to the prices of popular items being immutably the same in every shop. Since prices were printed on packs, and so well known in any case, no distributor was ever able to charge a higher price either. Distributors' profit margins were set by the manufacturer, and the trade had no option but to accept this margin or do without.

In the course of time it came to be thought repugnant that a retailer should be prevented from making a price cut when he felt able to, thereby depriving the public of the benefit of free price competition between shops. In Britain, resale price maintenance was made illegal in 1956, and the practice has by now come to an end everywhere else as well. Only in some very particular circumstances can an industry make a case for its continuance, on the grounds of price stability being essential for the provision of service to the public. (One of the very few areas where this exception was made in Britain is in the retailing of books and periodicals and newspapers.) In less developed markets the practice could never be enforced anyway, so that nowadays it would either not be legally permissible, or not feasible in practice, for a manufacturer to control the prices charged by a distributor to a user.

Having lost the power to control minimum prices, it is surprising how far manufacturers now seem to opt out of any concern at all for the price which the ultimate user will pay. Since they cannot actually control it, many manufacturers appear content to let the trade distributor decide for them what this price is going to be. There are of course many countries where the government itself controls *maximum* retail prices, and in these circumstances few distributors are likely to want to sell at less than the permitted price. Apart from this, the general rule nowadays is that a manufacturer who uses trade channels for his distribution cannot directly control either the price which the user will have to pay, or the profit which the distributor will be able to take. The most the manufacturer can do is to *plan* what the consumer price ought to be, and try to make arrangements which will enable it to be respected.

Many manufacturers publicise what has come to be known as the 'manufacturer's recommended price' or 'MRP'. Certainly this effectively prevents any retailer from charging more, but very often the MRP is not seriously intended as a price which any user will ever actually pay – merely as a notional figure against which the distributor can publicise spectacular price cuts. Special offers and price cuts may indeed be the very best way of selling the product at the optimum profit to all concerned, but it should be the manufacturer's objective to have as much influence over this process as he possibly can, rather than leave it entirely to the whim of the distributors. This implies that the manufacturer must make himself sensitive to the responsiveness not just of one market-place, but of two; that is, he must plan for the price awareness of the ultimate user, and also for the reaction of the distributive trade to the total reward it stands to gain from handling the product.

The basis of trade reward

Before considering trade reward any further, it is necessary to define exactly what it is. By trade reward is meant the ability of the trader to make money out of handling the manufacturer's product. It is not just some particular level of trade discount but all the aspects of the trader's relationship with the manufacturer which enable him to make money.

Making money in accounting terms means achieving an increase on the original investment . For the trader this involves four things:

1. *Net margin* – i.e. the difference between the net buying price and net selling price, less the costs of handling, stocking and selling the product.
2. *Volume sold* – in any given period, say one year.
3. *Rate of stock turn* – i.e. the number of times in a year the trader can sell his average stock holding.
4. *The amount of credit* which the trader gets from the manufacturer.

Net margin multiplied by volume gives the actual amount of profit in money made in a year. This is what matters to the trader rather than the percentage margin. A high volume at a low percentage margin can be much more profitable than a high margin product with only a low volume. Comparisons with the percentage margins offered by competitors are meaningless until sales volume is also taken into account.

The second question is how much investment must a trader make in order to achieve this total amount of profit. This means firstly how much stock the trader requires to achieve his annual sales volume; and secondly how much of his own money has to be invested in that stock. If the stock turns over rapidly and is rapidly replaced, the ratio of annual profit to stock value becomes high. If, in addition, long credit is given by the manufacturer, the trader has to lay out less of his own money and the ratio of annual profit to capital actually employed becomes even higher.

An example of how this works in practice is given in Table 5.1. Provided a trader can keep his stockholding at the minimum necessary for the maintenance of sales, the return on

Table 5.1
Trader's return on investment

Annual sales by trader	£10,000
Margin on sales	5%
Annual gross profit	£500
Average length of stockholding (say)	5 weeks
(i.e. stock turn is approx. 10 times per year)	
Therefore average stock value	£1,000

Return on investment per annum: £500 for £1,000 invested or 50%

investment becomes spectacularly high. Even these figures assume that the trader has paid for his stock in cash, and sold it for cash. If he got more credit from the manufacturer than he gave in turn to his customers the amount of his investment is less and his rate of return still higher. A useful way of calculating this is as follows:

Return on investment % =

$$\frac{\text{£ Profit}}{\text{£ Capital employed}} \times 100$$

But the right hand expression can be expanded by inserting £ annual sales on both the top and bottom line:

$$\frac{\text{£ Profit}}{\text{£ Capital employed}} \times 100 =$$

$$\frac{\text{£ Profit} \times 100}{\text{£ Annual sales}} \times \frac{\text{£ Annual sales}}{\text{£ Capital employed}}$$

Now: $$\frac{\text{£ Profit} \times 100}{\text{£ Annual sales}} = \text{Percentage margin on sales}$$

And: $$\frac{\text{£ Annual sales}}{\text{£ Capital employed}} = \text{Rate of stockturn}$$

Therefore return on investment can be quickly calculated by multiplying the percentage margin on sales by the rate of stockturn. Using the figures in Table 5.1 this would give 5% x 10 = 50% – an easier calculation than trying to find out total profit and capital employed.

It follows that the manufacturer can provide benefit to the trader in a number of ways and not just in the form of margin. Demand for the product on the market creates the volume which the trader needs. (A popular item brings in customers and generates profit on other items as well.) The frequency of the delivery and stock replenishment service which the company can offer increases the rate of stockturn. If the trader is given the opportunity of re-ordering monthly or even weekly, stocks can be kept low. If the manufacturer offers longer credit to the trader than the trader gives to his own customers in turn, still less of his own money is invested. At the extreme, the trader may sell for cash before having to pay the manufacturer for stock supplied on credit and thus make an infinite return on zero capital.

Traders habitually do not think this way, or pretend not to be able to, until it suits them. In making his proposition to the trade, the manufacturer must emphasise all these points rather than negotiate only on prices and margins. The manufacturer's proposition can still be an attractive one even with a low percentage margin. It is always incorrect to generalise that distributors in any given trade must have a minimum margin of some particular percentage.

Calculating distributor margins

The net price at which, on average, a distributor sells a product can only be ascertained by direct checking, with the distributor himself and with his customers; or by making the best possible estimate. Nevertheless, if the manufacturer is to exercise any control over what is happening to his distribution this kind of information must be obtained regularly. This is a job for the field sales force, if there is one. In addition to selling, the field force must act as the company's eyes and ears and bring back this kind of information as a matter of routine.

Monitoring selling prices

It is extremely difficult and time consuming to have to extract pricing information from reports salesmen send in on their visits to individual customers. Instead, it is much better to undertake a special survey from time to time on just a few key items whenever the need arises. (This can equally well include a few competitive items, as a cross check.) The survey must be completed over a short enough period of time so that the prices recorded are not affected by any general change in price levels between the first and the last. Each salesman should therefore be asked to collect the information in respect of all the customers he visits during, say, one week – which is not likely to amount to much more than 50. A specimen form is shown in Figure 5.1.

A separate form should be used for distributors in different classes of trade, such as supermarkets, small shops, wholesalers, specialist merchants and so on. The price being asked for each item is recorded against each distributor. Where the distributor quotes only one price to all customers and makes no exceptions (such as a supermarket) this is no problem. Where prices are open to negotiation, as with a wholesale merchant, an attempt must be made to find out the highest and the lowest prices actually charged in practice, and the range shown in the two columns provided. Similarly, some careful calculation must be done to determine what costs the distributor incurs in keeping the product in stock, in actively selling it, in providing any technical service, and so on.

Buying prices

The net price at which a distributor *buys* from a manufacturer should be obvious enough to that manufacturer from his own records. However, it is extraordinary how difficult it can sometimes be to disentangle exactly what this price was. The situation is often confused not only by list prices, invoiced prices, discounts, deferred rebates, and so on, but also by having to take a view on the time period over which the stock was purchased, and therefore what was the price, or the average price, over that period.

A more complex question may be that of special reductions in price made to the distributor, *which were intended to be passed on to the ultimate user*. This of course is one of the commonest ways of trying to promote the sales of a product to its users – when sales volume flags, make a special price offer. The only difficulty is, the special offer can only reach the consumer through the trade. There is much scope for misunderstanding with the trade as to their share in the offer. Is the trade supposed to keep some part of the price reduction, or to pass it all on to the user, or even to pass more on by making a contribution from its own normal profit? It is essential to have these points clearly settled at the time, and for actual performance to be monitored, not only to be able to assess the effectiveness of the price promotion as regards the consumers, but also to calculate correctly the total profit which the trade has been able to make out of handling the product. This issue is discussed in more detail in chapter 11.

In the short term, and with a product in good demand which the distributor cannot afford not to stock, his margin can temporarily be squeezed by forcing him to make a contribution towards a special consumer price reduction. But in the long term the amount of margin which has to be allowed in each trade sector must be calculated very carefully, in the light of the other factors, such as sales volume by the distributor, stockturn and credit, and against what is offered by the competition. These factors *together* with the margin must be sufficient over time to retain the interest and loyalty of the trade.

Inflation

A high rate of inflation can make calculations of profit extremely complex. In some countries, traders can speculate by holding stocks for sometimes only a few months and then selling at the increased prices caused by inflation, with an apparently enormous profit. Or they can undercut the increased price levels, apparently without loss. Even in Britain and other Western countries, the annual rate of inflation can easily exceed a trader's normal margin, so that the length of time an item is held in stock can have a great bearing on its profitability.

PRICE SURVEY

Class of Trade . . . . Week Ending . . . .

Salesman . . . . Territory . . . .

Customer Name	Product A		Product B		Product C		Competitor X		Competitor Y	
	Hi	Lo	Hi	Lo	Hi	Lo	Hi	Lo	Hi	Lo

Note to Salesman :

- Insert prices currently charged for each item by each customer visited this week
- Use the correct form for each class of trade
- Where there is a price differential for quantity or for customer, quote highest and lowest prices

Figure 5.1 Salesman's price survey form

In estimating real profit margins to the trade, either the buying or the selling price should be adjusted by the rate of inflation which has occurred between the estimated times of buying and selling. Alternatively, the buying and selling prices can be left unadjusted, and the cost of borrowing the money value of the stock held over the period taken into account instead.

It can (and does!) occur that the interest rate on borrowed money is actually *less* than the rate of inflation. When this happens, there is real gain to be made out of financial speculation in stock. A manufacturer can speculate in his own stock just as well as anybody else can, and the financial implication of letting inflation increase the value of stockpiling should be very carefully considered. Speculation by the trade should as far as possible be controlled through planned selling; heavy selling to the trade before a price increase is at the cost of future profit and is the same as giving the trade a special bonus.

Accounting conventions

In discussing trade reward it is worth looking at the ways in which the figures are usually kept in the manufacturer's own books. The value of sales made would in most companies be shown in the books as the actual cash value due to the company from its trade customers; that is to say, sales are valued at their net prices to the trade, after deducting any trade discounts allowed. There might be some exceptions to this. For example, if there were deferred rebates payable to some trade customers at the year end, these would probably not be deducted from the value of sales made at the time, but the actual payment would eventually be shown separately in the accounts as an item of cost. Similarly, special price reductions might not be netted off from the value of sales, but 'charged' as a separate cost to the prduct promotions account, like any other item of advertising and promotion. Thus the total sales figure shown in the books might not be *exactly* the actual net cost of those sales to the trade.

However, more importantly, what the manufacturer's accounts certainly will *not* show is the value of these sales *at the price charged to the user* by the trade, and therefore the total amount of margin retained by the trade. The consequence of this that the amount of 'reward' allowed to, or taken by, the trade in return for providing distribution does not show in the manufacturer's accounts as an item of cost at all. This is demonstrated by the figures in Table 5.2.

Consider what would happen if a manufacturer employed a large sales force and made all sales himself direct to users. Sales would be shown at the 'user' price, and the salaries of the sales force would appear as an enormous overhead cost. If instead the manufacturer makes all his sales through only a few distributors and needs hardly any salesmen to do it, sales will be shown at trade price, sales force salaries will be minimal, and there will be apparently a very low total cost of distribution. All that will show is a lower unit sales value and a lower gross margin achieved. But special trade prices and discounts to the trade *do* represent a cost, just as much as a sales force does. In estimating or comparing *total* costs of making sales and achieving distribution, the cost of 'employing' the trade should be taken into account, just as much as all other types of expenditure.

Trade pricing structure

Prices to the user have to be influenced (if not controlled) by correctly assessing the amount of reward required by the trade to perform the distributive function, and setting the correct level of prices and discounts accordingly. It is usually not too difficult to prevent the distributor from charging *more* than the planned price to the user, by the judicious encouragement of competition and by the publication of *realistic* recommended maximum prices. On the other hand, it is absolutely impossible to prevent a distributor from charging less if he chooses to. Provided mutual price cutting is not destroying a market, a manufacturer is usually not too unhappy at his distributors paring their own margins for the benefit of users. The process is however one which should be kept under control by setting the level of trade reward at a realistic figure in the first place.

Generally speaking, it will be insufficient for a manufacturer simply to have a single set of

Table 5.2
The real cost of distribution

		Percentage of manufacturer's sales value	
Price to the user	100		
Retailer's margin	20		
Price to retailer	80		
Wholesaler's margin	10		
Manufacturer's price to wholesaler	70	100%	Only this part shows in the manufacturer's accounts
Manufacturer's selling costs	5	7.1%	
Proceeds to manufacturer	65	92.9%	

According to the manufacturer's books, the cost of achieving sales is only 7.1% of sales value. But the total cost of moving the product to the user is 35% of the price the user pays.

prices and a single trade discount for all sales to all trade customers. In order to maintain a flexible control over the distribution process, a graded pricing and discount structure is usually necessary. The principal aims of differential trade prices and discounts are:

1 To stimulate extra sales to the trade
2 To motivate each sector of the trade to perform in the ways required of it
3 To preserve equitable prices in the different trade sectors.

Various ways of organising differential prices and discounts are discussed in the following sections. These are not exhaustive, as there is no limit to the ingenuity of sales management in devising ways of giving away money – but we shall try to cover the major considerations involved in establishing a trade pricing structure.

The quantity discount

Far and away the commonest practice in relations with distributors is to allow a discount in proportion to total sales. The biggest customer gets the biggest allowance. The object of giving a discount for greater quantities purchased is, or should be, to encourage the trade to buy more in order to sell more. The simplest way for them to do this is to concentrate on the products of the one supplier to the exclusion of his competitors. This aim is of course very desirable for the manufacturer, but in practice what is usually happening is that the sheer buying power of the larger customers has taken control, and the supplier is being obliged to accede to terms where the balance of advantage is far outweighed. Let us look first of all at the mechanics of the system.

1 A discount for total quantity purchased in a given period, say one year, is not necessarily related to any cost savings made by the supplier in respect of that quantity. There may be some marginal economies in longer production runs, and it is a great reassurance to have large, loyal customers, but in general the unit cost of the product supplied remains the same both for large and small customers.
2 Cost savings do result from larger indi-

vidual *deliveries*, but the annual quantity discount is earned irrespective of size of delivery. The customer is free to order as little and as often as he likes, increasing the demand on the supplier's services.

3 It is the larger customers who get the benefit of the quantity discount, which they then use to cut prices, increase their share of the market, become still larger and get still more discount.
4 The smaller customers without the price advantage are gradually eliminated and the supplier finds an ever larger proportion of his sales having to be made at high rates of discount and a lower profit.

Concentration of trade

This process is precisely what has been taking place in the structure of mass retailing throughout most of the countries of Europe at least since the 1960s. In the grocery business, the large supermarket chains have used their buying power to get ever keener offers from competing suppliers, and, with the removal of resale price maintenance,have been able to pass these on in the form of cut prices to the public. The smaller independent shops have been unable to compete, and have gone out of business in their thousands.

The public has of course gained from the process, at least as regards prices lower than they would otherwise have been, although at the cost of loss of convenience in the closure of thousands of little local shops. Insofar as lower prices to the public are made possible by the improved efficiency of the large supermarket, and by the rationalisation of the whole distributive process from manufacturer to retailer, this can indeed be welcomed as progress. The point to be made, however, is that in this instance much of the contribution to lower prices has come on a purely involuntary basis from the product manufacturer, in acceding to buying pressure from the larger multiples.

To quote Britain as an example, the profitability of practically all industry and commerce has declined since the 1960s, but it is notable that food manufacturers' profits have declined very much more than those of retailers in general. Between 1965 and 1977 real rates of return on capital employed fell in absolute terms as follows:

Retail distribution by 42%
All manufacturing industry by 54%
Food manufacturing industry by 67%
(*Source:* Monopolies and Mergers Commission Report on Discounts to Retailers, 1981)

By 1977 food manufacturers in Britain were earning on average less than 5 per cent return on capital after allowing for inflation; while retailers were earning over 10 per cent. (Same source.)

This has been a classic case of suppliers *not* retaining control of their distribution system, but being controlled by it. Even with hindsight the process may have been unavoidable, but much of it could be said to have started from the general currency of the simple idea that the large customer is entitled to ask for and to get a favourable discount for quantity.

Buying power: Robinson-Patman

The simple notion of a quantity rebate is clearly capable of some very potent effects, and governments in a number of countries have given their consideration to it. In the United States the Robinson-Patman Act of 1936 makes it positively illegal to give an extra discount to a customer merely on account of his size and purchasing power. To do so is considered to be 'discriminatory' against the smaller man who, to American thinking, ought to be allowed access to whatever supplies he wants to have on exactly the same terms as the most powerful corporation. What the Act actually says is that 'only due allowance for differences in the cost of manufacture, sale or delivery resulting from the different methods or quantities' can be used to justify differences in prices to customers. Conversely, any concessions must be accorded 'to all purchasers on proportionally equal terms'.

This thinking is held to very strongly, and the act is enforced with a good deal of vigour, so that American buyers cannot and do not seek to exercise their buying power directly on price, but instead use their ingenuity to find ways of getting large shipments, or of setting up special promotional 'deals' which escape the provisions of the act. The existence of Robinson-Patman has certainly not prevented the growth of supermarkets in the United States, but it is notable that the most flourishing supermarket in an area may still be a one-off establishment operated by an independent owner who with his limited total purchases is still fully able to compete with the largest of the supermarket chains.

The British Monopolies Commission

In Britain there is no actual legislation on the matter of bulk buying discounts, but since it has had such undoubtedly far reaching effects, the government in 1977 referred the whole question to the Monopolies Commission, which published its report on 'Discounts to Retailers' in 1981. The commission's basic conclusion was that, while the exercise of buying power in obtaining special discounts was considerable, the effect so far had been 'beneficial to competition and to the consumer'. However the commission accepted that in future 'the practice might encourage concentration in retailing to such an extent as to have harmful consequences'. No action was recommended for the present, but it was thought that any further concentration of the retail trade would have to be carefully watched. An interesting slant on the question of discounts for quantity in Britain is that government procurement departments are themselves often large scale beneficiaries – in many markets the government itself is a very powerful buyer, and is not slow to make use of this power.

The Treaty of Rome

The European Economic Community has two Articles, Nos. 85 and 86 in the Treaty of Rome, which prohibit 'dissimilar conditions to equivalent transactions' in respect of trade between member states. While not strictly applicable to trading practices within a member state, there is at least an implication that this ought to be the correct rule to apply. Both France and Germany in fact have national laws to much the same effect, at least in principle, but in practice they do not lead to the same rigorous control of discriminatory pricing as in the United States.

Practical considerations

Apart from the legal and ethical considerations, and any possible long term effects on the distribution system itself, there are a number of other purely practical inconveniences in the operation of a system of annual quantity discounts.

1. First and foremost, competitors retaliate. The system induces buyers to make all their purchases from one supplier so as to reach the maximum quantity on which to earn discount, rather than spread their purchases among several suppliers. Competition between suppliers becomes a life and death matter; either getting the entire supply contract or nothing at all. In complementary fashion, suppliers are often induced to increase the range of products they can offer, again so as to reach a total quantity more attractive to the buyer in discount terms. The single product supplier loses out.
2. The rate of discount given to large customers usually has to be kept confidential, and consequently the supplier is always vulnerable to the leakage of trade secrets.
3. The actual payment of total quantity discounts or rebates presents a problem. If the discount is deducted from each delivery as it is made there is no guarantee that the necessary total quantity will in fact be reached. If the discount is withheld until the necessary quantity *has* been reached, a lot of the incentive value throughout the year is lost.
4. Another problem with the deferred payment of a discount or rebate is that the buyer will tend not to take it into account in his current calculations of the cost of the product. When the retrospective rebate is paid as a lump sum, the buyer simply accepts it gratefully as a bonus to his general profit at the end of the year. The product itself is rarely given credit for the real profit it earns.

Discount for growth

A variation on offering discounts for the total quantity purchased is to offer a discount only for a specific increase in sales over the previous year or over a stipulated target. This is a more direct stimulant for growth in sales but it is subject to very much the same drawbacks as for total quantity discount. If the market is growing in terms of volume or value, or if the larger customers are increasing their market share, the company will again finish up paying higher rates of discount on an ever larger part of its sales, without any corresponding reduction in cost.

Alternatively, low-turnover customers may easily achieve a greater percentage increase, or even a greater absolute increase, than customers who have already been giving a large turnover. This may result in the smaller customer earning the larger discount.

Even more important is the problem of continuity. Should the discount for growth be paid only for years in which growth actually occurs, or should it continue to be paid forever just because growth occurred once in the past? As for quantity discounts, a discount which is withheld until the end of the year does not motivate; while if paid in anticipation of results it may well not be earned.

Discount for delivery size

It will normally always cost less per unit to sell and deliver in large quantities rather than in small lots. It takes a salesman no longer to write down a large order quantity rather than a small one. The cost of supervising the order, preparing invoices and other sales documentation will be about the same. Transport in bulk, in containers, in complete truck loads etc. is usually cheaper per ton than for small parcels. Therefore overall, there are significant cost savings to the supplier if he can deliver in bulk.

Furthermore, if business consists in the main of repeat supplies to regular customers, the supplier can make very considerable savings if he can persuade his customers to order more at a time, and less often. The total number of selling calls to get orders is greatly reduced, and a smaller sales force is required. While the total tonnage to be delivered may remain the same, the number of deliveries is also reduced and this will almost certainly represent some saving. At the same time, having been persuaded to buy more, the trade customer is motivated to sell more. It is very probable that creating a healthy pressure of stock behind the distributor will result not only in larger single deliveries but also in a larger total annual sales quantity as well.

A scale of discounts for larger quantities, ordered for delivery at one time and place, is therefore something which the manufacturer can offer out of cost savings rather than out of profits, but which will operate to encourage and reward the large scale buyer just as much as a system of discounts for total annual purchases. The large customer can, and should, order in larger quantities in any case. A well calculated range of delivery size discounts is likely to offer him much the same level of total reward as would have been available from an annual quantity discount, provided only that delivery quantities are concentrated.

Such a system can no longer be considered discriminatory, in that it makes the same advantages available to any trader who is able to order (and pay for) the quantities stipulated. Since the advantages are related to actual cost savings, the supplier is not 'showing favour' to particular customers out of his own money, as it were. Delivery size discounts are for example perfectly acceptable under the Robinson-Patman Act in the United States and indeed are the chief method of motivation of distributors. Since it is available to all traders, the discount scale can be published quite openly as part of the price list – there are no trade secrets. Finally, the discount is allowed against payment of the invoice for each delivery which actually qualifies. There is no need to estimate in advance what total annual sales will be.

Bulk central delivery

A very common option both for supplier and buyer is between having supplies delivered direct to all the latter's branches, or delivered instead in bulk to the buyer's own central warehouse or depot, for subsequent delivery to branches by his own services. In the normal way, the warehouse will have many other items to deliver at the same time, so that redistribution from the centre should result in fewer, larger single delivery drops at each branch. This applies in particular to multiple retail chains, both supermarkets and others. It is often the buyer who will take the initiative and represent to the supplier that central depot delivery is a much more efficient process and will be a considerable cost saving to the supplier. Even if the supplier is not proposing to make a regular feature of discounts for delivery quantity in his pricing policy, it is only prudent that he should work out in advance exactly what cost savings do exist at various levels of bulking of orders and deliveries. Otherwise he is liable to be faced with the need to respond quickly and under pressure of negotiations to a proposed price cut by the buyer which he has not had time to evaluate. Calculating the real savings available from bulk delivery is not a process to be hurried. It of course hinges on how much reduction in outgoings can actually be achieved when the number of small separate deliveries is cut. If actual transport costs to a third party are reduced, this is a real money saving. If the salesmen and the order office and delivery drivers merely have less work to do, no saving on account of larger deliveries is made, other than fuel costs, unless and until workforce numbers can actually be reduced, or employed on other useful work elsewhere.

Giving a better price for larger quantities delivered can still lead to the large buyer becoming in his turn more competitive and so gaining more market share. If in handling increased quantities the distributor's additional internal costs do not exceed the reduction in price from the supplier, then the whole distributive and logistic system has improved in efficiency to the benefit of the ultimate user. The only drawback to such a system is where the freshness of the product is of importance, and traders must not be encouraged to lay in excessive stocks which will then deteriorate, merely to earn discount.

As a general conclusion, the delivery-rated discount is the best all round mechanism for stimulating sales, motivating distributors and improving efficiencies, while still keeping a good control over the balance of the distributive system.

Distributor functions

When a manufacturer deals directly with only one level of distributor, the system of prices and discounts only has to take account of differences in size between them, not differences of function. This is the case when, for example, a manufacturer sells all his production directly to retailers, who in turn sell on to the general public; or to specialised distributors who sell on to industrial users. But when more than one level of distributor is used, and the manufacturer wishes to deal directly with customers in both categories, there has to be some mechanism for establishing a buying price differential between them. If a manufacturer sells in the main to wholesalers, but *also* directly to some retailers, then he must try not to undercut the wholesalers' prices to the rest of the retail market. For the distribution system to function correctly, the wholesalers' margins must be protected through their being able to buy more cheaply from a supplier than a retailer can when buying direct.

In some industrial markets with complex levels of distributors and dealerships, manufacturer suppliers sometimes try to establish a set of differential discounts based entirely on the *status* of the trade customer. If the customer can claim to be a main distributor, he is entitled to Scale 1 of discounts; if he is only a subsidiary dealer then he only gets Scale 2, and so on. In markets which are totally stable, this presumably works well enough, long experience having shown exactly what level of discount is necessary to one category of trader to protect his margins to the category below; provided each trader can be relied on to operate only in his own proper orbit.

The difficulty in less settled times and markets is to make a clear distinction between the different distributive functions at any given time, and to put a separate value on them. In the less developed countries this is particularly the case: 'wholesalers' are not above selling direct to the public when it suits them, and 'retailers' will always claim to be entitled to a wholesaler's discount. Many traders in fact operate both as wholesalers and as retailers. In more developed countries, one may again be up against the concept of 'discrimination' between customers if some are given more favourable terms than others.

Achieving differentials

If a system of discounts for total quantity, or for delivery quantity, is in force this may go some way to solving the problem automatically. The main dealer or the wholesaler should logically buy more than the small dealer or retailer, and so he should earn an appropriately bigger discount. But it is unlikely in practice that quantity discounts alone will always guarantee the correct level of price differential between wholesalers and retailers, and between main and subordinate dealers. In the retail grocery field in Europe, for example, any one of the larger supermarket chains, as a retailer, can easily outrank a grocery wholesaler in the quantities it buys – possibly even in any one delivery. To a very large extent, this superiority in quantity has in fact overcome the previous traditional differential which existed in prices to wholesalers, so that it is generally no longer possible for small retailers to buy from wholesalers at prices which will enable them to compete with large multiples. Since for the quantities they require the manufacturer will probably refuse to supply them directly at all, the small retailers have no escape route.

In order to get an insight into how the difficulty may be resolved, it is necessary to go back to the purpose of dealing through wholesalers or other higher echelon distributors in the first place. It is necessary to give such distributors preferential terms and so protect their margins not because of what they are, but because of what they are supposed to do. In other words, the intention is that the wholesaler, or main dealer, should perform an active function in *redistributing* the product, which the manufacturer would otherwise have to do for himself, and which he believes would cost him more. Therefore the redistributor should be rewarded for performing that function, and only insofar as he actually does perform it; and his pricing advantage over subordinate traders should be preserved by this means. Discounts should be made available only for the specific performance of relevant services, e.g. for conducting an active programme of selling, for carrying the total product range, for maintaining an appropriate level of stocks, or for achieving an acceptable standard of display.

Co-operation discounts

This is a most powerful motivation for distributors actually to perform the functions required of them. Instead of having to calculate the amount of discount differential which would be necessary to enable a wholesaler to resell to retailers profitably for both parties, and then paying this differential to those who claim to be able to do the job, the rate for the job should be offered to those who actually do it. This provides an automatic distinction between 'wholesalers' who are active sellers, merchandisers and promoters of a product range, and those who are merely passive suppliers when demand arises. It also solves any problems of distinguishing a wholesaler from a retailer; or of apparently 'discriminating' between one customer and another. As with discounts for quantity per delivery, this form of co-operation discount to redistributors is strictly related to actual costs saved by a company in not having to perform these functions itself. The notion therefore of having functional discounts, which are paid to dealers who have been selected for a particular role, is replaced by a system of co-operation discounts paid to those who do provide the particular service or range of services which has been asked of them.

Co-operation discounts can be deducted from the payment of current invoices by the dealer concerned, and this deduction can be allowed only for as long as the service is being performed satisfactorily; or else they can be paid by credit note issued after the service has been performed. If the reward for co-operation is expressed as a discount, i.e. in the form of a percentage of sales value, the total amount paid will be conditional on a satisfactory level of sales being achieved as well. The rate of the co-operation discount may have to be renegotiated year by year in the light of anticipated sales levels. Alternatively, a fixed amount payment for co-operation can be agreed, conditional on satisfactory performance and sales.

There is always scope for being a little generous in the co-operation payments that are made, where this is judged worthwhile in encouraging some promising trade customer to become better established, but this is an initiative which should always rest with the supplier. The trade customer should, as a golden rule, never be allowed to claim favoured terms as some kind of a right due to his position in the market hierarchy, but only as a return for the job he actually does.

Cash discounts

There is one further type of concessionary allowance to trade customers which is almost traditional, and that is the 'cash discount', or discount for prompt payment. The object of this discount is to encourage payment within the agreed credit or current account terms. If payment is required as cash with order or cash on delivery there is no need to offer a cash discount as incentive - you merely do not hand over the goods until the cash is received. But for the great majority of commercial transactions, it is necessary to operate on a basis of mutual trust through a current account. It would be impossible for both parties if each delivery had to be held up until it was completely checked and valued and the cash produced or a cheque made out. Standard practice is to allow the customer time to check his own records of receipts against the supplier's invoice, to check the prices and the invoice total, and to produce a cheque in payment as part of his stock accounting and book-keeping procedure. For a large trader such as a supermarket chain this may involve reconciling hundreds of deliveries made by each supplier to often quite distant branches. Most usually, a month seems to be regarded as a reasonable period to allow between supplying goods to a trade customer and getting payment for them. This length of time is by no means essential, however – at least one very large British supplier in the grocery field is able to insist on payment being made within *one week* of deliveries. Such is the popularity of the product that customers make a special effort to pay up on time.

Distortion of credit

Note that for the great majority of transactions it was not really part of the supplier's original intention to provide credit to his trade customers at all, that is, to use his own money to help to finance his customers' businesses. Thus the expression 'credit account' is a little misleading; strictly speaking it should be 'current account'. In practice, many suppliers find it convenient to close their ledgers once a month, send their customers a 'statement' of deliveries made during the month, and start counting the time allowed for payment from the date of the statement. This makes things easy for the accounts office, as all accounts become due on the same calendar date. For the customer who takes in supplies regularly throughout the month, the law of averages will apply. Half of his supplies will be delivered in the first part of each month, and half in the second part: so that for him the average date of supply will be the middle of the month. His average grace period before making payment will therefore be half the month in which supply was made, plus whatever further period is allowed from the month end. If this is itself a whole month, then such a customer will on average enjoy about six or seven weeks' credit before paying for his supplies.

A customer who is vitally concerned for his cash postition can go still further. By arranging to have all his supplies at the beginning of each month, and none at the end, he will be able to benefit from very nearly two whole months credit. Not only does this strain the manufacturer's resources, it may completely disrupt his production pattern as well. There are industries where all the customers are jockeying for position to get their orders accepted just at the end of each month so as to be delivered at the beginning of the next; with the manufacturer working flat out on overtime during that week, and having plant standing idle the rest of the time.

The first consideration therefore is to decide on what the 'normal payment' period ought to be, and how it should be calculated. There is actually no need for a whole month's transactions to be treated together; it is perfectly possible, especially nowadays with low-cost computerised book-keeping, for each delivery to be recorded separately and for the payment period, whatever it is, to be noted separately for each. Similarly, it is perfectly feasible for the trade customer to process each delivery as he receives it, and pay each within its proper time period, instead of bulking receipts and putting them aside to be dealt with at the month end.

Direct debiting

If the only consideration were to allow a reasonable time period for book-keeping by the trade customer, it would be perfectly feasible, and would simplify matters for both parties, to use the system of 'direct debiting'. This is the system operated by banks in very many countries including Britain whereby the trade customer gives a general authority to his bank to accept debits from and make payments to such and such a supplier, perhaps to within some overall limit. The supplier undertakes to raise a direct debit on the customer's account not less than *x* days after each invoice. Within that period, the customer should have had time to check for any errors in the delivery, or in the invoice, and make a counter claim. But the great majority of transactions would go through automatically, at precisely the agreed interval for payment, without the customer having to write out cheques, without the supplier having to chase them, or the banks having to clear them. This system exists, and is in use to a very limited extent between suppliers and the trade, but in a rational world it would become the rule rather than the exception. It remains a very worthwhile objective for the sales force to achieve in their negotiations with customers.

Reluctance to agree to direct debiting reveals how anxious trade customers are to be able, if necessary, to delay supplier payments and so stretch their finances over a difficult period. Some traders of course make a regular practice of it. They are expert at identifying the supplier who is a 'soft touch' and stretching their credit with him as far as it will go. Even the most respectable of businesses will make it a practice to work backwards from their bank position to decide which suppliers will be paid this month; and it is only the rarest of businesses which would borrow money specifically to meet payments to suppliers merely because they were 'due' at the first time of asking.

Deterrence

The aim of the cash discount therefore is to deter customers from exceeding the agreed payment period, and to penalise those who do. If a cash discount is going to be given, there is absolutely no question that list prices must first be increased by the amount which is to be discounted. There is always a creeping tendency to believe that the cash discount is somehow 'included' in the normal selling price, and does not have to be added in specially. Some (though very few) manufacturers have the courage to add the amount separately as a surcharge at the bottom of each invoice, rather like a deposit charged on returnable empties, stating clearly that this is the extra cost of delayed payment, which will be cancelled if payment is received on time.

If a cash discount is added, and made deductible, then obviously the amount must be substantially greater than the rate at which trade customers could borrow money for the period during which they hope they can get away with non-payment. Otherwise, offering a cash discount which is less than this is tantamount to issuing an open invitation to borrow money from the supplier at a favourable rate. Supposing that two and a half per cent discount is offered for payment within one month of the end of the month of supply, and one and a quarter per cent for payment within two months. The calculating customer will conclude from this that he can have up to two months' credit free; three months' credit for one and a quarter per cent; and four months – which can probably be stretched to six – for two and a half per cent. When bank overdrafts may well be 20 per cent per annum, this is not a bad propostition. Instead of bringing money in promptly, the cash discount may cause it to pour out.

Some suppliers of course may make a deliberate policy of offering financing facilities to their customers, as an aid to sales. The simplest way of doing this is for the supplier merely to act as an agent for a bank or finance house which will pay the supplier in cash and allow credit to the customer, at an appropriate rate of interest. If the supplier is quite sure he can perform this function safely and more profitably himself with his own money, rather than letting a bank take the profit, then the financing terms should be covered quite clearly and separately by some form of loan agreement or promissory note, with interest terms specified; and not mixed up with the pricing and cash discount terms for the goods themselves. Any legislation governing the granting of loans and credit facilities must of course be respected.

A case study

Brazil is a vast country; and in the cities of Sao Paulo and Rio de Janeiro it has some of the largest population centres in the world. Consumer goods manufactured in the industrial quarters of Sao Paulo have to be distributed and redistributed through many agencies until they reach the remotest villages of the Amazon Basin. In general it has not been possible for manufacturers to find out, much less control, what prices were charged for their products to the remote consumer. All they could do was to push their products to distributors located in the larger centres, and leave it to them to start the redistribution process, in which prices would find their own levels through competition. These distributors are also the source of supply for retail shops in the towns.

In recent years there have been two crucial developments. The primary distributors have grown and concentrated through mergers, until the average manufacturer may find most of his business going through only perhaps a dozen or twenty large concerns. At the same time, urban supermarkets have increased in size to rival anything commonly seen in Europe or the United States.

Originally, the distributive system regulated itself by means of the traditional scales of quantity discounts. The largest merchant got the largest discount and so could afford to resell at a profit to the smaller merchant, who could do no better by buying direct. The advent of the supermarket has upset this structure. The largest supermarket group can nowadays buy in quantities equal to the largest merchant. The supermarket does not resell to other traders, but directly to the public, and it does so at prices greatly below those charged in the small retail shops, which have had to buy through the chain of distributors. The result is that the more affluent section of the public, buying from supermarkets in high class shopping centres, pays much less for the same product than the poorer section, buying from shops and stalls in their shanty towns or favelas. The main thing which prevents them from storming the supermarkets is that they can only afford to buy the smallest size of everything which the supermarkets do not stock; and they also need a few cruzeiros worth of credit to the end of the month, which only the small shopkeeper will let them have.

To complicate matters further, many of the large distributors also own supermarkets, so that it would not be feasible for manufacturers to try to establish differential pricing between the two. There is no simple answer to this distributive chaos, in which manufacturers also have to contend with very high inflation and government control on maximum ex-factory prices. In an attempt to rectify the situation, the XY food products company is introducing 'second brands' of slightly more economical products, which will be sold only to distributors and on which special allowances will be given strictly in relation to distributors' efforts in actively selling to small shopkeepers in towns; and against an undertaking not to sell more cheaply in any supermarkets of their own. No supermarket will be refused direct supply, but no quantity discount will be given, nor of course will there be the special allowance for re-selling to other distributors. Early results suggest that these arrangements are pointing the way to a fairer distribution system.

Other discounts

Whatever arrangements are made for cash discounts, it should also be an absolute rule that all other forms of discount will also be allowed *only* if invoices are paid on the due dates. The terms of sale should stipulate very clearly that, for example, any discount for quantity is deductible *only* provided payment is made on time. If it is not, the amount of the discount is to be added back. Similarly for any discounts for co-operation – the first and most vital aspect of co-operation is that bills should be paid on time. If all customers who enjoy open credit accounts are also in line for other forms of discount, the fact of making these conditional on prompt payment may in itself be sufficient deterrent without having to calculate and apply a separate surcharge and discount for prompt payment in addition.

One last point on cash discounts – once they are offered for payments made by a certain date, few customers will ever be willing to pay any sooner. If, as is sometimes the case when dealing with small trade customers, the sales force is to be made responsible for debt collection, they will have little hope of collecting money or cheques if, when they make their call, the discount period has still a few days to run. Customers get into the habit of not making out a cheque until the salesman calls, and then arguments start over loss of discount, if the customer can blame the salesman for not coming on time. In this sort of situation, where the salesmen's visits are regular, there is a lot to be said for giving the salesman discretion to allow the discount, without being too rigorous as to time period, provided he gets payment for the last delivery on each new call he makes.

Discount formats

Once all the policy questions on discounts to the trade have been settled, there still remains the matter of working out the detailed rules, and checking their arithmetical implications. This deserves a great deal more care than it sometimes gets – a well intentioned scheme can produce the oddest results if no one checks what the effects will be over the whole range of figures. The following points are suggested for guidance.

Uniform rates

Whatever the other factors in the calculation of discounts, it is very worthwhile to keep to a single scale for all company products, if at all possible. This means that a single discount calculation can be made for the total quantity or value of an invoice. If different rates apply, invoices have to be analysed into different product groups, and separate calculations made, which can greatly complicate the accounting routine.

Inflation proofing

The constant reduction in the value of money means that the money value of customers' purchases will increase automatically for the same quantity of goods. If the discount scale applies to the money value of sales, the actual amounts paid will increase for no real increase in business. On the other hand, if the discount scale applies to the *quantity* supplied, then inflation has no effect, or may even bring about a reduction in the amount payable, as the following examples show:

1. *Discounts as percentages against value supplied*
   For example:
   1% discount on invoices over £1,000
   2% discount on invoices over £2,000
   With inflation, more invoices will come into the higher value brackets and the overall rate of discount given will *increase*.
2. *Discounts as values against value supplied*
   For example:
   £10 discount on invoices over £1,000
   £40 discount on invoices over £2,000
   With inflation, more invoices will come into the higher value brackets and the overall rate of discount given will again *increase*.
3. *Discounts as percentages against quantity supplied*
   For example:
   1% discount on invoices over 100 cases
   2% discount on invoices over 200 cases
   Since the rate of discount is not calculated on money values, it is *unaffected* by inflation.
4. *Discounts as values against quantity supplied*
   For example:
   £10 discount on invoices over 100 cases
   £40 discount on invoices over 200 cases
   Since the money value of the merchandise will have increased due to inflation, the rate of discount as a percentage will actually *decrease*.

Unit scales

Discounts expressed against a quantity scale protect against inflation, but if the product range has widely varying values or margins per unit of quantity, e.g. per tonne or per case, it may be impossible to offer the same rate of discount for all products. In this case, a scale of 'units' should be devised proportional to the value or margin of each product, and the discount paid on the total number of units. For example:

Scale of Units
1 tonne of Product A = 1 unit
10 cases of Product B = 2.5 units
etc. etc.
Scale of Discounts
1% discount on 10 units
2% discount on 20 units
etc. etc.

The unit equivalents have to be shown on invoices and totalled for the calculation of discount; note that this is still simpler than calculating a different rate for each product.

Cost savings

Where discounts are being offered against actual cost savings on for example larger quantities delivered, there should be no difficulty in deciding what the scale should be. A very careful 'model' has to be constructed of all costs of transport etc. from which the actual supply costs of any given quantity can be calculated. The discount scale should then be a mirror image of these costs, increasing as they decrease. The scale will start at the point where savings first arise, with an upper limit beyond which there are no more cost savings to be gained, and with pro rata steps in between. The same scale can also be continued downwards to determine the point at which a surcharge should be made or else a minimum order quantity set.

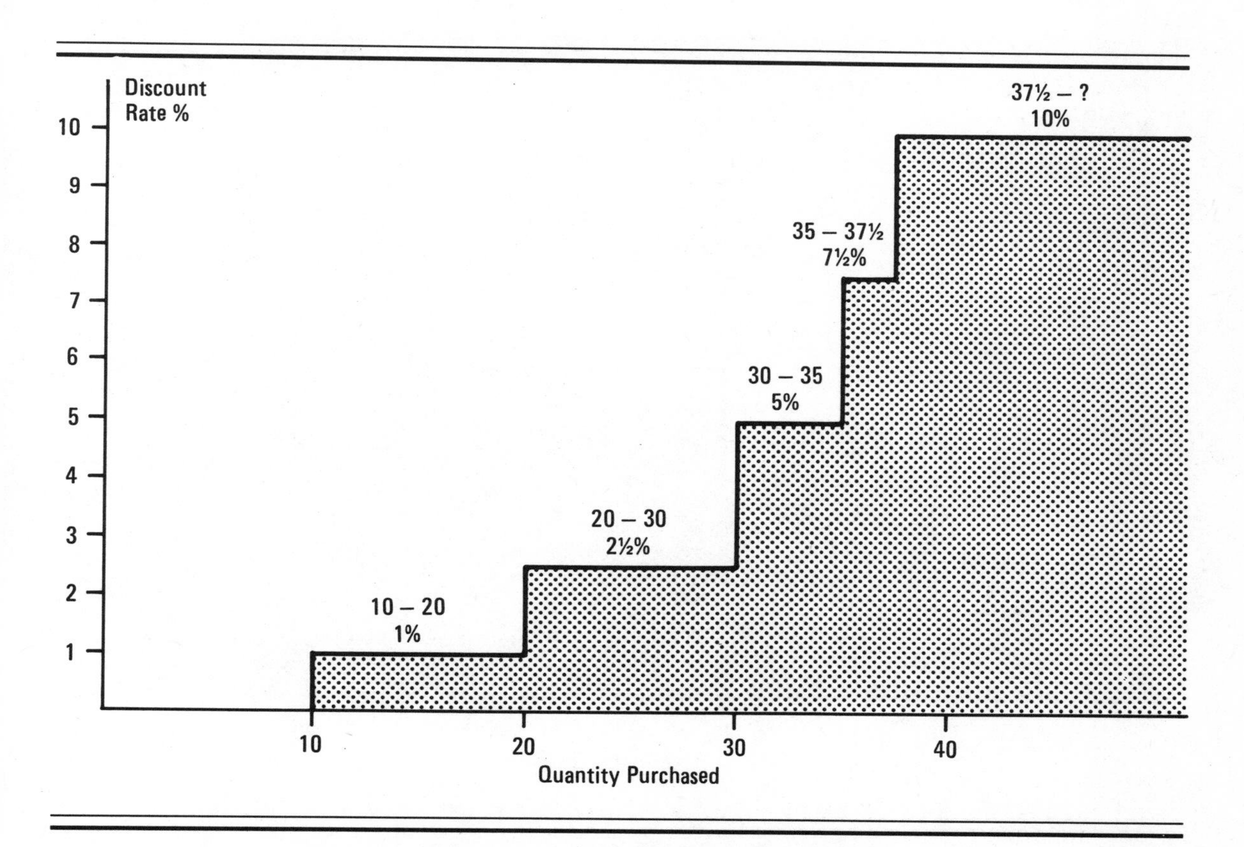

Figure 5.2 Progressive discount scale

Steepness and limits

Where discounts are not related to specific cost savings, but are in response to total turnover or other intangibles, then the effects of the discount scale have to be very carefully thought out. A view must be taken on what the maximum annual sale to any one customer is going to be. This can often be upset by mergers; if two large customers combine, they can face the supplier with a demand for discount at a rate implied by his scale but which he never contemplated actually having to pay. So the upper *limit* for discount must be determined, both as to the maximum rate to be paid and the point at which it will apply, e.g. 7½ per cent discount for 750-999 tonnes, 10 per cent discount for 1,000 tonnes or over.

This limit, together with the lower limit at which discount starts, will determine the *steepness* of the rate of rise of the discount scale and therefore presumably the degree of incentive to the customer to reach the next level. This steepness may be made uniform, or it may itself increase, or it may decline. If the rate of discount increases more steeply at each stage, it is said to be 'progressive'. If it increases less steeply at each stage, it is said to be 'regressive'. Figure 5.2 illustrates a progressive discount scale; and Figure 5.3 illustrates a regressive scale.

Uniform or regressive scales are certainly more usual, and accord well with a cautious approach. Progressive scales represent 'the sky's the limit' thinking; no discount is too big for a customer who can reach exceptional quantities. But even a progressive scale has to be given a top limit when there is no more margin available on the product.

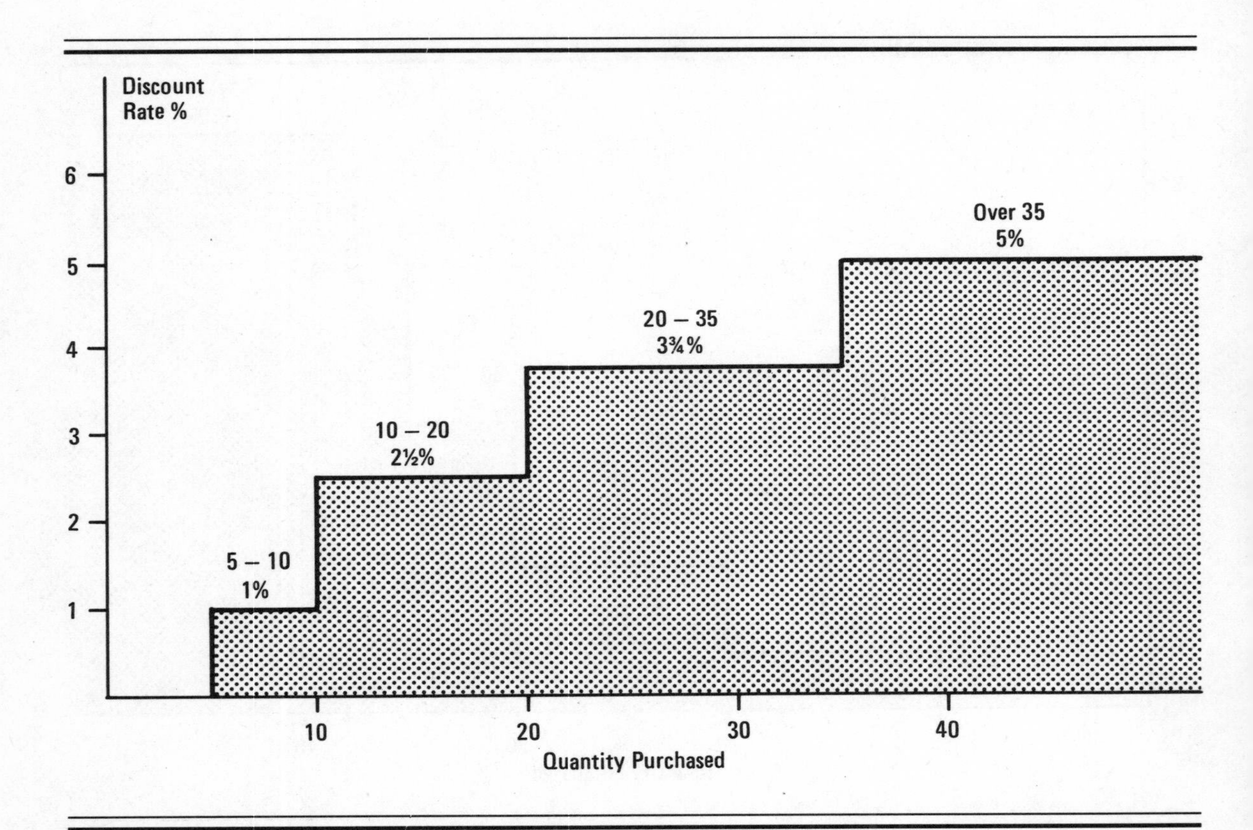

Figure 5.3 Regressive discount scale

When the limits and the shape of the steepness curve have been settled, it is necessary to check again carefully where on the scale each customer is likely to fall, and therefore what will be the amount of discount to be paid in total. This is usually an iterative process, in which a proposed new discount scale is tested for the results it will achieve both in total and for individual customers; to be revised again until the desired effect is attained.

Steps

If the discount on the *total* quantity increases as each quantity level is passed, the effect is to have a series of 'steps' in the scale. For example:

Deliveries of 1 tonne to 4.999 tonnes: 1% off total invoice
Deliveries over 5 tonnes: 2% off total invoice

This kind of scale produces the pricing anomaly that a quantity just above the step sells for *less* than a quantity just below the step, e.g.

4.995 tonnes @ £1,000 per tonne less 1% = £4,945
5.005 tonnes @ £1,000 per tonne less 2% = £4,905

It may be that this is precisely the effect aimed at, in order to give the strongest possible incentive to buyers to go for the larger quantity. But difficulty can arise if the supplier is unable to deliver the total quantity ordered – it is impossible to try to charge the customer more for delivering less. The anomaly can be minimised by having a discount scale consisting of a large number of very small steps, but this is inconvenient in practice.

Incremental scales

Anomalies can be avoided altogether by making the discount scale apply to the *incremental* quantity only. For example:

no discount off first 10 units
1% discount off next 10 units
2% discount off next 10 units
etc. etc.

This type of scale produces a smooth rate of increase in the discount allowed on the total quantity, without abrupt steps, as shown in Figure 5.4.

The figure also shows that with equal discount steps on the incremental quantities, the overall rate on the total quantity supplied will be half the level of discount, at the end of each increment. This makes it easy to calculate the discount scale required for a given level of total benefit.

To set an upper limit, the top discount step is turned into a 'ceiling'. The overall rate paid on large quantities will continually approach this ceiling, but never quite reach it.

Model trade terms

All businesses are different, but it is still possible to generalise about the objectives to be achieved by the terms offered by a manufacturer to his trade distributors. From what has been said already in this chapter, these objectives ought to be summarised as follows.

Consumer prices

The supplier should be well informed and have a strong influence over the actual prices charged by distributors, taking into account regional distribution costs and any other special factors.

Trade reward

Prices and discounts to the trade must be set so as to allow to each sector a level of reward sufficient to motivate it to perform enthusiastically the functions allotted to it, while respecting the resale prices planned for it.

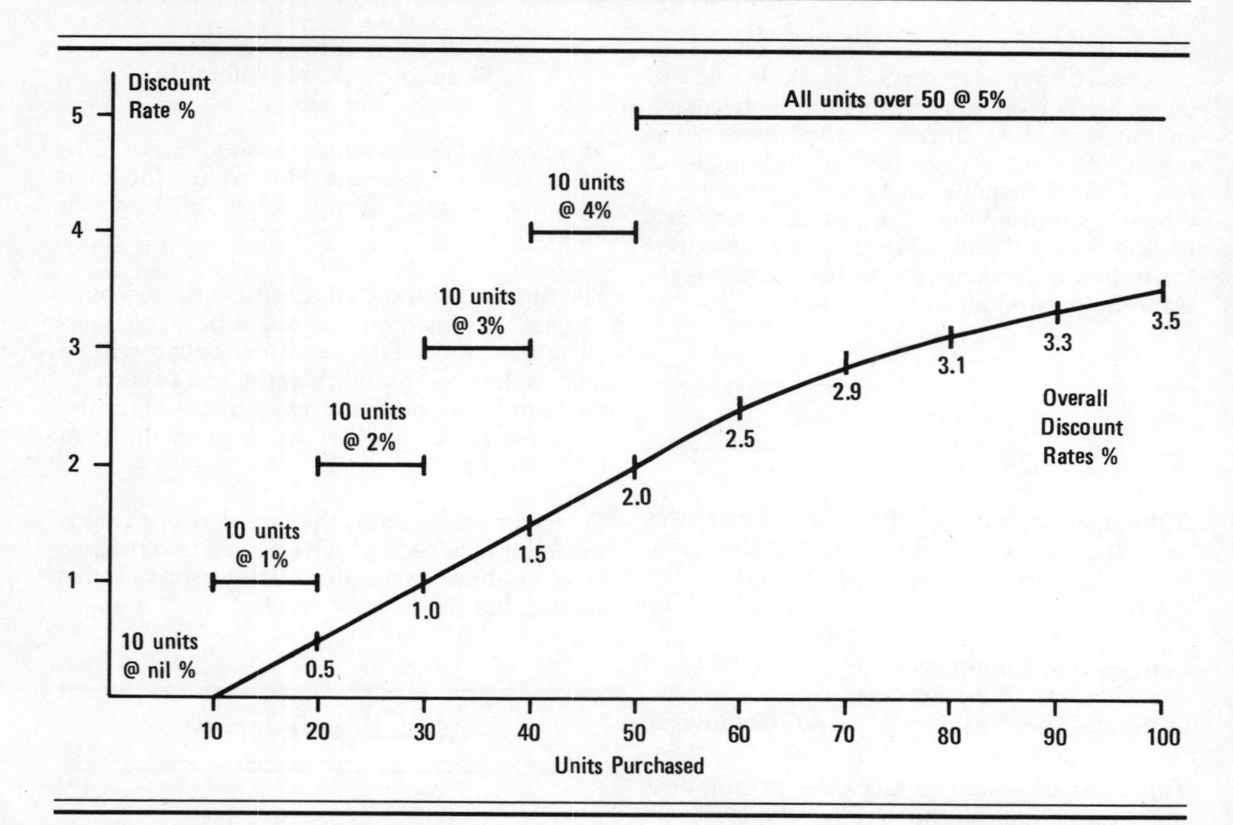

Figure 5.4 Incremental discount scale

Incentive

The discount structure should incite the trade to buy larger quantities in order to sell more. Such discounts must respect any local laws and feeling against discriminatory pricing, and should in any case be linked as far as possible to cost savings from larger deliveries. Discounts to large customers should not be just a surrender to buying power, and should not undermine differentials with other parts of the distributive structure. Ideally, terms should not have to be secret, but should be accessible to be viewed by all customers.

Functional performance

Trade sectors which have particular functions of redistribution to perform should be rewarded not against their status but specifically for the actual performance of services; such as stockholding, active selling, delivery and customer servicing.

Payment terms

Discounts and special terms should be made strictly conditional on compliance with the terms of payment laid down. Only if loss of these discounts is insufficient sanction should it be necessary to offer an additional discount for prompt payment, which must be additionally allowed for in prices to the trade.

Format and effects

The likely consequences of discount scales, both to the supplier and to individual customers, must be carefully estimated and anomalies checked.

Altering terms

It is one thing to lay down what should be the objectives of a set of trade terms, and possibly quite another to achieve them in practice. Most businesses will already have a set of terms established with their customers, and if these do not now fulfil all the objectives desired, the problem becomes one of how to implement change.

The purpose of altering trade terms ought to be to improve the total profit of the supplier, so the first thing to do is to make the best estimates possible of how customers would react to any proposed changes. If not all customers are going to be better off under a new scheme, it must be presumed that at least some of their business is at risk. For all principal customers and trade sectors, estimates must be made of anticipated sales volume at the new rates of discount which would apply, to see whether the total outcome is more profitable or not.

It will rarely be possible merely to announce a change in terms to buyers even when it is not necessarily to their disadvantage, and expect them to accept it without resistance. Much negotiation and compromise will be necessary and sometimes the risk of loss of business is too great to justify changing the trade terms at all. Implementation of revised terms can sometimes be made easier if combined with alterations in basic prices. This is one way in which inflation can be of service. If it is desired to eliminate some existing form of discount, the aim must be to increase basic prices at a time of general price increase (price control or other factors permitting) sufficiently to cover the cost of the existing discount as well. This discount can then be paid to everyone, and not just to those who formerly benefitted from it. The discount then becomes meaningless as such, and in due course it can be eliminated altogether in return for a corresponding reduction in list prices.

While old forms of discount are being extinguished in this way, new 'extra' rewards can be introduced. It may not be possible to cover all situations in this way, but every possible advantage should be taken of changes in basic prices to soften the blow of introducing new terms and discount structures and avoid the appearance of withdrawing any existing privileges.

Checklist 5

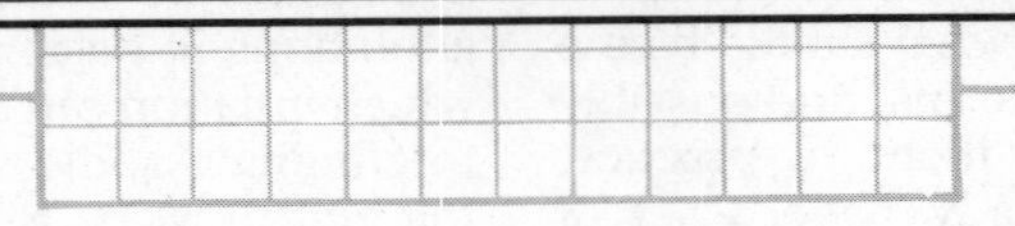

Terms for distributors

5.1 Consumer prices

(a) Are the prices charged to the ultimate user known? Are they planned by the manufacturer? Are they respected by the trade?
(b) Could a survey of consumer prices by carried out by the sales force? What would be the questionnaire format?
(c) If special promotional price offers are made, is the benefit intended to be retained by the trade, or passed on to the consumer? Is it passed on?

5.2 Distributor benefit

(a) What is known about the margins actually realised on company products by each category of distributor? Their rate of stockturn? Therefore their return on investment?
(b) Does the total on cost of moving products to the consumer through distributors seem a fair rate for the job? Could anyone else do it cheaper?

5.3 Discounts and terms

(a) How does the present system of discounts operate? Is it published? Are there special exceptions?
(b) Is the system inflation-proof? If not, how and when will adjustments be made to compensate for the effects of inflation?
(c) Does the system apply equitably? Overpay anyone? Underpay anyone? Create anomalies? Cause undercutting? Provide incentive for greater sales?
(d) What is the position on overdue payments from trade customers? Can slow payment be penalised?

6

Servicing and selling to the trade

Having decided which channels of distribution are to be used, and how they are to be rewarded, it is then necessary to consider two other aspects of dealing with the trade, which are very closely inter-related but nevertheless quite distinct. These are:

1. What kind of attention will have to be given to the practical needs of the trade, by way of providing services, assistance, support and supervision?
2. To what extent will active selling in to the trade be necessary and cost effective?

The two are inter-related in the sense that very often the same visit or the same activity can serve both purposes at once, so that it becomes easy to confuse the two objectives. Providing a practical service to the trade, such as for instance sending a salesman to check stocks, estimate forward requirements and make out a recommended order for replenishment, of course helps to sell at the same time. Calling regularly in order to increase the pressure of selling in itself provides a service – the trader is saved the necessity of keeping an eye on that portion of his stocks as he knows the supplier will do it for him. There may also be a third function involved, that of assisting the distributor to make sales in his turn to his own customers. However difficult it may be to distinguish the different functions that are being performed on any one occasion, it is still essential to have a clear idea in the first place of exactly what objectives are to be pursued in making contact with the trade. Only then is it possible to decide what kind of resources to use and what level of cost is justified.

How much effort?

On occasions a supplier may decide that no level of effort towards the trade is required at all. He may feel that his product is in such demand with users that no selling in to the trade is necessary. Consumers will be clamouring for supplies from the trade, and creating such a strength of demand 'pull' that there is no need for any additional supply 'push'. In these circumstances there may be no need to provide any services to the trade either. They can be left to their own devices, and those that look after themselves best will get the largest share of the profitable business which is on offer. The supplier's attitude can be strictly one of 'If you want it, come and get it'. The case study overleaf illustrates this point of view.

The functions of selling

Most suppliers will, however, find themselves faced with the need to decide exactly what kind of functions are likely to be worthwhile in support of dealings with the trade. We say only 'likely' at this stage, since a final decision can be taken only when the costs of proposed dealings are known. At this stage it is only necessary to take a view, in the light of experience, on what would be effective. Action can fall into three principal categories, each of which shades into the next; (a) selling in to the trade; (b) servicing

A case study

That this is no mere theoretical approach can be shown by the instance yet again of the animal feeds business in Britain in the early 1970s. We have cited a couple of object lessons from this industry already, and on this topic it provides yet a third. Having as we have seen decided to make all its sales through agricultural merchants, and none directly to farmers, the newly-merged AB feeds company concentrated all its marketing efforts on the farmer users. Advertising in the specialist media was backed up by a programme of regular visits to farmers, by way of offering specialist advice on livestock feeding, and of course encouraging the use of the AB brand. This campaign of farm visits was almost intensive enough to have supported direct dealing with farmers in the first place. It was also extremely effective; the farmer is a busy man but he is always very willing to stop and talk about his own animals to someone who is knowledgeable and understanding. Adding to this the very skilful use of a presence at agricultural shows and semi-social gatherings, the AB company was highly successful in getting its products accepted by the user and creating demand. The message to the farmer was simply that he would find the product stocked by all merchants; or else that he should tell his regular merchant to get it for him.

As far as the merchants were concerned, the message was that the mill gates were open at 6 a.m. every day, and that they should send their vehicles to collect what they needed. Normally orders were placed a little in advance and made ready for the collection time, but the company was also perfectly prepared to supply anyone purporting to be a merchant who arrived with cash to take delivery on the spot. A system of differential discounts was allowed, based on annual sales quantities, so that the largest merchant got the highest profit and could quote the keenest prices. This in itself was largely sufficient to deter small cash buyers, or even farmers themselves, from trying to purchase direct, as they could usually get just as good a price from a large merchant.

Here was a case of a supplier feeling secure enough in his consumer franchise to take the distributive trade for granted and let it look after itself. The sequel? After several years, it became apparent that the simple quantity discount structure was not making the market self-regulating as intended but was turning merchants more towards competing with one another rather than supporting the AB product against the competition. Merchants began to have a positive interest in offering their farmer clients something 'different' rather than the well-known AB brand, on which some other merchant was sure to be offering more of a cut price. Market share began to be lost. By degrees, the AB company had to respond by specifically choosing distributors on a semi-exclusive basis, each with his own shared territory, and cutting out indiscriminate supply. Support services were provided to these distributors, both to improve their own businesses and to back up their selling efforts to farmers. The company's own farm visits were no longer made in isolation, but as part of a planned programme in support of the appointed distributor. From having concluded that the distributive trade would fulfil a function automatically, and that no servicing or selling to it was required, the AB company was forced to the position of seeking support from it as an active ally, and giving it all the support possible in return. This too is likely to be the conclusion of the majority of suppliers seeking market distribution.

the trade and (c) supporting the trade in selling out.

Selling in to the trade is certainly the primary function, although not necessarily the most important. Again, there are several levels to distinguish, which will have a bearing on the kind of personnel needed to carry them out.

Major negotiation

Major negotiation will be concerned in the main with whether or not a given distributor is going to handle the product. The ostensible bargaining point may only be price, but if behind it there lies the threat of business being discontinued in case of disagreement, then the negotiation is a major one. It would also cover such matters as the settlement of a new distributorship agreement, discussions on a product to be 'tailor-made' for the trade, and so on.

The two points about major negotiations are that they are likely to require the presence of someone of rather higher calibre than a salesman; and that, by definition, they do not occur regularly (unless there is an annual bonus scheme in operation). Therefore this is not so much an activity that can be planned for, as a necessity that may arise at any moment and for which adequate resources must be held in reserve. Either senior management must be prepared to step in whenever required, or as outlined in chapter 4, the task can be delegated to an account manager.

Introductory selling

This is where the function of the sales organisation really is to make a sale. The need may arise comparatively rarely, essentially when a distributor has to be persuaded to begin buying for the first time. This ought to be either when an altogether new distributor customer is being recruited, or when a new line is being introduced to an existing distributor. Either way, the full powers of salesmanship (by which we mean insight into the customer's needs and how they can be met by the product) must be brought to bear. Clearly it is essential to assess very carefully the extent to which this capability will really be required. In a developing market situation, where new outlets have to be found, there will perhaps be predominant need for prospection and introductory techniques. In a stabilised market, one would not expect to have to re-sell the trade every time on the merits of the product. If one did, there would have to be something wrong with the product. The need is to decide whether this kind of selling will have to be the norm for the entire sales force, and to recruit accordingly; or whether it will be required only exceptionally, when perhaps a few senior men can look after it.

Maintenance selling

This is far and away the principal task of a sales force in charge of market distribution. The situation is one where the distributors called on have by and large already accepted the product, and the point at issue is not 'whether' but 'how much'. Naturally, at any moment an existing distributor customer may fall to the competition and stop buying; at which point all the techniques of selling to convince may be needed to get his custom back again. But most of the time selling to maintain the business of an established distributor calls for different techniques. The attitude of the distributor is usually the disarming one of 'You don't have to convince me – convince my customers'. Salesmanship of a particular kind is needed to maintain the pressure in a diplomatic way and try to gain a steadily greater share of the distributor's business away from competition. If the distributor is already working exclusively for the supplier, the pressure must be on him to increase his aggressiveness in the market. Doing this will inevitably involve providing training, example and assistance and so will merge into the provision of service in general. The extent of the need for this kind of selling pressure on the distributor network must again be carefully assessed. Describing it separately from introductory selling is not to downgrade its importance, merely to ensure that the need for it is correctly identified and quantified. The task is not just to maintain the existing level of sales; but to maintain relationships and thereby ensure growth.

Routine order taking

This description applies to situations where the supplier is sufficiently confident of having retained the distributor's commitment, and is concerned only to remedy his forgetfulness or preoccupation with other things by calling regularly to work out his order for him and save him the trouble of mailing it. A vast amount of routine contact with distributors is in fact at this level and for a great deal of the time it is all that is required. Obviously it is essential to identify accurately the cases where routine order taking will suffice, both to avoid giving less attention than is due in other cases, and to benefit from any cost saving in using less highly qualified personnel where possible. To be realistic, there is precious little of the selling function in this kind of activity, and little to distinguish it from a routine service to the distributor, albeit one which will err on the side of the supplier when it comes to order quantities. The role can very well be combined with maintenance selling. One selling visit can alternate with several order taking visits, which are sufficient to keep the account going in the meantime. Telephone contact can often do the order taking job, always assuming the order is not too complex, and that the distributor customer actually does know what he needs.

Both routine order taking and maintenance selling can as a rule be scheduled – the tasks are recurring ones and the *frequency* with which each is required must also be assessed with care. Essentially this will depend very much on logistic issues: the amount of stockholding the distributor will carry; therefore the frequency at which replenishment is required; thence how often orders must be obtained; and finally, how many such occasions can be left to an order taker rather than a salesman.

Physical distribution

A major form in which service has to be provided to the trade is the physical delivery of supplies of the product. This has to be organised in such a way as to provide an acceptable frequency of supply and an acceptable response time to orders, at the minimum cost to the supplier. An initial choice is whether to pass on the problem in whole or in part to transport contractors, or for the supplier to provide his own service. Either way, the requirement on the strategy planner is the same, to work out and specify what is the realistic level of delivery service which it will be justifiable to provide to distributors. It is not in the scope of this book to deal with the science of physical distribution, which is an entire subject in itself. Simply because it is so complex, ranging from the design of warehouses and the calculation of stock requirements to the planning of routes for vehicles, there is a tendency for physical distribution questions to be left to specialists, who then are inclined to determine what is to be done as well as how to do it. It is essential for trade marketing management to remain firmly in control of the objectives to be met, and the kind of service required, and to communicate these clearly to those responsible, whether an outside contractor or colleagues within the same company.

Service level

The first thing to settle is the so-called 'service level', i.e. the extent to which the supplier can meet incoming orders from available stock, or within so many days from receipt. Normally this is expressed as a target percentage for each product. Sometimes the percentage is used to refer only to the numbers of *orders* for the product which have been met in full, irrespective of quantities involved, but it is usually more informative to take total quantity into account. It is not very helpful to have a statistic which says that 99 out of 100 orders were met, if the 100th that was not met was for as large a quantity as all the others put together. The object of setting a service level is merely to have a reasonable definition to those concerned of what is wanted and a reasonable measure of how far it is being achieved. It may even be appropriate to measure service level against the sales which were *forecast* for the period, as well as against actual orders which were received. The forecast is the only target which those responsible can work to, and it is only fair that their performance should be judged against this, rather than against an actual level of demand which they were not told to expect.

As with the level of distribution availability referred to in chapter 2, a realistic service level can only be set in the light of experience, and 100 per cent, or even 99 per cent, is not realistic. Achieving a service level of course involves every function throughout a manufacturing company, production, purchasing, personnel and finance. The two essential points are that, firstly, the joint product and trade planning processes must make the predictions of what quantities are likely to be required; and secondly, trade marketing management must lay down the level of performance aimed at. In doing so, they make themselves responsible for the level of costs involved. Ability to meet all orders on receipt is very largely a matter of investment in a sufficiently high level of stocks to cater for all possible fluctuations in demand. In the same way as product marketing management must agree with trade marketing management what level of distribution availability in the trade is cost justifiable, so must trade marketing management agree with their production and stock control colleagues what level of supply availability is cost justifiable.

Delivery time

Given that the product is available from stock when the order is received, the total time required to put it into the hands of the trade customer will be a function of:

1 The actual transportation time
2 The frequency with which transport to that destination can be made available.

If a transport contractor, such as a railway, provides a daily service to the destination required, then the frequency problem is to all intents solved, and delivery time involves only loading and transit time. (But even a daily frequency is not always sufficient – suppliers of drugs urgently required by pharmacies have to be prepared to make several deliveries a day to the same destination.) If there is no such frequent service the question is how soon can a trip to that area be organised. Without going into all the complexities, this depends very much on whether the transport service, whatever it is, is working in a purely reactive fashion to demand, or whether it is trying to plan ahead and schedule its routes. In the former situation sufficient reserves of vehicles have to be available. One can visualise the transport manager receiving a pile of delivery instructions at the end of the day, calling his drivers in, and saying: 'Right, boys; this is where we have to go tomorrow' – regardless of the fact that they had already been there yesterday and will probably have to go there again the day after. As a rule, this will be a much more expensive approach to giving delivery service than if journeys to particular areas are scheduled at regular intervals, and orders are held over until the next scheduled departure.

Scheduled deliveries

Trade marketing management must consider very carefully how far it would be appropriate to schedule deliveries to their distributor customers, and what consequent maximum delays to deliveries would be acceptable. It is immaterial whether the transport service is being provided by the company itself or by outside contractors; in the latter case it is even more important to specify exactly what system is to be operated, since the contractor will certainly charge accordingly. Clearly, the frequency and time lag on deliveries are very much bound up with what arrangements are to be made for selling in to distributors and soliciting their orders, which as we saw before are in turn bound up with their stockholding and financing needs. A general rule would be that at least the previous order must have been delivered before the next one is asked for – it is quite impossible both for the salesman and for the client, not to say for the credibility of the business, to have to take into account a previous order not delivered while trying to get the next one. It is possible to go even further. If orders are being collected from customers on a regular, cyclical basis, then this of itself may provide an outline schedule which the delivery services can follow. Deliveries to the areas which salesmen have visited can be timed to be made a few days afterwards, giving sufficient time for the orders they have obtained to be made up ready for despatch.

At its most sophisticated, this issue may even have to be resolved by comparing the real costs of travelling salesmen versus delivery services, and deciding which one to optimise at the expense of the other. This might mean turning the question on its head and deciding that salesmen should call at times most convenient for the scheduling of subsequent deliveries. In some companies there can be long arguments over whether the delivery van should follow the salesman, or whether the salesman should run ahead of the delivery van. The point is that delivery services are very much a part of the selling strategy of the business and the level of service to be provided must be discussed and agreed by trade marketing management. Thereafter the specialists in physical distribution can be left to work out how best to provide it, in terms of warehousing needs, local depots, vehicle routeings and so on.

Other services

Other forms of service and support to the distributive trade will be more completely the responsibility of the sales organisation itself. Under the heading of direct assistance to the distributor in running his own business will come:

1 Ensuring that his stocks are properly controlled, stored, rotated ('first in, first out') and re-ordered.
2 Instituting proper administration and records, of his own customers, of sales statistics, of complaints and claims and so on.
3 Providing training to his staff, whether as salesmen or as product specialists.

Activities more directly concerned with helping the distributor to sell on the product range to his own customers will include:

1 Setting up displays, installing advertising material, advising on layout and decor, supervising promotions and (in self-service establishments) carrying out 'merchandising' – that is, ensuring that stock is brought forward to the shelves, properly priced, given adequate shelf space, made clean, tidy and attractive (more is said about this in chapter 11).
2 Giving product demonstrations or sampling to the distributor's customers.
3 Backing up the distributor's own sales efforts by accompanying his salesmen, giving on-the-job training by example, or calling separately on his customers to reinforce calls already made.

Finally, there are the unglamourous tasks which the sales organisation must carry out for its own account; such as the reporting of market activity and competitors, the reporting of the results of promotions, the keeping of records on sales and customers, and possibly even the collection of cash.

Resource requirements

Once a view has been taken on the different forms and levels of selling and servicing to be adopted, the next thing to be considered is the *kind* of manpower resources which will be required to perform them. Delivery services are likely to be a special case, in that resources will be provided by an outside contractor, or at least by another department of the company; but all other requirements will have to be met by the sales organisation itself. Immediately the question of specialisation arises. For all the various tasks to be performed, how many differently qualified groups of people are needed? Some of the main needs for specialisation of staff are discussed below.

Different product groups

One of the commonest reasons for specialist divisions in a sales organisation is that the product range is too diverse to be handled by the one group of generalist sales people. Each product group is said to require a special understanding in order to be discussed properly with prospective customers. This may be true, but the proposition has to be questioned very thoroughly, to see if the logic holds up. First of all, are the products really so technical that the same salesman cannot have sufficient knowledge of them all? In his selling interviews, particularly with distributors, are issues of deep technicality in fact going to come up? It may be possible to isolate the need for expert specialism to a very small group of technicians, on call when needed, while day to day concerns are dealt with by generalist salesmen. Or it may be that the real problem is not so much the technicality of the products, as that the total *number* of them is too great for one salesman to discuss in one selling interview, or for the customer to listen to. The customer on his side may go in for product specialisation, so that the salesman for different product groups would have to talk to quite different people in any case.

If the different product groups are sold largely to different groups of customers, then specialist salesmen in each group can make their calls without overlapping visits to the same customers. The total amount of work to be done is the same as if one group of salesmen called on all customers, except only that the time spent on travelling will be greater. If each salesman has to visit only some of the customers in an area, leaving the others to other specialists, then his customers will tend to be more spread out than if he had to visit everyone; with consequent increased distances and travelling time between them.

Where the different product groups are sold to the same customers – as is often the case with distributors – then specialist sales forces will be calling a second time on each other's customers. This is extremely wasteful, unless particularly good reasons can be found to justify it, such as that customers themselves prefer it, and react favourably. More commonly, the opposite will be true – a busy customer prefers to get all his dealings with one supplier disposed of at one time.

A solution to the difficulties of a large and diverse product range can sometimes be found along the lines of dealing with different items on different occasions in a cyclical pattern, so that each gets the same amount of attention at the same intervals; combined with having real specialists available for technical questions or in case of trouble.

Different trade categories

A second cause for specialisation is the converse of the above, whereby the trade customers for the same group of products may themselves be so different as to require a completely different selling approach, and therefore separate specialist groups of salesmen to deal with them. Where a manufacturer is selling the same products to different classes of users, the salesmen concerned may well require special knowledge of the users' technical processes, and therefore the appointment of separate groups of specially qualified salesmen can easily be justified. But when the argument is that a different kind of salesman is required to deal with wholesalers compared to retailers; or with pharmacies as against supermarkets; or with builders' merchants rather than do-it-yourself shops – then the facts have to be checked on very closely. Certainly, when segregating salesmen according to the type of outlet called on, there is no overlapping of calls, and so no extra expense on that score, but average travelling time will again be increased and complications may be introduced into the sales organisation for no good reason. Any increase in effectiveness through allowing salesmen to specialise according to type of trade customer would have to be fully proven in order to justify the undoubted extra cost.

Different selling functions

If real differences can be identified in the *tasks to be done* in the course of selling interviews, these may provide compelling reasons for specialisation in the sales organisation. The previous two situations, specialisation by product and specialisation by customer, are really only particular cases of different tasks being required; and this can occur even when the products being discussed are the same, and the customers are of the same class. So it is generally more useful to look for genuine differences in the kind of work to be performed, rather than outward differences in the surrounding circumstances.

Differences in selling and servicing functions have already been described, and one of them – major negotiation with important accounts – already identified as justifying the appointment of specialist account managers rather than being left to generalist salesmen. It remains to see whether there are any other areas of dealing with distributor customers that really would be better handled by different groups of people.

Sales support

A distinction is often possible between real salesmanship, and the order taking or support role. If there is a large element of routine or even manual work, such as stock counting, display building or merchandising, involved in keeping distributors serviced, then it may seem worthwhile not to waste the time of a fully qualified salesman on such tasks, but to use lower cost manpower hired specially for the purpose. It is however necessary to be sure that the saving in rates of pay outweighs the cost of organising and splitting the work between two or more people.

Subordinate tasks of this kind can often be done by junior or trainee sales staff, and the work provides an excellent training ground for eventual salesmen. But if there are insufficient numbers under training at any one time, it will be necessary to hire less qualified staff specially for the purpose. In some countries 'general help' of this kind is available from agencies, who undertake to find the staff and get the work done for an inclusive fee. Otherwise, the selling organisation has to try to find the right kind of secondary employees in exactly the right numbers to provide sales support where and when it is required.

Staff hired for simple tasks can be paid less than salesmen, but this will be a cost saving only to the extent that they can be kept fully and productively employed. The need for sales support work and assistance to salesmen is likely to arise in quite a patchy fashion both in place and time, so that compiling work schedules to keep secondary staff fully occupied may be quite complex. If such staff can be employed on a part time basis only, it may be easier to engage them only for when they are required, without idle time or excessive travelling between jobs. Part time staff usually also imply less liability for social costs and job security than do full time employees.

Organising and controlling casual staff takes a lot of time, and supervision costs must not be underestimated. Sometimes it is quicker for a salesman to do a job himself, rather than arrange for an assistant to come and do it and then have to check on the work afterwards. Either the assistant follows the salesman around wastefully until he is needed, or the two must arrange how and where they are to meet, and what jobs the assistant can get on with in the meantime. Having said that, however, using secondary support staff as and when required can add enormously to the flexibility and scope of a selling organisation. The effective range of a first class salesman is greatly increased if he can merely make a note of all the secondary tasks which can be done later by an assistant, and get on to the next customer. Since support staff can perfectly well undertake routine order taking duties, by using them it is possible to extend direct selling coverage to smaller outlets which it would not otherwise have been economical to service direct.

To sum up therefore: at this stage the whole range of desirable activities in regard to the trade should have been reviewed, and a provisional choice made from among methods of negotiating, selling, supporting, servicing and supplying to distributors; as well as deciding on the different kinds, groups, and grades of staff which would be necessary. It now remains to calculate what the costs will be.

Time standards and costs

Knowledge of the costs of proposed selling and servicing activity will demonstrate whether or not the activity is justifiable in the light of sales expectations from the customer. For example, suppose that to get the business of a certain class of distributor it would be necessary to send a salesman every two weeks to discuss an order, plus an assistant to check stocks and build displays, and that the sales potential through that distributor is £*x* a year; would it be economic? If not, would visits at a lesser frequency still bring in enough business to make it economic? To calculate the costs of selling activity it is essential to know how much *time* each activity will require, on the part of each category of staff, in the circumstances which apply to each particular customer. Accurate timing estimates not only enable each kind of activity to be costed, but also show the total numbers of staff required in each category, once the total amount of work has been added up. This calculation is basic to the proper planning and control of sales force activity.

It is very common practice for sales force performance to be controlled, and the cost of selling calls calculated, purely on the basis of the average number of *calls per day* which can be achieved. If all calls are in fact being made on exactly the same kind of customer, for exactly the same objects, then it may be perfectly valid to say that all calls can be treated alike and that all salesmen should be able to make the same number of calls per day – which is the same thing as saying that all calls take the same average time. But where calls and customers are different, this approach can be seriously misleading. An average conceals differences. If we merely count the average number of calls made per day, we make no distinction between the cost of a salesman spending hours with one customer, and ten minutes with the next. In order to assign costs correctly, and so decide what strategy to adopt, there is no alternative to finding out as accurately as possible how much time is needed for different customer related activities.

Standard times

Deciding how much time is required for a specific task is known as setting a *standard time* for it. This concept is very generally understood and accepted as regards repetitive work in a factory, using the techniques of work study. By this process, an experienced observer notes how long it takes a man to do a particular job, say the assembly of some component; judges what rate he is working at, whether fast or slow; and from this computes the time which would be required by a man working at whatever is regarded as the normal pace. This standard time for the job is then made the basis for bonus payments to those who produce more in the time, and so the actual time set can become very contentious. What is not generally in dispute is that it is possible to set a standard time which will be applicable to every occasion the job is done, since the job itself is the same every time.

Applying the concept of standard times to the work of a sales organisation if often a good deal more difficult to accept. Salesmen and sales managers rightly object that every selling visit to a customer is different, that it is impossible to know in advance how long it is going to take, and that a sales interview with a customer cannot simply be ended when the fixed time is up. All of this is very true, but it is still possible to make very practical use of the idea of standard times for sales force tasks.

The first thing to be clear about is that in this context a standard time can only be the *average* time required for a particular kind of selling job. If we observe dozens of salesmen making hundreds of calls on very similar customers, covering much the same topics each time, and the average of all the times taken is 30 minutes, with the majority of individual timings all clustering around the 30 minutes mark, then we can begin to say not unreasonably that probably the average time required for such calls will continue to be 30 minutes in future. If similarly we find that with a different type of customer the average is 45 minutes, then it is not unreasonable to allow 30 minutes for calls on the one type of customer, and 45 minutes for the other. This is all that is meant by standard time allowances for selling activity.

The time actually required on any one occasion may vary. All that the standard time predicts is that over a month or over a year, the time taken on average will come out close to the standard. If the salesman is given work based on a fixed daily total of standard times, he may have to work for a greater or less time on any one day, to get all jobs completed, but he can expect that his hours of work will balance out in total over a period.

Setting standards

In order to set standard times, it is necessary to begin by observing accurately how the workforce is performing at present. In a completely new situation it might be necessary to set standards purely by guesswork in the first place, but then to amend them by actual observation as quickly as possible once the workforce has settled down.

To arrive at standard times for selling jobs, the first thing is to ensure that the sales force is performing its tasks *correctly*, and at an acceptable *rate*. This should in any case be a normal part of the supervision of a sales force, through regular accompaniment and on-the-job training by local management to correct any inefficient practices. There are three things to look out for:

1 Any tasks or practices which are unnecessary must be eliminated.

2 The remaining tasks which are necessary must then be done in the most efficient manner, to avoid waste of time.
3 Salesmen must work at an acceptable pace without slacking, and be prepared to go on doing so for the proper number of hours per day.

Making observations

Once all these conditions are fulfilled, it is possible to begin to observe and record how much time is being taken to carry out sales calls on different types of customer, in different situations. This is not a difficult job to do, provided supervisors who accompany salesmen follow a careful routine. Figure 6.1 shows a format in which observations can conveniently be recorded, for results to be extracted afterwards.

It may look complex, but is in practice very simple.

The record to be kept is in the form of a 'log sheet' on which all activities and times throughout a salesman's working day are noted. A salesman's day can be considered to be made up of only three different kinds of activity:

1 Selling calls on customers
2 Driving (or other travelling) to, from, and between customers
3 Everything else, which we can call 'interruptions'; e.g. meal breaks, telephoning, administration work and so on.

Therefore the daily record form contains three columns, one for each of these kinds of activity. In each column, the activity can be further defined by a series of code numbers; e.g. each call or customer can be given a reference number, interruptions can be coded from 1 upwards to describe what they were about, and so on. Figure 6.1 shows how these are entered.

The information required is the number of elapsed minutes spent on each activity. Since it is confusing to work out elapsed times in one's head while keeping an eye on a salesman, it is much safer to record the actual time by one's watch at the start of each event. That way, no time goes unaccounted for – the finishing time of each event must be the starting time of the next one. Therefore in the left hand column of the form goes the actual observed time of day at the *start* of each event. The type of event, and the coding for it, is noted in the corresponding column. When that event ends, and the next one begins, the time is again noted on the next line of the left hand column. Subtracting the two times of day gives the number of elapsed minutes for the first event, which is entered in column 2.

Since for many of us it is somehow easier to subtract 'downwards' rather than upwards, Figure 6.1 shows the record being kept from the bottom of the form up. Each time figure is then subtracted from the one above it. This is not obligatory, however, and the record can be kept the other way round if preferred. (But do remember that subtracting times is not the same as subtracting decimal numbers – subtract the hours figures first, multiply by 60, then add to the upper minutes figure before subtracting the lower one.)

From a set of records of this kind it is then an easy matter to carry out a subsequent analysis on the following lines:

1 Average length of the working day, start to finish, and average starting and finishing times.
2 Average times spent on travelling, to and from first and last customers, and between customers.
3 Average times spent on breaks, administration work and other interruptions.
4 A listing of actual times spent on sales calls, each identifiable through its reference number.

Call time distribution

The next stage could be attempted scientifically, by those with a taste for statistics and computing; but in practice a trial and error approach will serve equally well. What one must now do is try to find whether there is any correlation between particular *types of call* on *types of customers*, and the lengths of time which have been observed. At the extreme, if one were to find that all calls congregated closely

DAILY LOG SHEET

Observer A. Brown Salesman B. Jones Date 12 Dec

Time at Start of Activity	Elapsed Minutes per Activity	Selling Calls : Customer Reference	Driving : Type Code	Interruptions : Type Code
1006		A19		
0952	14			9
0940	12		2	
0905	35	B62		
0850	15		2	
0845	5			2
0800	45	A123		
0730	30		1	

Driving Codes :

1 = to first customer
2 = between customers
3 = from last customer

Interruption Codes :

1 = meal break
2 = telephoning
3 = administration
9 = any other

Figure 6.1 Sales force timing record

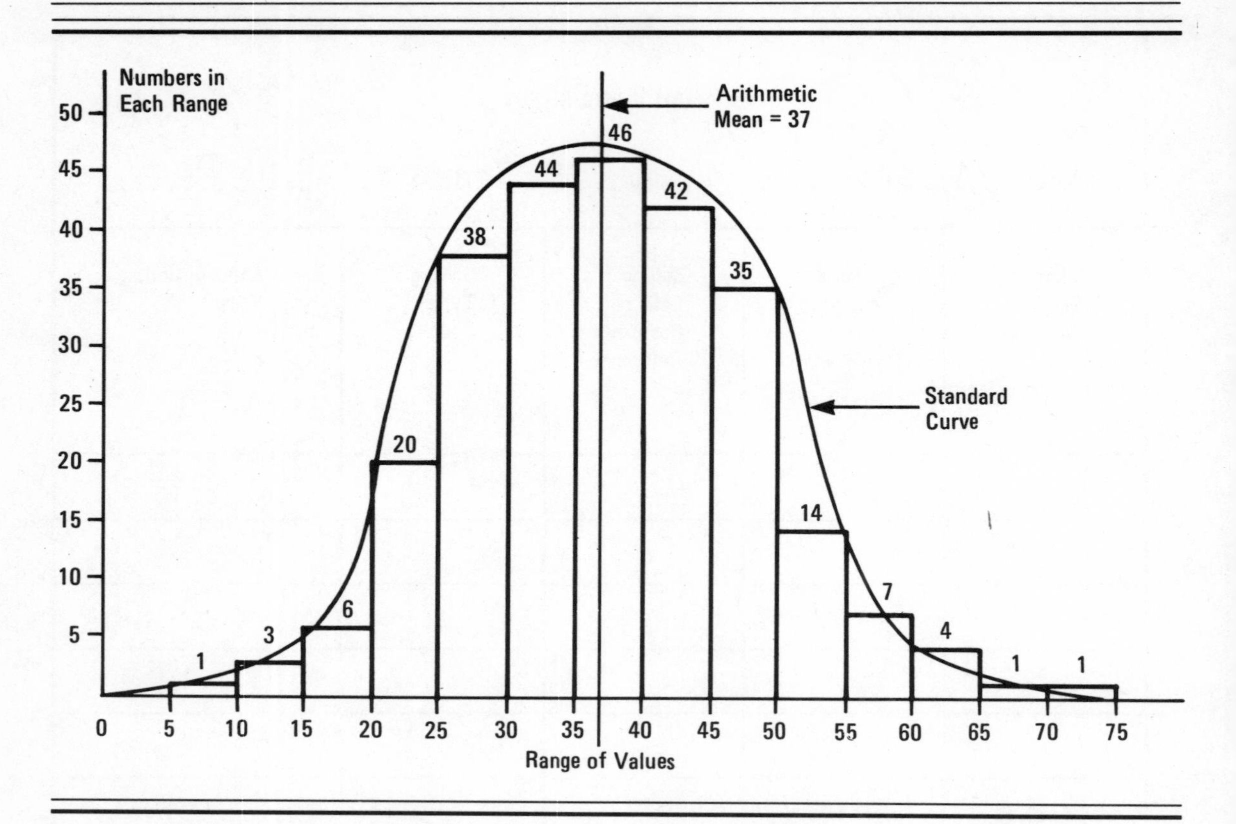

Figure 6.2 Normal distribution chart

around the same average time, then it would be fair to conclude that there was no significant difference between calls, and that the same standard time could be allowed for all of them. This is unlikely however. More probably, it will be found that when calls are grouped according to certain key features, each group forms a more or less consistent distribution around its own average, which is significantly different from other groups. To put it mathematically, what one is looking for in each group is a 'normal' distribution with a low standard deviation about its mean.

A normal distribution of results is one which, if plotted in bar chart form as in Figure 6.2 produces a 'bell-shaped curve'; that is, equally spread on either side of the average or mean, and declining first rapidly then slowly outwards.

If one visualises water being sprayed from a hose towards the centre of a row of very tall jars standing side by side, one would expect the jars to fill up very much in this pattern – the slight randomness of the spray on either side of centre would fill the jars at the side less than the ones in the middle, just as shown in the bar chart.

The best way to go about this in practice is to put together calls believed to be similar as to key features, and then judge by eye how close the timings seem to come to this ideal. One is not looking for minor differences after all, only major groupings. A useful tip is to discard the highest and lowest times in a group, on the grounds that these are most likely to be due to unusual circumstances; and then see if the rest of the grouping is consistent. Differences in average call times might be expected under the headings of:

1 The type of visit: was it scheduled, by appointment, on prospection, abortive?
2 The type of customer: are selling calls different according to whether the customer is a retailer, a wholesaler, a main distributor, a sub-stockist, or so on?
3 The size of customer: does the size of

his business make a difference to the length of the selling call?

4 The work to be done: are certain jobs, e.g. stock counting, building displays, needed on some calls and not on others?
5 The frequency of call: do calls take less time when they are made more often?

At the end of this process, it should be possible to put together a very simple table of standard time allowances for the main distinguishable groups, which might look something like Table 6.1.

Table 6.1
Standard times for calls

Type of call	*Standard time*
Wholesalers, over 1,000 sq.metres weekly calls with stock check	90 minutes
Same but without stock check	40 minutes
Direct buying retailer, with merchandising	30 minutes
Support call, small shop, with display check	15 minutes
etc.	etc.

Projecting forward

As with nearly every procedure mentioned in this book, setting standard times is an iterative and circular process. There would be no point in going to all this trouble merely in order to put on record and make official exactly what the sales force is already doing. It is necessary to start from what the sales force is doing at present, but in the expectation that some changes will have to be made. Keeping in mind the original objective, which is to refine the strategy of getting distribution through the trade, the intention is to find out:

1 What exactly does the sales force do, how long does it take to do it, and therefore what costs are being incurred in each trade category?
2 What should the sales force be used to do in future?
3 What would that cost?

Therefore, having worked out standard times for current activities, in all probability it will be necessary to amend them and project them forward to cover slightly different ways of working in future. The observation exercise is very likely to reveal that disproportionate amounts of time are being spent on certain activities. Remember that, to quote Northcote Parkinson, 'work expands to fill the time available'. If a salesman has a whole morning available for a job, he will do nothing else that morning. It may be thought, for example, that 50 minutes is too long to spend on checking stocks in a wholesaler, that it is simply not worth it. The concept of standard time allowances implies balancing what could be done against the benefit the company may get from it. Salesmen, and even customers, may have to be told that such and such an activity must only take so long in future. When a salesman finds himself overrunning the time allowed, he must diplomatically get himself out of it, or at least make sure he does not spend so long next time. Standard times have to be set, based on the evidence of current practice, amended for any proposed ways of working in future, which in turn will take some account of what is economically justifiable for that class of customer.

Driving and interruptions

To complete the quantification of sales force work, standard times should be set for travelling, and for the 'interruptions' that have to be allowed for. These standard times will in general be the averages that have been found by observation, again amended insofar as ways of reducing the time required can be found. For example, if excessive time seems to be spent on driving between customers, perhaps the route planning can be improved – see chapter 8. Time spent on administration can perhaps be reduced by better systems – see chapter 10.

In calculating standard travelling times it may be necessary to distinguish between one region and another, and between cities, towns and rural districts, finding as different average for each. Results should look something like Tables 6.2 and 6.3.

Table 6.2
Standard driving times

Region A:		
to and from first and last customers		30 minutes
between customers:	in towns	8 minutes
	in country	15 minutes
Region B:		
to and from first and last customers		45 minutes
between customers:	in towns	10 minutes
	in country	20 minutes
etc.		etc.

Table 6.3
Standard interruption times

Personal breaks and meals	60 minutes
Administration, daily reports	30 minutes
Contingencies	10 minutes
etc.	etc.

Commuting to work

Finally, the norm must be set for the length of the salesman's working day. This will depend on what, if any, time is allowed for travel between his home and the first and last customers each day. In some situations, it may be possible to take the view that a salesman should travel to his place of work, i.e. his first customer, in his own time like everybody else; and that therefore his working day should be counted only from the first to the last customer irrespective of the time taken to get there and back. If distances are very considerable, it may be necessary to make separate allowance for this, but making the working day longer in proportion, counting from leaving home to returning home.

Productive time

It is then possible to work out how much *productive time* is available in a salesman's standard day; that is, the time available for selling visits to customers, plus the unavoidable time spent in travelling from one to another. A specimen calculation is shown in Table 6.4.

The amount of time spent on driving between calls depends on how many calls are made in a day. It is therefore not possible to set a standard amount of between-call driving for a day, and deduct it from the productive time, as we do for the other fixed time allowances, since we do not yet know how many calls are to be made. Therefore the only way to deal with between-call driving time is to add it to the standard time for each call, according to where the call is located. Thus, using the examples given in the tables, if we have a wholesaler call with stock checking located in a town in Region B, the total standard time for the call will be 90 minutes plus 10 minutes driving, or 100 minutes in total. The number of calls which can be made in a day is then the number whose standard times including driving can be fitted into the total productive time available.

To be completely accurate, the number of between-call driving allowances should be one less than the number of calls in a day. Since in practice we are adding a driving allowance to every call, the equivalent of one allowance should strictly speaking be deducted from the driving home time or the other fixed allowances.

Figure 6.3 will make this clear. However, as this is likely to be only a matter of 10 or 15 minutes in a whole day, and we are not working to that degree of accuracy, the issue is not of vital importance.

Costs per man

Once all these standard times have been fixed, it is possible finally to calculate the cost of per-

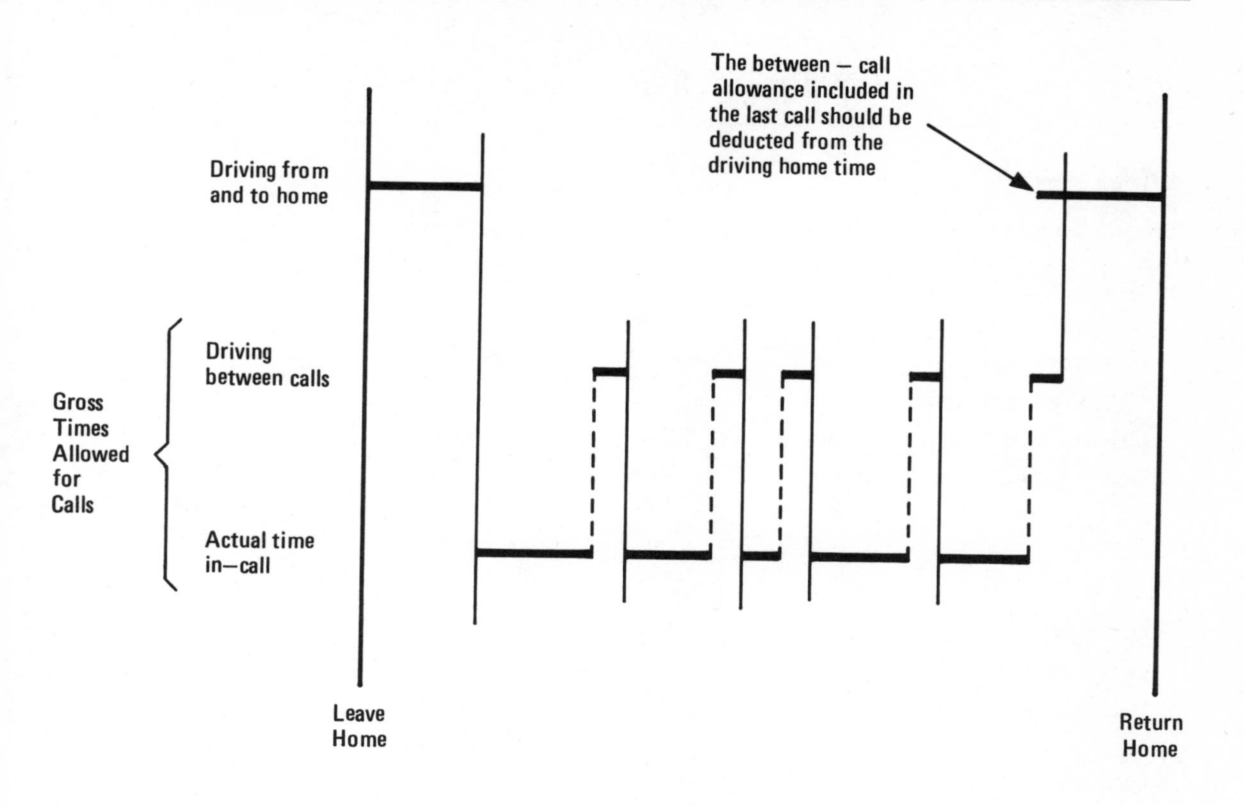

Figure 6.3 The between-call driving allowance

forming the various selling and servicing tasks that are being planned. The cost of an activity will be the time it takes, multiplied by the cost per hour or per minute of the person who does it. However, calculating the hourly cost of an employee does require a little care.

For the salesman, or whoever else is to do the job, take the annual cost of employing him: salary, bonus, pension contribution, social security payments, depreciation of car, running costs of car, other travel costs, meal expenses, hotel expenses, etc. Next consider what, if any, overhead costs are incurred solely on account of the salesman and which would not arise at all if there were no field sales force. In this category will come any sales managers engaged entirely in supervising the sales force, the costs of any area sales offices and so on. People like the sales director should not be included, on the grounds that there would probably still have to be one even if there were no field sales force. Take the annual cost of all these direct overheads, divide them by the number of salesmen, and add this equal share to the cost of each salesman. Divide the total cost of a salesman by the number of working days in a year – after holidays, average sickness time, sales conferences and so on – to get his cost per working day.

This cost must be absorbed by the *useful* tasks done in a day (hence this kind of calculation is known as absorption costing). In the case of our salesman, the only tasks which can be considered useful are his selling calls on customers, inclusive of between-call driving. On the assumption that his available productive time each day can be kept fully occupied with such calls, then his total daily cost can be spread over the daily productive time. This would mean dividing the salesman's daily cost

Table 6.4
Productive time available

Grade 1 salesmen	*Region B*	
Standard working day @ 10 hours		600 minutes
Deduct:		
Personal breaks	60	
Administration	30	
Other interruptions	10	
Driving time to first customer	45	
Driving time from last customer	45	
		190
Balance available for calls and between-call driving		410 minutes

by the total number of productive minutes to get his cost per minute. Table 6.5 gives a fully worked example of a calculation of costs per salesman minute.

These calculations assume that the whole of the available productive time per day can be kept fully occupied, which may be quite difficult to achieve. If only a smaller time on average can be utilised, the usable productive time must be set correspondingly lower, thereby increasing the standard cost per minute.

Cost per activity

The true cost of a sales call on a customer, or any other form of service, can therefore now be found by multiplying the standard time, inclusive of between-call driving, by the standard cost per minute of the person performing it. Using our previous examples, a support call on a small shop in the country in Region B would cost 15 plus 20 minutes multiplied by 22.22 pence, or £7.78. A call on a wholesaler in a town in Region A would cost 90 plus 8 minutes multiplied by 22.22 pence, or £21.77.

Marginal costing

Once all of a salesman's costs have been absorbed by fully occupied productive time, anything else which he can still manage to do in a day would not then incur any salesman cost. Suppose that around 410 minutes productive time is available, but only 380 minutes on average can be kept filled with productive work; and this latter figure is used for costing. This would leave an average of 30 minutes a day of 'spare' time, free of cost. Such time can then be used for other jobs which would not justify the full normal cost of doing them. Some tasks can therefore be undertaken on the basis: 'The salesman is there anyway – he has nothing else to do – it costs nothing to do it'. If a salesman has 30 minutes or more in hand at the end of a scheduled day, it would be ridiculous for him to go home early just because his costs for the day have already been covered. He may be able to use the time to call on less important customers, or give some assistance to his larger customers which would not normally justify his full costs.

Work done on this kind of 'marginal cost'

Table 6.5
Salesman costs

Average salary		£8,000
Bonus, pension etc.		2,000
Average car and travel costs		5,000
Costs of field supervision:		
Area Managers	£100,000	
Offices etc.	150,000	
	£250,000	
No. of salesmen: 50		
Share of supervision:		
£250,000/50		5,000
Total direct cost per man		£20,000
Working days per year: 225		
Cost per working day:		
£20,000/225	£88.88	
Usable productive time per day: 400 minutes		
Cost per productive minute:		
£88.88/400	22.22 pence	

basis must be watched very carefully to ensure that it does not encroach on time which could in fact be spent on tasks that could justify the full cost. The aim must be to keep available time filled to the maximum with cost-paying jobs, so that the overall cost rate per minute is kept down; rather than letting only a few large jobs absorb all the costs, and allowing a lot of other unimportant work to be done free. A good rule of thumb is to beware of work being done *regularly* on a marginal cost basis. If it can be scheduled regularly, this implies that the time involved could equally well be scheduled for something more important instead.

Checklist 6

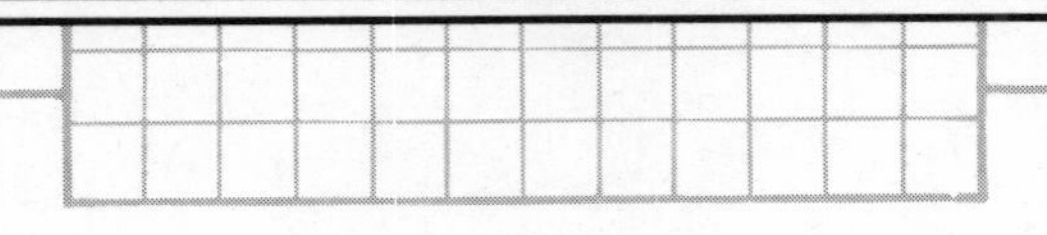

Servicing and selling

6.1 Functions

(a) In dealings with the trade, can differences in selling function be identified? Are they adequately provided for?

(b) Have performance levels for physical distribution service been defined? For service level? For delivery time?

(c) Are deliveries scheduled by destination? What is the maximum time-lag before despatch? Could costs be reduced by scheduling?

(d) What specialisation by function is there among sales staff? What could there be? Is there scope for sales support staff? How could they be organised?

6.2 Costing

(a) Are costings available for the different levels and functions of selling and servicing? On what basis are they calculated?

(b) Do standard time allowances exist for selling activities? How were they arrived at?

(c) Has current sales force performance been observed? Could observation and analysis be undertaken?

(d) What kind of deviation occurs in practice from any timing standards laid down? From any proposed new standards?

(e) How much productive time is available? How much is being filled?

(f) What are current total costs per year/day/hour/minute for each category of selling staff?

(g) To what extent are activities being justified by marginal costing?

7

Planning sales action

Using the methods described in the previous chapter, the true cost of performing each different kind of selling action or service to customers can be determined. The next step is to decide exactly which customers should be receiving which kind of treatment, in the light of what it is now known to cost, and of their actual or potential sales performance. At the same time the total cost of the projected selling programme can be calculated, and compared to what is thought to be acceptable. As before the whole process is iterative, proceeding by trial and error until the most cost-effective solution possible has been reached. Being iterative, the repeat cycle can be entered at any stage.

Hitherto, the logic of the planning sequence has been described as if a completely new programme of trade marketing distribution were being launched. Starting from first principles, a plan of campaign would be worked out, a suitable selling force recruited, and the whole strategy set in motion. Occasions for starting from scratch in this way will of course be comparatively rare. Much more common will be the situation where an existing sales force is pursuing a selling programme with existing customers, and the need is to review it and improve it. Exactly the same planning principles can still be applied; the only difference being that they can be used to audit the effectiveness of the existing situation.

Identifying customers

The first essential is to be quite sure that all customers or potential customers who are worthy of being contacted are known and identified. The numbers and nature of these selected contacts will depend on the selling strategy which the company has in mind at this stage: to which kinds and levels of trade distributors are direct sales to be made; and whether support action of any kind is proposed for any other levels which do not buy direct. If a company is to sell direct in the first instance to only a few main distributors, and not itself to intervene in the market in any other way, then its list of contacts will not be too difficult to identify. Companies selling direct to the retail market, on the other hand, will have many thousands of outlets to consider.

The universe of potential contacts to be considered must not consist only of those customers whom the company happens to know already. One of the commonest faults of salesmen is to go on calling on their 'friends' who can be counted on to do business, and to ignore the more difficult outlets which 'never buy anything'. A company then has knowledge of only a quite arbitrary section of the market, and is totally unaware of the existence of the remainder, which might in fact yield good business if approached properly. Discovering the rest of the customer universe can be quite a lengthy and difficult job. Trade directories are a standard source, and sometimes mailing lists can be bought from specialist firms. Often the only way to track down potential outlets is to use the sales force to carry out a special survey of its own, with each salesman checking out his own area, town by town and street by street, to note down names and addresses.

Where support calls are to be made on outlets which are, or should be, customers of the main distributors, the latter should be persuaded to provide copies of their own customer lists for the purpose. Distributors, wholesalers and so on are often very reluctant to do this, on the grounds that it gives away their trade secrets and might lead to customers being taken away from them. The concern is natural and distributors will have to be reassured that the information really will be used only to help them in their own efforts and not used to their disadvantage. In any distributorship agreement, a clause should always be put in requiring the distributor to provide if required full details of customers for the company's products, both to assist any support activities and to provide continuity in the event of the distributorship being given up for any reason.

If at the planning stage it is neither practical nor economic to collect the actual names and addresses of all potential points for sales force contact, then at least an estimate should be made of the probable numbers in each category in each location. Government and local authority statistics on, for example, the total number of retail shops in an area may be of some help in this. By whatever means, a very complete assessment must be made of the total area from which to select the targets for sales force activity.

Classifying customers

Most businesses classify their customers in their records, if only by some obvious characteristic such as 'class of trade' – wholesalers, retailers, supermarkets, co-operatives, independents, multiple chains and so on. These classifications while valid enough are often not very helpful in pinning down exactly how the customers are to be treated, particularly when the categories are not mutually exclusive – for example a supermarket may also be part of a multiple chain, and at the same time a co-operative. None of these descriptions in any case defines exactly what kind of selling attention should be given. The kind of classification required for planning purposes must be such as to enable the planner to judge what kind of selling activity is likely to be effective and at the same time cost-justifiable. There are probably at least four headings to be considered:

1 The type of business, that is what it does, rather than how it is legally constituted.
2 The criteria as found by observation for the time required for sales calls, e.g. size of business, kind of work to be done.
3 Current sales performance, if any.
4 Sales potential.

Looking at all these together should make it possible to say exactly what kind of selling programme would be appropriate for the customer: what forms of action, by which class of personnel, at what frequency, and with what time allowances. From the work already done on costings in the previous chapter, it is now also possible to say exactly what this will cost.

Sales potential

Of all the foregoing processes, estimating the sales potential of a customer may well prove the most troublesome. Nevertheless it is extremely important to try to make a fair assessment of this, as it is absolutely central to the whole philosophy of strategic selling. If selling efforts are to be planned purely in the light of sales already being made, the company is certainly reinforcing its successes, but doing nothing specifically for further development. To a very large extent, effort must be concentrated where the prospects lie, which is not necessarily where sales are coming from at present. Therefore sales potential should be estimated, as much for existing buyers as for prospective ones who have not bought anything yet.

'Potential' in practical terms means the sales which could possibly be obtained in the coming year from a customer, given proper selling efforts and a certain amount of good fortune. For existing customers, this will be not less than what is being obtained at present – unless it is known that the customer is going out of business. The question is whether the customer is capable of buying more than at present. If so, how much? Is the potential for increase of customer A greater than for customer B? In the case of prospects who are non-buyers at present, the question is whether they could be persuaded to start. If so, what could be hoped for in the first year?

Generally, it is not worthwhile to try to look further forward than a year, since in a year's time the planning will be reviewed in any case and the prospects re-assessed. The people best qualified to judge a prospect are those who are closest to them; that is, either the salesmen in the field or their area supervisors. Involvement of the field force in the planning process should be put on a formal footing, and its views called for annually in the form of reports on customer prospects. Quite apart from the invaluable information to be obtained, this kind of participation pays dividends in higher morale and greater sense of commitment to objectives which they have themselves suggested.

Matching action to prospects

For each category of customer, the current level of sales and the prospects for increase allow a view to be taken on what the plan of action by the sales force should be. To some extent the argument is a circular one. We have already seen in chapter 6 that the amount of time required for a selling call on a particular type of customer tends to be dictated by the characteristics of the customer himself, largely irrespective of the amount of business done, or in prospect. It is on this basis that standard time allowances for calls can be set. So if a particular class of customer is to be contacted at all, it may look as if the amount of time the sales force will have to spend is predetermined, and that there is little room for discretion on what the plan of action should be. On the other hand, we should like, as far as possible, to relate the amount of sales effort to the value to us of the customer.

Room for discretion does normally exist, however, in a number of ways. First, there is the matter of how many services are to be given in the course of a selling call. If the call is to consist quite literally of nothing more than a discussion of the available products and an attempt to book an order, then this certainly is an irreducible minimum. But there could be a lot more than this. Should the salesman give product demonstrations? Either to the customer or to the customer's customers? Is checking of stocks appropriate? Should there be any staff training or assistance with record keeping or building of displays? Should all this be done by the one salesman, or is there scope for sending in a sales assistant as well? On all these points the planner can exercise judgement on how much effort to put into a customer category, depending on what is to be obtained.

Secondly, there is the all important question of frequency. This is the factor which most directly affects the cost of sales and service. If the frequency of calls can be reduced by half, so too is the annual cost in salesman's time. As we have seen, the frequency of sales calls to get replenishment orders is dictated by the customer's policy on stock investment, and by the logistics of supply. In all cases it is a desirable objective to extend the frequency as much as possible. When dealing with a prospect who is not yet buying at all, the question of stock and logistics does not arise, and the frequency with which calls are made can be set entirely at discretion and according to the importance of the prospect. Similarly, other services given to existing buyers which are not related to the replenishment cycle can be set at a frequency proportionate to actual sales and prospects.

Lastly, there is always some leeway in the standard time allowance for any one activity within a selling call. As mentioned in chapter 6, when setting standard times there arises the question 'Is it worth it?'. It can be decided that a particular service should be given, but to spend only a limited amount of time on it. Assistance with a display might be in order, but for not more than ten minutes, while another more important customer might be given half an hour. This kind of approach to salesmanship is merely to formalise the old sales manager's injunction: 'Call there and try to get an order, but don't waste too much time on them'.

Pulling all this together, the form and extent of action planned for each distinguishable category of contact should be entirely a matter of judgement by the strategic planner, in relation to the objectives sought in the trade, and to the sales potential of each group. Once this is decided upon, the man hours required for each type of action will then follow from the standard time allowances agreed; and the cost in turn derives from the man hours.

A selling programme

We now come to the crucial part of the whole process of planning a strategic selling programme. It should now be possible to summarise plans for action in the form of a table showing the different target categories of customers and the programme intended for each. This will take one stage further the application of standard times for calls which began with the examples given in Table 6.1 in the previous chapter. Table 6.1 showed, as a result of direct observation, how long certain types of call were taking. What we are going to produce now is a table of exactly what type of customer should get what kind of calling programme, which will then also show how long these calls are going to be allowed to take. A specimen is given in Table 7.1. This example assumes that there are two categories of selling staff, salesmen and assistants, and the annual man-hours required of each are calculated.

The standard call times used in such a table should be the gross times, inclusive of the allowance for between-call travel, so that the man hours figure will represent the total requirement of productive time for one customer of each category in a year.

Calculating costs

Once such a table has been produced, it finalises the criteria which are required for customer classification. We know now which customer features are relevant to the selling programme and which are not. The next stage is to apply these classification criteria to the entire list of prospective contacts which have been identified, and to find out how many there are in each category. Multiplying the customer numbers per category by the annual man hours requirement for that category, and by the hourly cost for the appropriate grade of selling staff, gives the first approximation of the total cost of a proposed selling strategy.

An example of this calculation is given in the first part of Table 7.2. Using the same customer categories as determined in the previous Table 7.1, let us assume that there are 195 wholesaler customers in the first category. Each such customer is going to require 34.7 man hours in a year from salesmen, and 52 man hours from assistants. If salesmen have been calculated to cost £13.33 per productive hour, and assistants £9.50, the proposed selling strategy for these 195 wholesaler customers will cost a total of £186,527 as shown in Table 7.2. Similar calculations are made for all other categories of customer, and the grand totals of man hours and annual costs arrived at.

Before going any further, a very necessary cross check must be performed as shown in the second part of Table 7.2. Our calculation of total cost depends on the accuracy of our previously calculated cost for a productive hour of a salesman's time. Any error in this has now been multiplied several thousand times. Therefore it is vital to recheck the calculation by another route. The total number of man hours required should be translated into the number of real people that this would represent; and the total costs of such a selling organisation estimated again in terms of actual salaries, bonuses, travelling costs, supervision and so on. There is certain to be some discrepancy with the previous result. A difference of one or two per cent is immaterial, but any more substantial difference must be tracked down between the two sets of calculations and adjustment made before going on.

Judging cost-effectiveness

Building up a strategy in this way is bound to be very much a trial and error process. The first results of the projection are only too likely to produce an unacceptably high level of cost in relation to estimated sales, either for individual categories of customer, or in total. It is then a question of reviewing the provisional plans which have been made to see if less could be done, at lower cost, while still achieving the sales target. Alternatively, if the full-cost selling programme were to be carried out, could it possibly result in yet higher sales? The aim must be to assess the point at which sales and costs are in the best possible relationship to one another, i.e. where costs are at their lowest as a percentage of sales. It is very unlikely that sales will increase exactly in step with any increase in selling effort and in selling cost. The position is more likely to be as represented graphically in Figure 7.1.

Table 7.1

Customer classification and callage programme

Customer category	Type of call	Standard Call minutes	Call frequency per year	Man hours per year: Salesmen	Man hours per year: Assistants
1. Wholesalers, current buyers, potential over £50,000	a) Salesman: direct orders, promotions	40	52	34.7	
	b) Assistant: stock checks, stock records	60	52		52
2. Wholesalers, non-buying, potential over £20,000	Salesman: prospection, presentations	30	26	13	
3. Small shop, indirect buying, potential over £1,000	Assistant: display check, transfer order to wholesaler	15	13		3.25
etc.	etc.				

Table 7.2
Calculation of costs

Customer category	Nos. in Category	Man hours/year per customer	Man hours/year per category	Hourly cost	Annual cost
				£	£
1. Wholesalers, current buyers, potential over £50,000	195	a) Salesmen 34.7	6766	13.33	90,197
		b) Assist's 52	10140	9.50	96,330
					186,527
2. Wholesalers, non-buying, potential over £20,000		etc.	etc.	etc.	
Total man hours (say)		Salesmen	63875		851,454
		Assistants	27690		263,055
TOTAL COST (say)					£1,114,509

Cross check:

No. of man hours in a year: 1500

No. of Salesmen required = 63875/1500 = 42.58 Rounded up = 43

No. of Assistants required = 27690/1500 = 18.46 Rounded up = 19

Total costs of sales force comprising 43 salesmen + 19 assistants:-

Salaries: 43 @ £8,000

19 @ £5,000

Supervisors: etc. etc. etc.

TOTAL COST (say) £1,200,000

Discrepancy with previous calculation: 7.7%

Above a certain level, any increase in selling effort will produce less and less response in the form of increased sales, so that the percentage of costs to sales value will rise. Going the other way there will also be a point where, if selling effort is reduced any further, sales will fall off quite disastrously, and the cost percentage will again rise. Judging where these levels are must be part of the expertise of sales management, who have to be prepared to stake their reputations, and perhaps more, on the results to be achieved by any given level of selling campaign. The target level to be adopted for sales must of course also be agreed with product marketing management, as part of the joint planning process. It may be justifiable in the end to go for sales at a level which is above the optimum in selling costs, if at that level some other economies are possible elsewhere, perhaps in production costs. It may even be justifiable in terms of social cost, such as the avoidance of redundancies in

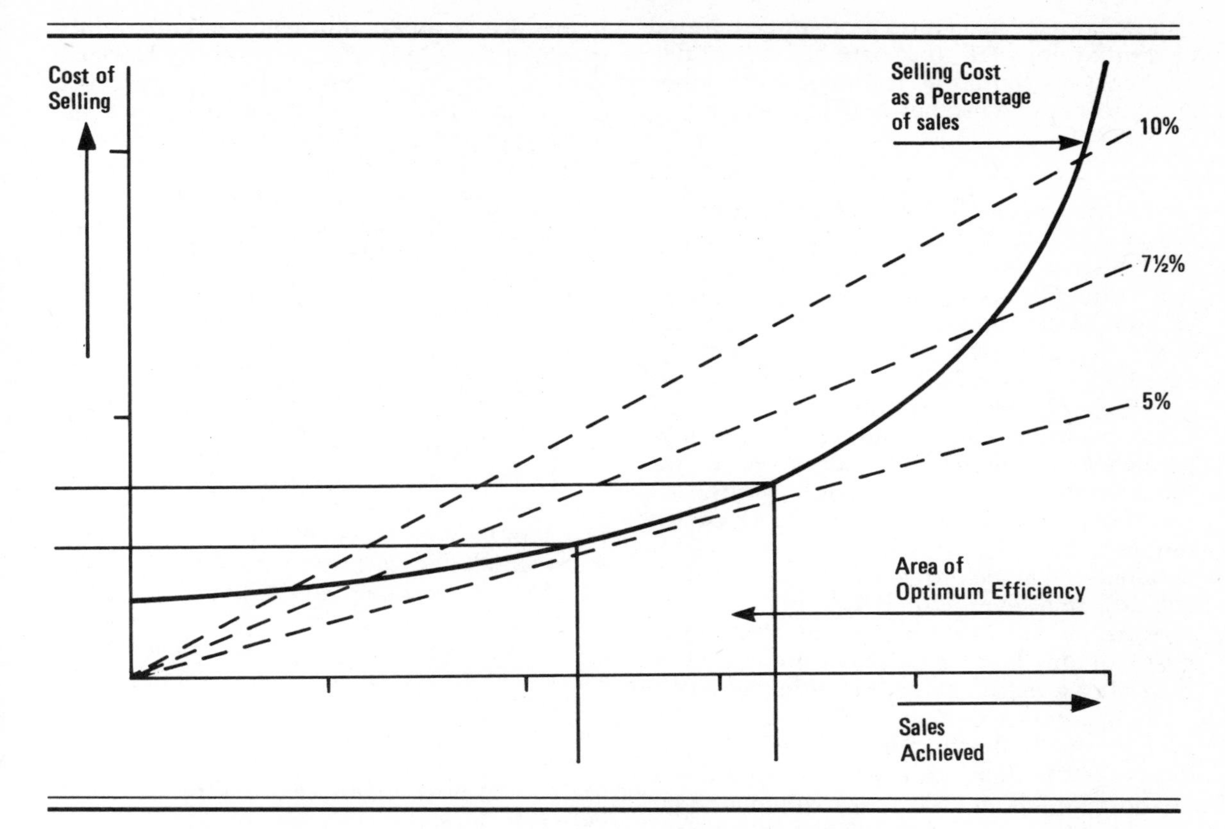

Figure 7.1 The result of selling effort

the workforce. But whatever the criteria used, it is the task of sales management (or trade marketing management) to judge what will be the outcome of a given selling programme with a known cost.

Consistency and market sampling

Selling effort should be applied consistently and logically to the distributor market as a whole, and not just to arbitrarily selected parts of it. On the face of it, all distributors in the same category as to type and size and potential should receive the same treatment. Sales forces are often found to be calling on, say, 200 outlets of a certain type, when there are at least 2,000 in total, all apparently similar. The question then is, why those 200? If it is economically justifiable to call on them, why not call on all the others and make sales to them as well? If that would not be economic, what is the justification for calling on any of them? This type of situation often arises from the salesman's propensity, mentioned earlier, to go on calling only on his friends and familiars, and the planning process must ensure that this is corrected.

There can of course be a case for calling only on a *sample* of a trade category at any one time, rather than on the whole of it, either on the basis of devoting only a limited amount of development expenditure to that part of the market, or because selling resources are limited for the time being. In such a case, the sample can best be drawn in rotation from the sector as a whole, so that in time effort is spread over as large a part of it as possible. This method is particularly applicable to support calls on indirect buying outlets, where the effects of support activities should linger for some time, while the sales force moves on to another area. The same thing applies to calling on sales prospects: if after a prolonged period of trying to break in there are still no results, the prospect should be left for another year, and effort applied somewhere else.

Minimum economic customers

Any cutting back that is necessary in the overall level of selling effort should be made consistently within each category, in line with the expected sales potential. At this stage, the question of the limit for a minimum economic customer will probably come up. This will be the level at which the gross margin on the customer's business, after direct production costs, will not even cover the cost of the minimum amount of selling effort required to obtain it – let alone provide any net profit. Calculating this level should be quite straightforward. If, for example, a customer's business can only be obtained by sending a salesman once a month to get his order, which in terms of productive time would cost, say, £100 a year; and if the margin on products after direct costs is 20 per cent; then clearly sales of anything less than £500 a year will incur a net loss. It is this kind of calculation which may finally determine which category of outlets cannot be sold to direct, but must be left as indirect customers for other larger distributors. Alternatively, it may indicate the level at which only telephone selling should be used.

This calculation will show the absolute minimum level for doing business. When a reduction in the total cost of selling effort becomes necessary, it may be appropriate to raise this minimum level, and cut out another tier of direct contacts whose contribution, although positive, produces very little net profit. Resources should be used in the most cost-effective manner possible, in sectors which offer the best prospects of a return on sales effort invested.

Reviewing present effectiveness

None of these planning processes can be regarded as permanent. After a year, say, it will be necessary to monitor the results achieved from whatever plan was made, and go through the whole process again.

In practice, in an existing selling situation, this is where the sequence is most likely to start. Sales management inherit existing customers and contacts, with a sales force operating to an existing policy, and the need is to find ways of improving sales effectiveness. A first stage then is to look at the various categories of customer who are currently receiving different levels of sales treatment, and to see whether these differences are justified by the results being achieved in each case.

Where the current selling programme has been arrived at by a logical planning process, the categories of customer receiving different sales treatment will already be known – they will be the categories defined in the 'classification' process and used to specify the selling programme in each case. With an existing situation which has not been formally planned it will first be necessary to discover who is receiving what forms of attention. To be able to do this it is essential to *know exactly* what the sales force is doing, and this can be surprisingly difficult to be sure of in many situations. The ways in which sales force activity is controlled and reported on may not make it easy to discover how resources are being allocated between different customer groups. One of the major benefits of a time study of the sales force by direct observation as described in chapter 6 may well be that it provides this information for the first time. As well as showing how much time is spent on individual calls, such a study will also reveal in sample form how much time is being given to one category of customer compared with another.

Analysing activities

The object then is to construct a table similar to Table 7.1, but working backwards from the levels of attention actually being given – i.e. by which grade of sales staff, for how long, at what frequency – to discovering which customers currently benefit at each level. A specimen of the kind of results which should be found is given in Table 7.3.

From the information which has already been worked out on costings, it should be quite simple to calculate the total cost of the selling effort expended on each group. What is now necessary is to find out what each group is

Table 7.3
Analysis of sales callage

Type of callage	Type of customers receiving	Customer numbers
1. Weekly calls, with stock check and merchandising, average time 60 minutes	Mainly supermarkets, department stores, some pharmacies	512 (see list A*)
2. Weekly calls, without stock check, average time 25 minutes	Mainly wholesalers	89 (see list B*)
3. Fortnightly calls, direct order, some display, average time 15 minutes	Independent retailers, pharmacies	3,500 app. (no detailed list)
	etc.	etc.

* Note: these would be lists of actual names and addresses

producing in sales; what this is on average per customer; and what is the distribution of sales among customers. Obtaining this information in an existing unplanned situation may be somewhat laborious. It is not very likely that the existing accounting or computing systems will be able to select the groups automatically from the descriptions given, and there is probably nothing else for it but to go through customer records individually, putting each in the correct category of selling programme and extracting the sales figures required. Of course, once a proper classification has been set up, the company's information systems should be geared accordingly, so that sales results can be extracted automatically in each category in future.

Analysing results

Once customers have been sorted out according to the selling programme they receive, the current sales performance in each group can be analysed, and a very interesting picture usually begins to emerge. It can now be seen for the first time exactly how much selling effort and cost is being put into each category, compared to the value of sales being got out.

Frequently, the disparity between different groups of trade distributors will be very striking. In Table 7.4 we take the selling programmes which were identified in Table 7.3 and put against them the total costs as well as the total value of sales derived from each callage category.

These figures are hypothetical, but they will serve to illustrate the kind of comparison that can be made. The first callage category is that of customers receiving weekly calls, with stock checks and merchandising, each call taking on average 60 minutes. There are 512 such customers and the total cost in sales force manpower can be worked out as follows:

Cost per salesman minute	£0.22
Minutes per call	60
Calls per year	52
Number of customers	512

Multiplying all these together gives £351,436 per year expended on this category of customer. If the total cost of the sales force is, let us say, £1 million per year, then this category of customer is absorbing 35 per cent of the total selling effort.

Let us further assume that the company's total

Table 7.4
Comparison of selling effort to sales achieved

Callage category	No. of customers	Callage cost	Per cent of total cost	Sales in category	Per cent of total sales
			35%	£5 M	25%
1. Weekly,	512	£351,436			
× 60 mins.			2½%	£3 M	15%
2. Weekly, × 25 mins.	89	£25,454			
3. Fortnightly, × 15 mins.	3,500				
	etc.	etc.	100%	£20 M	100%
Grand totals		£1 M			

sales are £20 million a year, and that this first category of customer is producing £5 million of these sales, or 25 per cent of the total. We can then see that in this category, 35 per cent of total selling effort is producing 25 per cent of total sales.

The same calculations can be applied to the other categories. Category 2, wholesalers, is absorbing only 2½ per cent of selling effort. If we assume that total sales in this category are, say, £3 million, then we would be getting 15 per cent of our total sales for 2½ per cent of our selling effort. And so on, for each category.

Disparity of effort

It will almost invariably be found that there is a considerable disproportion between the various groups as regards the amount of effort put in and the end result obtained. Not infrequently this approaches Pareto proportions – 80 per cent of the selling effort may be producing only 20 per cent of sales. Sometimes this state of affairs can immediately rectified, sometimes not. It is of the utmost importance however to be aware of what is going on, and if some group of customers is absorbing what seems to be much more than its proper share of selling effort, there should be a very clear justification for it. At least one would hope to find that the high level of selling expense was balanced in some other direction. In chapter 5 it was pointed out that financial reward to the trade is another form of cost of selling. If one trade group is being given less reward than others, in other words gets less favourable prices or lower discounts, then a higher cost of field selling effort to that group may well be admissible.

We are still not finished with our analysis of the different sales callage categories. Where a category is producing a disappointingly low return in sales for the amount of selling effort being put in, the next thing to examine is whether this is true for all the customers in the category, or only for some of them. To do this it is necessary to look at the distribution of sales among the customers making up the category. If there are only a few of them, they can listed individually in ascending order of sales. If the category is numerous, it is better to subdivide it into groups according to sales turnover, and show the numbers of customers in each turnover bracket. Table 7.5 shows the kind of results to be obtained by taking the first category of customers in Table 7.4 and breaking them down by turnover.

There were 512 customers in total in this category producing £5 million in sales, or £9,765 each on average. How closely are they grouped around this average? Not very closely, it seems. While there are 63 customers producing over £20,000 a year in sales, there are 153 producing less than £5,000, and 3 producing nil – but these are still receiving selling attention at the rate of one hour a week. Since this level of attention costs nearly £700 a year, many of the customers in this category may be causing a net loss.

Sales potential again

Individual accounts which are so far below the norm should be reconsidered very carefully to see if it is worth going on at the present rate, or if the amount of effort put in can be reduced to a more acceptable level – in other words, should they be transferred to another category. Reviewing accounts in this way will inevitably come back to the question of sales potential in each case. If the customers were to be re-arranged not by actual sales results, but by anticipated sales potential, would the picture look any better?

Unless there is a potential and a prospect of achieving sales greater than at present, there would be no point in going on devoting selling attention to a customer at a level which is uneconomic or nearly so. This is obviously the case with a prospect who is producing nil sales at present. Effort is being applied in the hope of a breakthrough, and is justified so long as there is reason for the hope. There is therefore nothing alarming in having small numbers of 'nil' customers in the sales callage programme – in fact having none would be more alarming, as it would indicate that no development of new customers was being undertaken.

Customers in the lower brackets of sales results should therefore be reviewed to check that development potential really is there and

Table 7.5
Distribution of sales per category

Category 1 – Supermarkets No. in category 512
Total sales £5 M
Average sales £9,765

Distribution of sales:

Sales of:	No. of customers
nil	3
Below £5,000	153
£5,001 – £10,000	160
£10,001 – £15,000	109
£15,001 – £20,000	24
Over £20,000	63
	512

that effort is not being wasted on unpromising material. In many cases it will have to be admitted that there is not much more to hope for, and that selling and servicing attention really should be reduced, as far as there is opportunity to do so. By degrees, it may be possible to transfer customers into categories of selling programme which much more closely match their sales potential, if not their current level of sales. As this process nears completion, the subdivision of customers will come closer and closer to the ideal form of 'classification' by sales potential illustrated at the beginning of this chapter in Table 7.1. In other words, having started the action planning and re-planning cycle with a review of an actual 'as is' situation, we still in due course come round to the point of instituting a new classification system in the same way as would be necessary for a brand new selling campaign. This classification will form the basis for the next review of results against expectations, and so on.

Review against potential

The annual review of results will now begin to reveal how far sales expectations per category of customer have been reached. Once customers have been assessed as to their sales potential, and selling action planned accordingly, it becomes natural to look at results using the same classifications. By a process of evolution extending probably over several annual cycles, customers should have been regrouped into categories which are more and more based on their sales potential, and less and less according to the arbitrariness of the selling programme which they happen to receive. When this stage is reached, the average of sales results and the distribution of results about the average can be examined in relation to the potential that was assumed for each category in the first place. This is the ultimate in the sequence of action planning and review.

An illustration of this comparison is given in Figure 7.2. On the left hand side of the figure is listed the classification of customers which we assume has now been adopted, based on an assessment of potential combined with type of business in each case. Against each is shown the number of customers and the selling programme planned, in terms of callage and costs.

The first thing to monitor is how far the planned selling programme has actually been carried out in each case. If the attention planned has not in fact been given it will not be surprising if the results are not achieved either. Sales force activity must be controlled and reported on in such a way that its achievement of work plans can readily be checked – more of this in chapter 10. Achievement of workplan could be measured in terms of planned calls actually made, or in man hours actually spent against man hours planned per category of customer. By way of illustration in Figure 7.2 the callage achievement is shown as a percentage of actual to plan.

In the right hand portion of Figure 7.2 the sales results in each category for the previous year are summarised in the form of a distribution table of the numbers of customers in each turnover bracket. Displaying results in this way shows immediately how many customers in each category have failed to come up to expectations. Two questions then arise:

1. Is the estimate of potential for these customers still thought to be correct, and should the programme of selling effort still be persevered with in the hope that this potential will be realised?
2. Or should the estimate of potential be reduced, and the customer accordingly relegated to a lower classification, with a correspondingly less expensive selling programme?

Whichever course of action is chosen the objective is the same, to reduce to the minimum the numbers of customers year by year who produce less than the potential attributed to them, after a level of selling effort commensurate with that potential. When this stage has been reached, selling action can truly be said to have been planned and made effective.

Plan				Actual						
Customer category/ potential	No. in category	Selling programme planned		Achievement of selling programme	Distribution of sales :— customer numbers per turnover range					
		Hours	£000s		Nil	Below £5,000	£5,001 to £7,500	£7,501 to £10,000	£10,001 to £15,000	etc.
1. Wholesalers, potential over £10,000	54	2200	30	83%	6	12	7	8	21	
2. Wholesalers, potential £5 – 10,000	126	2500	34	89%		14	63	46	3	
3. Pharmacies, potential over £5,000		etc.		etc.			etc.			

Figure 7.2 Review against potential

Checklist 7

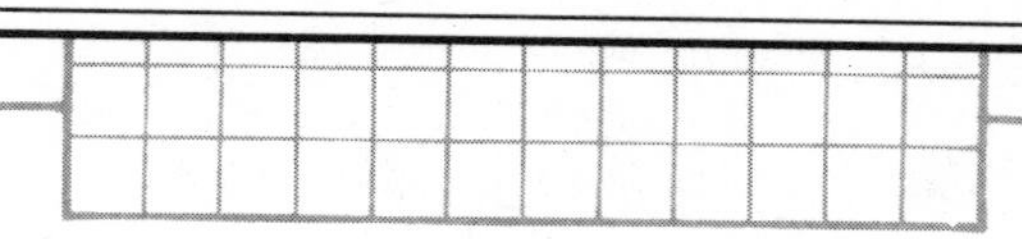

Planning sales action

7.1 Customers

(a) Have all possible outlets for distribution been positively identified? What means are available to identify those who are not currently customers?
(b) Are outlets also identified which would not buy direct but through other distributors?
(c) What is the present basis, if any, for customer classification? Does this help to define appropriate selling action?
(d) What if anything is known as to the sales potential of current customers? Of others?

7.2 The selling programme

(a) To what extent could the amount of selling effort be related to the business done, rather than to the circumstances of the customer?
(b) What would be an ideal programme of selling effort, in relation to customer type and sales potential? Would the total cost be justifiable?
(c) What is the cost of existing selling effort, as a percentage of sales?
(d) Can selling effort be applied consistently to each level of the trade, or is it necessary to apportion it in some way?
(e) Has the minimum level for an economic customer been calculated?

7.3 Existing situation

(a) Is it known how sales force time is being allocated between different types of customer? How could this be analysed?
(b) Is it possible to analyse sales results in these different groups?
(c) How does the percentage of total selling effort relate to the percentage of total sales in each group? Can any disparity be justified? Or rectified?
(d) Do low performers in each group have a sales potential which justifies continuing the present level of selling action?
(e) How many non-buyers receive regular sales attention?
(f) Is it possible to review sales results against sales expectations for each group?

8

Deployment of resources

By the processes described in the previous chapter, a detailed selling programme should have been planned, reviewed and checked so that the company's selling resources in the form of salesmen, supervisors and assistants will be used to the best advantage. Customers will have been identified according to category and a programme of selling activity determined for each, in relation to their to their circumstances, their current business, and their estimated potential. It now remains to translate these plans into action.

The selling cycle

Plans have hitherto been looked at on an annual basis, as being the period most suited to the analysis of costs and sales. When it comes to controlling actual sales force activity, it is much more convenient to reduce plans to the level of their *repeat cycle*, that is, the period in which all planned activity is due to occur at least once, so that in subsequent cycle periods all activity will repeat itself identically. There is no point in planning a salesman's entire year, day by day, when it is enough to plan it for one cycle and repeat for the others.

The length of the cycle will depend on the call frequencies which have been planned. In most businesses it is usually desirable for both supplier and customers that sales calls and other activities should be exactly equally spaced out, since their timing ought to be constant in relation to lengths of stockholding, delivery time lags and so on. Sometimes it is preferable for calls to take place always on the same day of the week. Therefore it is not usually convenient to use the calendar months as cycle periods, being of unequal lengths – the same maximum number of calls simply cannot be achieved in each calendar month. One of the most convenient cycle periods to adopt is that of four weeks, of which there are then thirteen in a year. This is very suitable when calls have been planned on the basis of one call every one, two, or four weeks. If calls are planned at more than a four-weekly frequency, the cycle will have to be longer. Awkward combinations of frequency should be avoided if possible. For instance if calls are to be at three and four week intervals, the repeat cycle to contain both frequencies would have to be twelve weeks, of which there is then not a whole number in a calendar year.

If there are only a few calls to be made at the longer intervals it may be acceptable to have a shorter basic cycle, but with some calls occurring only every second or third cycle. This produces planning complications, but may be preferable to having to plan a very long cycle in which the great majority of calls occur several times over. Some businesses may wish to make a regular call on some customers, but only perhaps once in six months. It would be ridiculous to make the planning cycle this long for the sake of just a few exceptional contacts.

The sales cycle therefore should be set so as to facilitate planning in the sales department, and should not be unduly influenced by conventions in the rest of the business. The accounts department in particular will probably have quite different requirements for accounting periods, but this need be of no concern unless the sales force is involved in the collection of payments on monthly terms – this was mentioned in chapter 5.

Table 8.1
Calculation of total workload

		Man hours	
		Salesmen	Assistants
Category A			
No. of customers: 435			
4 Salesmen calls per cycle:			
Standard call time	45 mins.		
Average between-call travel	10		
	55 mins.		
Man hours $= \dfrac{435 \times 4 \times 55}{60}$		1,595	
2 Assistant calls per cycle:			
Standard call time	30 mins.		
Average between-call travel	15		
	45 mins.		
Man-hours $= \dfrac{435 \times 2 \times 45}{60}$			652.5
Category B			
No. of customers: 118			
2 Salesmen calls per cycle:			
Standard call time	35 mins.		
Average between-call travel	10		
	45 mins.		
Man hours $= \dfrac{118 \times 2 \times 45}{60}$		177	
etc.		etc.	
GRAND TOTAL		(say) 7,225	3,628

How big a sales force?

Working from the selling programme for each customer category, the first task is to compute the total workload for all customers in terms of man hours per grade of selling staff for a complete cycle (or for a year if need be). The number of customers per category is multiplied by the planned call frequency per cycle and by the standard call time, inclusive of between-call travel allowance, to give the total requirement in productive time for each category. All categories are then added. The form of calculation is illustrated in Table 8.1.

Calculating staff numbers

From the study of sales force timings which should have been carried out, the available or usable amount of productive time per man per day is also known. Multiplying by the number of working days in a cycle gives the productive time per cycle. Total productive time required divided by available productive time per man gives the minimum number of men required to fulfil the programme. This calculation is performed in Table 8.2.

In making this calculation it is wise to double check that no work requirement has been

Table 8.2
Calculation of staff required

1. Salesmen

Usable productive time per salesman-day: 400 minutes

Working days per cycle: 20

Productive time per salesman

per cycle: $\dfrac{400 \times 20}{60} = 133.3$ hours

Total productive time required per cycle (from Table 8.1):	7,225 hours
5% extra allowance for contingencies:	361
	7,586 hours

No. of Salesmen required:

$\dfrac{7,586}{133.3} = \underline{\underline{57 \text{ men}}}$

2. Assistants

etc. etc. etc.

overlooked. For instance there may be a certain amount of unscheduled work from time to time, in setting up promotions, or conducting special surveys, or prospecting for new outlets, which cannot be specified in the selling programme. All that can be done is to estimate the average amount of time likely to be absorbed per cycle on such tasks, and add it to the total productive time required as a contingency. Available productive time per man should have been calculated *after* allowing for unavoidable absences due to holidays, sickness, attending conferences and training sessions. These items do not have to be allowed for again but should be checked to ensure they are realistic. Only then can the required establishment of selling staff be regarded with confidence.

At this point, the total cost of the programme should be checked once more, by a different calculation. Hitherto total costs have been estimated using the computed cost of one man hour or one man minute of productive time – see chapter 6. It is now possible to verify this from another direction by taking the actual numbers of men required in each grade, and adding up known salaries and other costs. To a large extent it may be possible to do this from the current payroll for known individuals. The two calculations should of course agree. If they do not, it is 'back to the drawing board' – a mistake has been made somewhere. There must of course be whole numbers of men (and women) employed, except in the case of any part time sales assistants, who can be counted as fractions of full time employees. Very likely the need to round up will mean employing and paying for more man hours than the theoretical minimum required.

Starting from an existing situation it is perhaps unlikely that the staff numbers ideally required will correspond to the numbers a company has actually got. Nor is it usually possible to hire and fire salesmen at a moment's notice. A company may therefore have to continue for an appreciable time with staff numbers quite different from the requirements of the selling programme. If this situation promises to be prolonged, it may be necessary to go back and revise the selling programme again to fit the staff numbers available. With insufffi-cient salesmen, the least rewarding categories of customer can have sales calls withdrawn, or minor services elsewhere can be temporarily abandoned. If there is a surplus of salesmen, they will have to be kept occupied, until they can be redeployed or their numbers reduced, by increasing the sales attention given to some categories of customer.

Seasonality

Calculation of the total workload may be complicated by the question of seasonality. The workload on a sales force throughout the year is rarely completely constant. Either there will be some feature of the product which makes it more in demand at certain times of year, or annual holiday arrangements may affect the rate of supply to the trade. In some situations this may materially alter the workload on the sales force either by increasing the length of time required for individual calls, or by increasing the number of calls to be made.

A company must do whatever it can to counterbalance seasonal changes in workload by changing other factors which are within its own control. Any promotional programme can be scheduled for the less busy periods, as can salesmen's holidays. Once as much smoothing as possible of the workload has been achieved, the calculation of normal workload should be made at a point above which any extra requirements will not be more than can be covered for short periods by extra work and overtime on the part of the salesmen. It would be uneconomic to have an establishment calculated for maximum peak load, if it were then underemployed for most of the rest of the year. Peakload can sometimes be accommodated more efficiently by hiring temporary staff or agency assistance when required. Very occasionally, opportunity arises to take on work during the slack season on behalf of some other supplier with an opposite seasonality problem. In Britain, one of the organisations which supplies ice cream to the shops in summer takes on the job of distributing frozen turkeys for Christmas.

Temporary disruption

Temporary absences or public holidays of only a day or two can have a very disruptive effect on regular workload, especially if this is planned on a repeat cycle by day of the week. If Monday is a public holiday, what is to be done with all the customers who normally receive regular calls on Mondays? Certainly what should not be done is to postpone all the rest of the regular calling pattern by one day so as to catch up with the day that was lost, thereby upsetting everyone. As far as possible this kind of disruption should be foreseen at the previous scheduled visit, and a forward order taken, or other arrangements made to cover the gap. Salesmen can find the time to telephone unvisited customers the day before or the day after, to confirm last minute requirements. Supervisory staff can undertake special visits to compensate. Whatever is done, the regular work programme should be adhered to on all available working days, so that changes from schedule affect as few customers as possible. Once it is settled exactly how such missing calls are to be covered, the calculation of workload can be very slightly adjusted accordingly. For instance, if there are ten days public holiday in the year, and the calls missed on those days are to be taken care of by supervisory management afterwards, then there is that much less total workload for the salesmen. The total workload capacity of each salesman should already have been reduced by the fact that he will not be working on those days in any case. The division of workload by work capacity to give the number of men required will then have taken these holidays correctly into account.

Location of workload

When the total workload of the entire market for all categories of staff has been established, and the exact numbers of staff required worked out, the next task is to discover exactly *where* all these staff have to be put to work. The workload requirement has been calculated in total, without regard to where it is located – whether spread evenly throughout the market or, as is more likely, concentrated into lumps at the urban centres. The staff numbers computed as being sufficient will be able to cover the work only if each is assigned to a territory whose workload will add up to exactly what one man can perform in the productive time available. This assignment or deployment to territories must be carried out separately for each different grade of staff, such as salesmen, sales assistants or merchandisers; and is crucial to the efficient employment of selling resources. There are basically two ways of going about finding a solution to this problem of territory building. One is by trial and error. The other is more scientifically, by actual plotting on the map. Each method has its advantages in different circumstances, and at times mixtures of both are required.

Trial and error territories

The trial and error method is, having computed the number of staff required, to appoint each to a 'centre', with only loosely defined boundaries at this stage. Centres will be chosen because they contain some important customers to begin with, and because the spacing looks right compared to customer numbers in the area. All known customers then have to be divided between salesmen, working more or less by eye and apportioning the intermediate locations to one salesman or another until each has a 'rough and ready' territory surrounding his centre. It is then up to each man to work out the best schedule he can to try to fulfil the planned selling programme for the customers he has been allocated, and see whether he can maintain the schedule in practice. During this period salesmen must be supervised very thoroughly, to ensure that at least the major customers in each territory receive regular attention, and to form a judgement on how far any salesman is overloaded or appears to have time to spare. By degrees, customers will have to be transferred from one salesman to another to try to even things up. If the centres were chosen shrewdly in the first place, this may be merely a matter of adjusting the boundaries between the centres, without more major changes. But if the disproportion of work between salesmen is more serious, and differs from one area of the country to another, then it may become necessary to make more radical changes, creating a 'knock-on' effect from one territory to the next. Some salesmen may have to be moved to new centres altogether. The disruption and length of time involved in getting such a system to settle down may prove extremely costly in practice.

In a pioneering situation in which the final customer pattern has not yet emerged, and most of the work to be done is of a prospecting nature, this approach to territory building is the only one available. In these circumstances there is nothing else to be done other than appoint salesmen to promising areas, making their first task that of finding customers for themselves and building up their own territories accordingly. Each salesman works out from his centre until he literally bumps into his surrounding colleagues. The process is competitive and is none the less efficient as a result. Nevertheless it is still extremely likely that in the end there will be a highly inequitable division of workload between one salesman and another. The salesman with the less demanding territory will adopt an easier pace, or spend more time on less important outlets. His colleague in a more promising area may work harder but still leave a higher proportion of prospects unattended to. Quite different standards of service to customers may grow up in different parts of the country.

Plotted territories

The second, more formal, approach to territory building consists of *calculating* what the workload is for each customer, and *plotting* its actual location on the map. Thereafter, territories can be put together, each containing exactly the correct total amount of workload for one man, with no need for trial and error in practice.

Sophisticated companies, with sales planning departments and computers at their disposal, will find this method easy to follow but there is nothing in it which is impossible for those who have to use manual methods and a pocket calculator. The only proviso is that the great majority of customers and prospects must be known and their locations identified – if potential customers have still to be tracked down this must be done first by means of special field surveys, and more permanent sales territories created afterwards.

Location codes

When there are more than just a few hundred customers in total, it is first of all necessary to adopt a system for combining them into small groups for the purposes of location, since it would not be feasible to pin-point them all on the map individually. Location grouping can be quite simple, merely a matter of putting together all customers with an address in the same town or the same district. But as customer numbers become larger, more sophisticated method may be needed, which will key customers into smaller and more defined map areas. Various means exist for doing this.

Postcodes

The postal coding system can be used, if there is one. Many countries in Europe and also the United States have systems whereby a code is assigned to each district, street, or even individual address to facilitate mechanical mail sorting and delivery. To take the British system as an example, the postcode consists of letters and numbers which define first a main geographic area, then a district within the area, next a sector within the district, and finally the delivery round of an individual postman. There are 120 main 'areas', which are broken down into 2,688 'districts', in turn comprising 8,883 'sectors'. Figure 8.1, reproduced by permission of the Post Office, shows the boundaries of the main 'areas', which are denoted by the first two letters of the postcode. The subsequent figures of the postcode subdivide each area into its constituent districts and sectors. Thus the characters in the postcode, taken in succession, identify an address to an ever more closely defined location on the map.

An advantage of the system is that, at each level, the areas enclosed represent roughly equal volumes of mail deliveries, and therefore roughly equal levels of commercial activity. As a means of dividing up customers, therefore, postcode divisions are likely to yield a more equal split of numbers than areas which are merely of equal geographic size.

The point of using postcodes instead of ordinary addresses is, firstly, that the location can be found on the map in a logical rather than a random manner; and secondly that customers can be put into contiguous groups according to postcodes in a way which cannot be done using place names.The system is in the public domain, and can be freely used by anyone without cost. As a rule every commercial customer knows his own postcode and prints it on his stationery, but even if he does not, it can readily be obtained by looking up the published directories giving postcodes for every postal address in the country. Any customer can then immediately be located to a small defined area on the map.

Telephone areas

As an alternative, in countries with automatic telephone systems, it is often possible to use the telephone area dialling code as a means of locating customers. First it is necessary to check whether the telephone authority is able and willing to provide a map of the areas covered by each dialling code. Given this, it is an easy matter to locate each customer according to his telephone number. At first sight this may seem no different from locating customers by name of town in the first place. Two possible advantages are that in large towns the telephone system gives a more detailed breakdown of location; and telephone numbers lend themselves more readily to sorting by computer than the alphabetic names of towns and districts.

Map co-ordinates

Many countries use similar systems of geographic grid co-ordinates or map references to divide up the country into one kilometre squares or smaller. Use is more widespread in some countries than in others; but in Britain for example the national grid lines are shown on all popular maps, and grid references for thousands of place names are published in a number of gazetteers. It is not too difficult to look up the official map reference for every

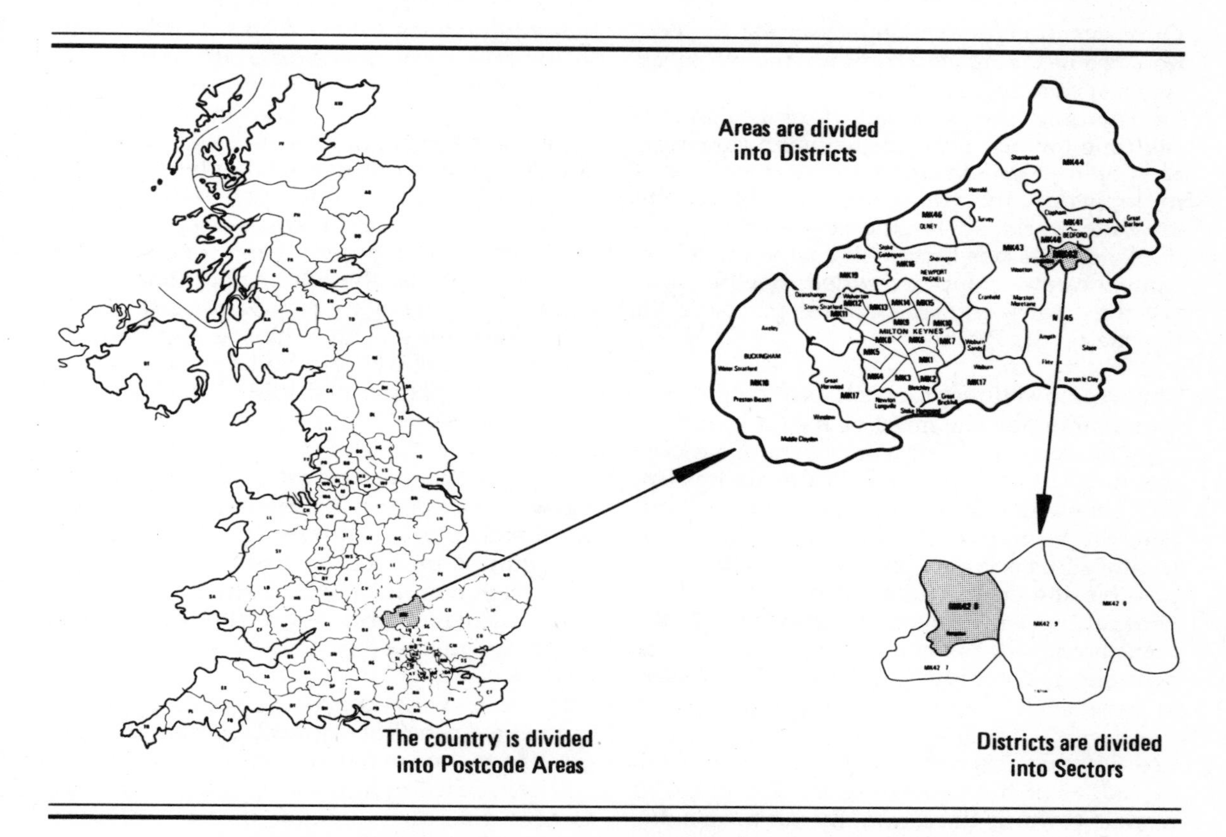

Figure 8.1 The British postcode system

known customer, which will then pin-point him with navigational accuracy to within a kilometre or even 100 metres. The main advantage of this system is that the grid reference numbers are geometrical co-ordinates; that is, each number specifies its own position on the map from the point of origin of the system. All customers whose map references lie within a certain numerical range are therefore known to be located within a certain square on the map. These squares can be chosen to be of any convenient size, such as one kilometre square, ten kilometres square, or practically anything in between. The system lends itself to the sorting of customers into the correct numerical sequences by computer, so that a list of the customers in each chosen square can rapidly be produced, and the workload per square calculated.

Aggregating workload

Once customers have been grouped by location, the next step is to compute the workload for each customer in the same way as was previously done for workload in total. Standard call time for that class of customer plus average between-call driving time for the region is multiplied by the number of calls per cycle to give the workload for the customer in standard minutes per cycle. All customers in the same location group are added together, giving the total workload minutes per cycle for that particular location.

The workload figure for each location group is then marked on the map, by means of pins or flags or numbers. The work norm of productive time per man per cycle is already known. The object then is to add together work locations on the map so as to form a complete sales territory for each man, containing as nearly as possible the correct total workload minutes, while at the same time making sense from the point of view of travel – that is, as compact as possible, and without any impassable barriers to travel such as rivers without bridges.

In doing this, it is generally better to start from the edges of the country to be covered, and work in towards the centre. By this means, the last territory will be a compact space left in the centre, and if it is too big or too small, some adjustment can be made outwards again in the neighbouring territories. Working the other way round can mean finishing up with disjointed strips all round the edges to be made into the final territory. Some regard must also be paid to where salesmen live, or where they could be persuaded to move to. Ideally a salesman will have least travelling to do if he lives within the boundaries of his territory but this is not absolutely essential. As mentioned in chapter 6, a salesman can live elsewhere if he chooses as long as he travels to his territory in his own time every day.

Revising territories

Once sales territories have been established by the calculation method, it should be possible for salesmen to take them over and perform all the tasks required without any need for trial and error or re-shuffling. Territories should remain valid until there is any major change in the customer list, or in the selling programme. Selling strategies are due for revision annually in any case and sooner or later this is bound to lead to the need to alter territories. Requiring one salesman more or one salesman less to fulfil the selling programme will logically entail adjusting practically every other territory to fit him in, or to get him out. Some industries are particularly prone to losing trade customers at short notice, and to gaining new ones. For any of these reasons, the whole allocation of territories may have to be re-arranged at any time, and done quickly. This will apply whichever method of territory building is used, but with even less time available to allow the trial and error, evolutionary method to take its course. A likelihood of changes being required is a still stronger argument in favour of having the whole process systematised, with customers already permanently assigned to their location groups by code or map reference. New customers can quickly be added, new workloads calculated, and new territories compiled whenever the need arises.

Companies with an existing selling operation in the field can evolve gradually from trial and error to the arrangement of territories by calculation. Starting from the existing list of customers for each salesman, his individual workload per cycle can be calculated as explained before: for each of his customers, multiply the standard call time plus driving allowance by the number of calls per cycle, and add together all his customers. Results are likely to be startling. Experience suggests that where territories have been allowed to evolve over time, or have been put together by arbitrary means, differences in workload of over 100 per cent will be not uncommon. What this means in the case of overloaded territories is simply that a large part of the work never gets done. The task then is to make adjustments between territories so as to eliminate some of the grosser anomalies; and in due course work towards having all territories based on a proper computation of workload.

Sales by territory

It needs to be underlined that nothing in the process of territory building is designed to produce territories with equal *sales*. Unless all customers are identical, it is obvious that territories will not necessarily contain equal numbers of customers, and this is accordingly not a method for putting together territories. Similarly, the customers in each territory will not necessarily produce the same amount of sales. It was the theme of chapter 7 that selling effort should be applied as far as possible in relation to sales potential, rather than actual sales, but that even then the time required from the salesman could not be kept strictly pro rata to the worth of the customers.

Territories should be constructed to provide equal amounts of *work* and it is a matter for management judgement what results that work is expected to produce at any given time. It is for this reason that the payment of salesmen directly by results, in the form of a commission on the sales made to 'their' customers, is so apt to cause difficulties. Some territories are bound to be richer than others in the commission they yield, quite irrespective of the salesman's personal efforts. Sales can be as much due to some other action on the part of the company as to any triumph of salesmanship. When it comes to re-allocating territories, salesmen will be most reluctant to give up high volume customers. Whatever method is chosen to remunerate and motivate salesman, it should not be one which restricts management's freedom to allocate workload equitably and in accordance with the selling strategy.

Journey scheduling

When territories and lists of customers have been established for each member of the field selling force, the business of planning is still not entirely complete. It still remains to work out a schedule for making all the calls required in a territory and preparing a detailed journey plan for getting from one to the other.

This is a task which is frequently left to the salesman himself to make the best of, on the slightly specious grounds that he knows the territory better than anyone else and is familiar with all the routes and travelling conditions. More truthfully, the job is often left to the salesman since no one in the central sales planning department would know how to go about it. When a salesman has in fact been assigned to a brand new territory created by planning methods as described above, it is a little unfair to expect him to tackle his own journey planning without any guidance. Also, if it appears in the course of supervision that a salesman is spending excessive amounts of time on between-call travel, and that some calls are being left unmade in consequence, it is essential for the head office to have sufficient knowledge to intervene and put matters right.

Whoever is responsible for producing it, the journey plan for each territory must be put down on paper and adhered to thereafter. If it cannot be adhered to regularly, then it must be changed, but again put in writing. Only in this way is it possible to ensure that all calls have been planned for, that repeat calls are regularly spaced, that customers know when to expect a call, that at any time the company knows where the salesman is, and that support activities by sales assistants or by telephone contact can be made at the proper time.

Choosing days and districts

Good journey planning starts with choosing the best *day* for visiting each customer, such that all the calls for any one day lie as close together as possible. The shortest route between them usually then becomes fairly obvious.

Planning should be done for one complete selling cycle, which by definition will include at least one call on every customer. Usually it does not matter *when* in the cycle a call on a customer is made, as long as the repeat sequence is equally spaced. There are two exceptions to this, however. One is when sales promotions also occur every cycle, and there is pressure to visit at least all the major customers early in the cycle with details of the latest promotion. The other is when territories have been changed and journey plans revised: a customer's place in the new schedule must be governed by when he last had a call under the old schedule.

When all calls on all customers are to be made at the same frequency, journey planning is at its simplest. The sales cycle itself should then also have this frequency, so that each customer requires just one call in the cycle. All that then needs to be done is to allocate each day of the cycle to a different district, with just enough calls in each district to fill one working day. Each district is visited in rotation. Travelling on each day is restricted to within one district and is so kept to a minimum.

As far as possible the districts to be visited each day should be spaced out so that the salesman is due to be back in a neighbouring district to the one just visited on the same day of the week a week later. This is done by using the same day of each week to visit neighbouring districts, rather than working round the whole territory in strict daily sequence. Figure 8.2 shows how a territory is first divided up into five segments, one for each day of the week, and then these segments are in turn divided into districts, one for each week in the cycle. In consequence the salesman is never absent from any part of his territory for very long at a time and in an emergency he can call back on any customer a week or so later without having to deviate very far from his planned journey for that day.

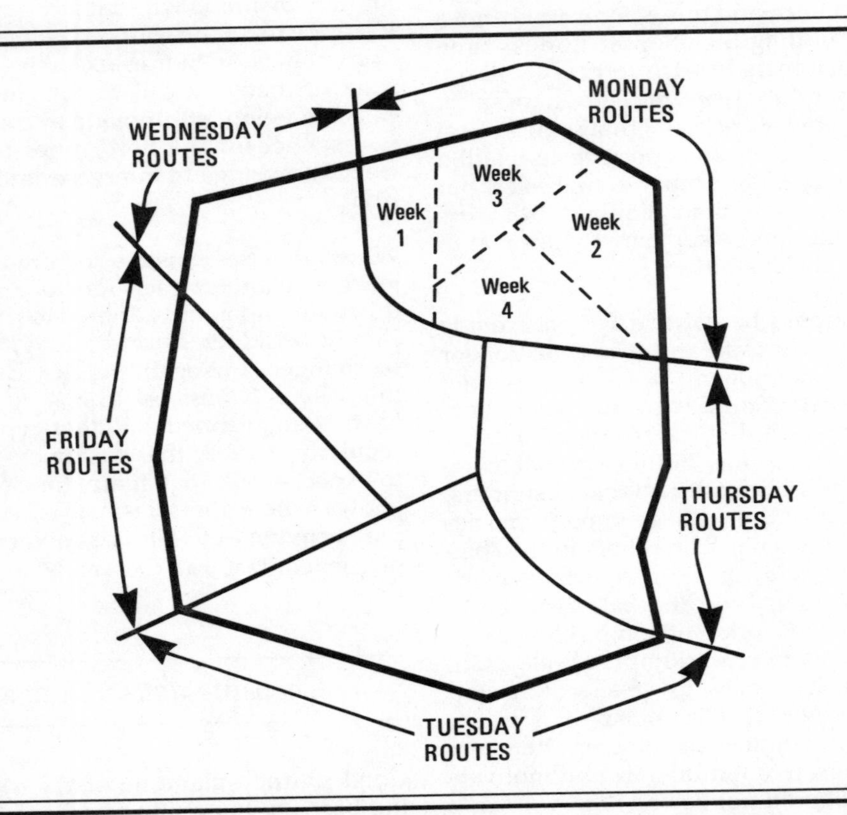

Figure 8.2 Journey plans for a four-week cycle

Mixed call frequencies

Complications arise when customers are not all to be visited at the same frequency. For instance in a four week cycle some customers might be due for one call, some for two and some for four. The repeat calls must also be equally spaced; that is, they must be made on the same day of the week at one week or two week intervals. Once again, the object is to divide the territory up into five segments first of all, one for each day of the week as was done before. Only this time, it will not be possible to keep to quite separate districts for that day in each of the four weeks of the cycle. Instead, there will have to be four quite different

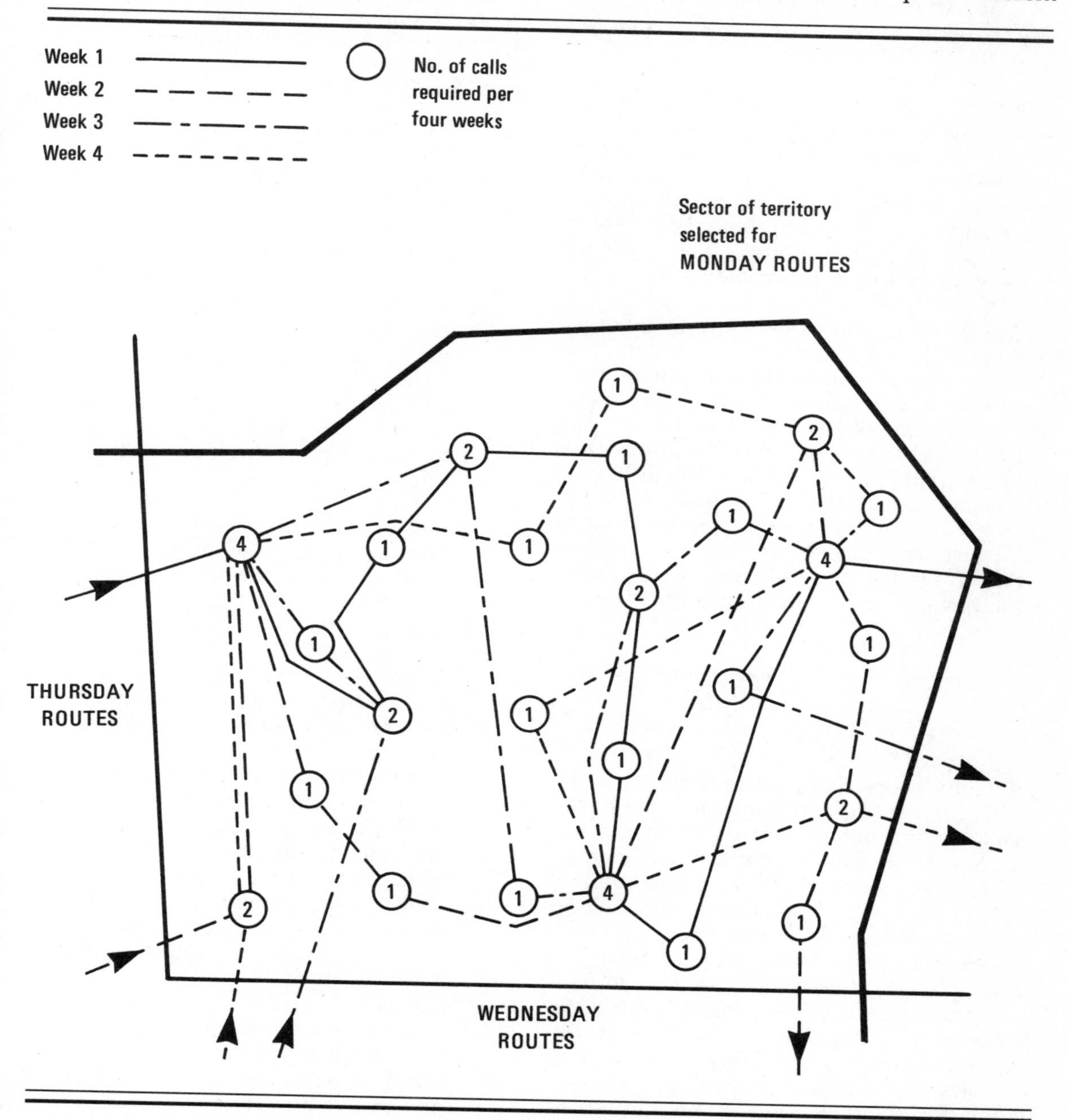

Figure 8.3 Route planning for different call frequencies

weekly journeys for that day, which *overlap* one another so as to give the necessary number of repeat visits to the right customers. Out of the four journeys which have to be planned:

1 Calls to be made weekly will appear on all four
2 Calls to be made every two weeks will appear on two out of four
3 Calls to be made every four weeks will appear on only one.

Figure 8.3 shows a segment of a territory which has been selected for visiting on,let us say, every Monday of a four week cycle. Within it are 25 customers, of whom: (a) 3 require 4 calls per cycle; (b) 6 require 2 calls per cycle and (c) 16 require 1 call per cycle. These customers are marked on the map, with the number of calls to be made shown for each.

Thus, 40 calls have to be made in total. To keep matters fairly simple, let us assume that all the calls will require the same amount of time and that therefore 10 calls a day will be made on each of the four Mondays in the cycle. What we now have to do is to work out four different journeys, each of 10 calls, keeping each journey as short as possible, while giving the correct number of repeat visits to each customer. Figure 8.3 shows one way in which this can be done, although there will be a staggeringly high number of alternatives.

Time constraints

Difficulty occurs in practice in trying to decide which segment to adopt for each day of the week, and it is only rarely that a neat and tidy division can be made in the way we have assumed. Daily segments may have to overlap, as there may be a compelling reason why on one particular day a salesman has to go back into an area which has already been visited on a previous day. One such reason could be if the customer is imposing constraints on the day or time of day when he is willing to receive calls. Busy supermarkets do not wish to see salesmen on Fridays when they are preparing for the weekend. Some businesses close on certain days of the week. Eventually it may become literally impossible to meet all time constraints simultaneously and customers may have to be asked to co-operate in finding some compromise.

How to plan journeys

Keeping track of all these conflicting requirements can only be done by adopting a step-by-step process for planning journeys. For a territory with complex requirements the procedure should be as follows:

1 Prepare a card for each *call* that has to be made, showing the customer's name, address and reference number, the standard time allowance for the call including average between-call travel, and any restrictions on acceptable days and times for the call. Show how many calls per cycle are to be made on this customer and, if more than one, which are the cards for repeat calls, e.g. '1 of 4', '2 of 4' and so on. A specimen of a set of cards is shown in Figure 8.4.
2 Set out on a table a series of boxes, one for each day of the journey cycle, arranged in weekly rows.
3 Put up on the wall a map of the territory with all customers marked in their locations by reference number.
4 Start with the customer having the largest number of calls in the cycle and the severest restrictions on acceptable call times.
5 Choose an acceptable day of the week for the first call on this customer. Put the card for the first call in the box for that day in the first week.
6 Put the cards for the remaining calls on the same customer in the boxes for the same day in subsequent weeks, ensuring equal spacing between them.
7 Take the next most difficult customer and repeat the process.
8 Progressively, put less difficult calls into acceptable boxes that still have room for them.
9 Each time a card is about to be added to a box, check two things:
a) That the total call time of all cards in the box will not exceed the available productive time for one working day.
b) That, by reference to the map, all the calls in the box are situated as close together as possible, so that travelling

distance between them will be at a minimum.

10 When all cards have been fitted into boxes, prepare a journey sequence between all the customers in each box to give the most compact route overall.

If the job is done well, the routes for the same day in each week of the cycle will tend to congregate in one segment of the territory, as indicated in Figure 8.3, with the minimum of overlap with the journeys on other days. This is the test of travel distance having been minimised.

There is no denying that planning routes in this way can be very time consuming and frustrating, but there is no other systematic way of going about it. It is really most unlikely that a salesman will go to all this trouble for himself unless he is guided, supervised and assisted by his head office, which must therefore be prepared to take the job on. Failing this, salesmen will simply never get their routes properly worked out and will miss calls as a result.

The objective of efficient route planning is not merely to save a few per cent of the fuel costs involved in travelling, but to ensure that the complete selling programme is in fact carried out using no more staff than necessary.

Computerisation

For those who like to take a problem to its logical conclusion, it will be clear that there is a certain circularity about the salesman's routeing problem. It is necessary to start by assuming that between-call travelling time can be kept to a certain average figure, and then to work out actual routes which it is hoped will come within this figure. When salesmen are being required to make a large number of short calls in a day, the accuracy of between-call travel times can become very important. The ideal would be to try to calculate the *actual* journey time involved in getting to each prop-

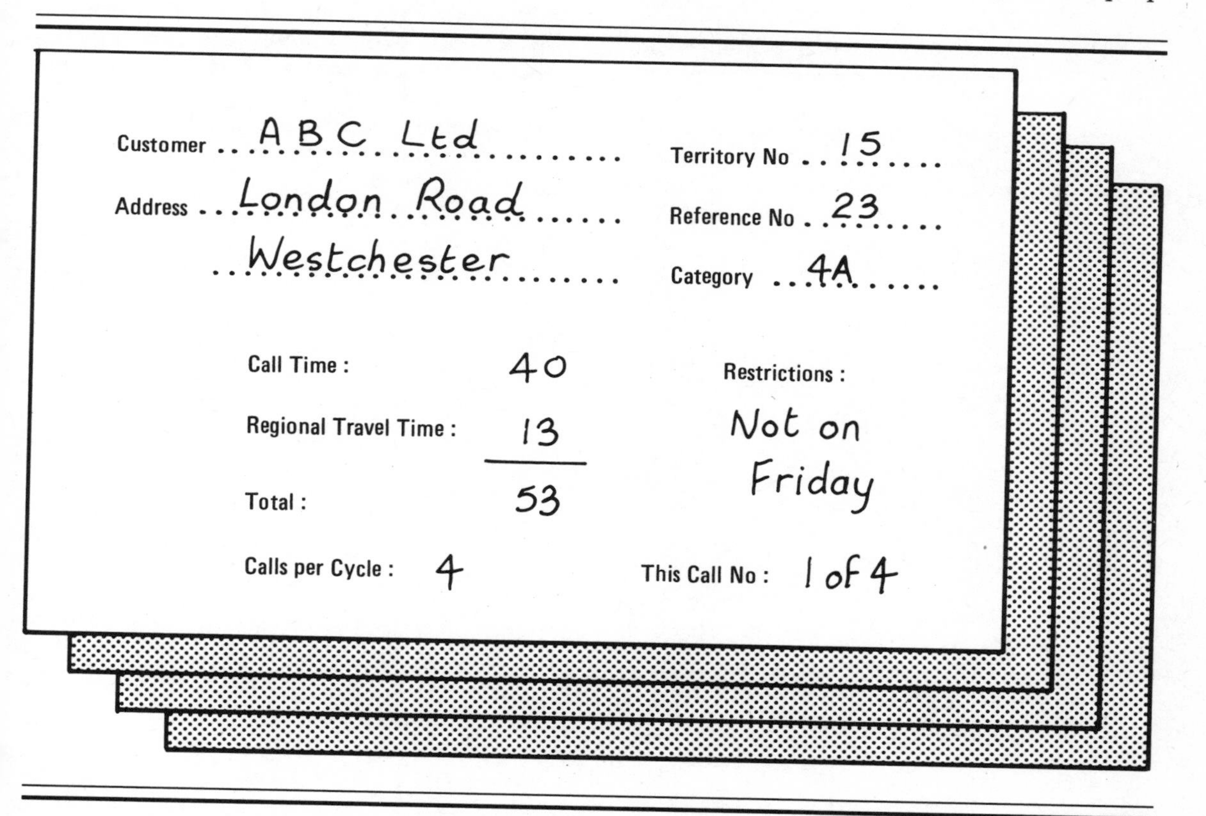

Figure 8.4 Journey planning cards

osed new call from the last one, and to build up the working day accordingly. Unfortunately the computation involved in such an exercise makes it quite impractical by manual methods. This makes it sound like an ideal problem to be dealt with by a computer, and indeed computerised systems for the purpose have been developed, although the problem is by no means simple even so. To be of the greatest value, the computer first of all has to have stored in memory complete details of the actual network of roads, from which to work out the travel time required between any two customers. Accurate map references for all customers must also be fed in. This demands a great deal of preparatory work, but thereafter, using mathematical formulae and several iterations, these systems are able to reach a high degree of optimisation of routes. Companies which employ a high level of resources in calling on customers to complicated schedules could well benefit from adopting this degree of sophistication in journey planning.

Irregular calls

In all the foregoing planning it has been assumed that all the calls required by customers are regular ones, which can be scheduled at fixed intervals with a standard call time allowance. Certain types of customer may require calls from time to time, when some particular need arises, but not regularly. This could be especially true of calls to service equipment, or calls to collect overdue payment, or in answer to specific enquiries or complaints. Some provision for such calls ought to be made in the journey plan, even though they do not occur regularly. A possible approach is to make some estimate of the *probability* of a call being required in any given journey cycle. Suppose on average a call on a customer has been required hitherto in one cycle out of four, then there is a one in four probability of a call being required in the next cycle. On the day on which a journey is being made to that area in any case, a time allowance can be given for calling on this customer, but at only one-fourth of the normally required time. If there are a number of such calls for which provision is made on the basis of probabilities, there is every prospect that cycle by cycle they will balance each other out, and that the total time allowed will not be far away from the time actually used. Prospecting for new customers who are not even known yet can only be allowed for by giving the salesman spare time on certain days. Alternatively time can be given when the salesman is already due to visit areas where there might be the prospect of new customers.

Checklist 8

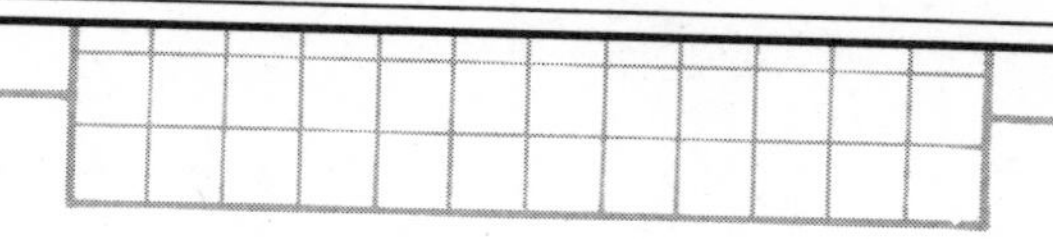

Deployment of resources

8.1 Planned workload

(a) Is there a fixed length cycle for the planning of sales activity? Does all activity occur at least once per cycle? Is there anything which cannot be planned on a cyclical basis?
(b) Is it possible to calculate a 'standard' workload for the sales force(s) for a total of one cycle? Is there a workload norm per man? How do actual staff numbers compare to the calculated requirement?
(c) How are seasonal effects on workload and temporary disruptions taken care of?

8.2 Territories and journeys

(a) On the basis of calculated standards, what range of difference in workload exists between the territories of individual salesmen?
(b) Can the location of customer workload be plotted on the map? With sufficient accuracy? And clarity? Could this be made the basis for designing or revising territories?
(c) Do salesmen have fixed lists of customers? Fixed territory boundaries?
(d) Are there fixed daily journey schedules for each salesman? Are they adhered to? Are they feasible? Comprehensive? Who designs them? Is it known where salesmen are on any day?
(e) How far can customer calls be planned on a regular basis? What is the range of frequency for calls? Are there restrictions on acceptable calling times?
(f) Does salesmen's daily travel time between customers seem excessive? What can be done to monitor it? To improve it?
(g) Would it be possible to introduce systematic planning of daily journey schedules? By head office? By salesmen themselves?

9

Organising the sales force

Organisation structures seem to have a fatal attraction for some businesses, which become ever more entangled with re-organisations intended to remedy the problems caused by the last re-organisation. Much misplaced ingenuity goes into producing complex webs of inter-relationships with everyone having some form of responsibility to or for everyone else. An organisation structure should reflect quite straightforwardly the functions which people are expected to perform; and the more clarity there is about what these functions are, the less confusion there will be in working out an organisation structure that will help rather than hinder.

Sole responsibilities

Functions in a selling organisation fall broadly into two categories: those which are clearly the responsibility of the sales department itself, and of no one else; and those in which some other parts of the company are also involved, but where the sales department must take a share. In respect of the first category, the sales organisation operates in a self-contained manner and can structure itself to suit its own concerns. When functions have to be shared with other groups, a structure has to be created which will form an effective interface with them and facilitate co-operation.

Before becoming involved in the detail of an organisation structure, the key questions are: who is to do what, and to whom are they to be answerable for it? The principal areas for which the sales organisation is solely responsible in this way are all discussed in detail elsewhere in this book and can be summarised as follows:

1 Managing and implementing the field selling operation to customers. This is the primary task of a selling organisation and its main reason for existence. The operatives are the salesmen and other selling staff in the front line, and the management of them will be carried out by delegation through the various levels of central, regional and local supervision, sub-divided as necessary into specialist divisions.
2 The account management of major customers, whether single entities, or multiple branch operations spread over a wide area. It is the size of these areas of operations which determines whether such customers can be managed at local level, or whether this can only be done at regional or even national level in order to ensure co-ordination of activity in all the locations affected by negotiations.
3 Pioneering work, prospecting for new outlets, conducting surveys, selecting special distributors for appointment, negotiating territorial agreements and the like.
4 The management of what is generally known as sales operations: that is, the particular form which a selling campaign is going to take, the detail of promotions, the specific selling activity, and the programme of events.
5 Sales planning and development; which will include the identification, classification and review of the customer universe, followed by the correct deployment of the sales force in relation to its targets and its workload.
6 Establishment of an efficient system for

administration, routine and information, and its proper management thereafter.

The importance of these functions has to be assessed to determine how many people are required for each, or whether some are only a part time job. Quantifying the workload for field selling has already been dealt with, and the other functions have to be evaluated as objectively as they can be. Once this has been done, responsibilities can be assigned to individuals by inclusion in their formal job descriptions.

Shared responsibilities

Among shared responsibilities is the most important one of all, namely that shared with product marketing management for the total sales volume and profit contribution of the business. Means of assisting this process organisationally will be looked at later. Other shared functions which are likely to exist will include:

1 Physical distribution
2 Production planning
3 Credit control

Physical distribution

As was pointed out in chapter 6, it is the selling strategy of a business which determines the kind of physical distribution services which must be provided, and those services are a very important element in the total strategy package. Choice of market distribution method – direct sales to a multitude of small outlets, or only through a small number of main distributors – will dictate whether or not a company has to make widespread deliveries of small orders, involving regional supply depots, and a large transport fleet; as opposed to bulk shipments direct from factory to only a few locations. Sales policy on service level and speed of delivery will affect the size of stockholdings required. Once the sales department has specified these requirements – taking full responsibility for the cost consequences involved – many businesses find it appropriate that the actual management of physical distribution should be done by a separate, specialist department. Warehouse operation, and the supervision of a transport fleet are seen as too much of a distraction for managers whose primary concern is making sales. Since the control of stock levels is very much a financial and cash flow concern, responsibility for physical distribution is often vested in the financial or accounting management of a company. Even when sales management are thus relieved of the day-to-day burden of managing physical distribution, they must continue to keep the closest watch on what is actually done, and to have a close co-operation with those responsible for doing it. It is to his familiar contacts in the sales organisation that the customer will complain if deliveries go wrong; and the sales organisation must be sufficiently knowledgeable to respond correctly and take the right action. If in a region there is both a sales manager and a depot manager, there must be the clearest understanding between them of the policy that is going to be followed in distribution matters, and of what demands on distribution are going to arise as a result of the selling programme.

Production planning

Sales management are the people who have the means of making the most immediate impact on the level of sales volume at any given time. The actions of product marketing management in promoting the appeal to consumers are likely to be longer term in their effects. By actively speeding up the process of getting orders, sales management can do a great deal to bring forward sales volume from a later to an earlier period; and vice versa, can unobtrusively postpone it when immediate supply is embarrassed. Selling tactics therefore impinge most directly on the production planning process, which extends all the way from the purchasing of materials to the scheduling of plant and labour. Longer term production planning is in any event completely dependent on the sales forecasts which sales management jointly with product marketing management have been responsible for producing.In the shorter term, sales management must maintain the closest understanding with their production colleagues so as to be continuously aware of any limitations or surpluses in production, and also of the likely consequences for production of any proposed selling or promotional campaign. It is a sales responsibility to try to minimise peaks and troughs in the sales figures so as to avoid costly overtime in production, followed by over capacity and idle plant. Provision must be made for regular liaison with the production function.

Credit control

No sale is complete until it is paid for. In this most fundamental sense, sales management and front line salesmen must have a responsibility for the credit commitments they undertake and for the due payment of debts. The keeping of customers' accounts and the routine of requests for payment will normally be entrusted to an accounts department, but there must be complete understanding and agreement between sales and financial management as to how these routines will operate. Sales management become involved in credit matters in the following ways:

1 The credit terms offered to the distributive trade are a vital part of the total trade reward package, as discussed in chapter 5. The implications for company finances must be fully worked out between sales and financial management, so that cash flow can be correctly predicted at all times, and sales management do not find themselves suddenly faced with a finance director's ultimatum to bring down the level of debts before the company goes bankrupt.

2 Credit limits for individual customers also have to be agreed between sales and financial management. Nothing goes more against the grain than for a salesman to have to relinquish a sale because it exceeds a credit limit; therefore the salesman and the accountant must fully understand one another on this score. Assessing the financial standing of a customer through bank references and trade enquiries is a job for the accountant. Sizing up the way in which a customer is trading should be the skill of the salesman. A customer who is going over his credit limit because he wants to buy more from you and less from your competitors has to be distinguished from one who wants more credit from you in order to pay his debts to someone else. The sales force and the accounting service have to pool their information to arrive at a jointly agreed limit, and then stick to it. Of course, as long as a customer pays on time, the bigger a credit limit he uses the better.

3 When a customer exceeds agreed limits or fails to pay, the action to be taken must be fully co-ordinated between accounts and sales. At what point is credit to be stopped and orders refused, and who is to tell the customer? For that matter, who is going to tell the salesman? Whatever happens, it must not be the customer who is the first to tell the salesman that credit has been stopped, when he calls in all innocence to get the next order.

4 If cash and debt collection is to be made a job for the salesman, due allowance must be made for this in assessing his workload and in working out appropriate call cycles and dates. It is no good expecting a salesman to collect money before the credit period is up. Nor can he be expected to call back out of journey sequence merely to collect money – unless it is the kind of emergency for which some provision should have been made in his workload planning. If the salesman does not collect payment as routine, but is only asked to intervene when there is a difficulty, there must be a very efficient routine for notifying him in good time to make the necessary changes to his schedule.

Organisation structures

An organisation structure with its different levels of jobs and its lines of responsibility is then an attempt to summarise for practical purposes what have been identified as the necessary functions, and how they are to be allocated. It must not become an excuse for compartmentalisation and it does not do away with the need for the whole sales department to work together as a team without too narrow a concern for personal responsibilities. Nevertheless these responsibilities must be clearly thought out, so that on the one hand all functions are properly taken care of, while on the other hand those who are made responsible for a function are given the authority to carry it out. An organisation structure has to take into account the three things which are essential for making a human organisation work harmoniously:

1 The allocation of responsibilities
2 The authority to control
3 The span of control.

Complication in the structure of a sales organisation nearly always arises as a result of specialisation in one form or another. The question of specialisation has already been discussed in detail in chapter 6; in what follows some of the consequences of it will be examined.

Since product marketing and trade selling inter-relate so closely, it is not really possible to consider an organisation structure for the one without at the same time showing where the other fits in. This aspect of the shared responsibilities of sales management is therefore included from the start, but otherwise only the direct functions of the selling department need be considered at this stage. The integration of the trade selling structure into the wider company functions is something to be looked at a little later.

The unspecialised structure

Taking the simplest case first, that of a sales organisation which is not subdivided in any way into specialist groups, but which sells a total list of products through a single field force to customers as a whole, the organisation structure can be quite simply a single pyramid extending from the head of the selling function down through its various levels, to the front line salesman. The number of intermediate levels required will be dictated by the number of salesmen in total and by the geographic spread of the operation. It will probably be necessary for the head of sales to delegate responsibilities first to a number of regional managers who may in turn each control managers in charge of smaller areas and so on down to individual salesmen. Figure 9.1 illustrates this very basic organisation structure. The arrangement is ideally simple with clear lines of responsibility and each man responding directly to only one immediate superior.

The span of control, or the number of subordinates whom one manager can manage,should be decided as far as possible by actually working out what the superior will have to do. If an area manager or supervisor is intended to accompany each of his salesmen once per cycle, visit major customers himself, conduct area meetings, prospect for new customers, and do some administration work, it should be a simple matter to calculate how much time he is going to have available and therefore how many salesmen he can control effectively. The same applies at other levels of the organisation. When the workload becomes too much for one man, he must be given an assistant, or an additional colleague at the same level, with the work redivided. What must be avoided is the 'one over one' situation, in which a manager is given one subordinate but with all his duties apparently to be delegated through that subordinate, and no direct contacts with any of the rest of the organisation. Work then tends to be duplicated by both manager and subordinate, rather than shared. Duties must be split in some manner, with the subordinate having a clearly delegated area of responsibility which he can attend to on his own.

Board accountability

Still referring to Figure 9.1, the head of selling, or more accurately of the trade marketing operation, collaborates directly with his colleague in charge of product marketing in developing a joint strategy, the trade aspects of which are then implemented uniformly throughout the selling organisations in its regions, areas and territories. Similarly the head of product marketing implements the product aspects of the strategy through a team of product group managers and possibly individual brand managers. Both departmental heads will be responsible for their policies at board level in the company. This may be through being board members themselves, with the respective titles of marketing director and sales director; or they may be merely senior managers who report both to the same board member, who might be the chairman of the company, or a director responsible both for product and trade marketing. Whether a joint strategy is better served by having both the product and the trade functions separately represented at board level, or whether both

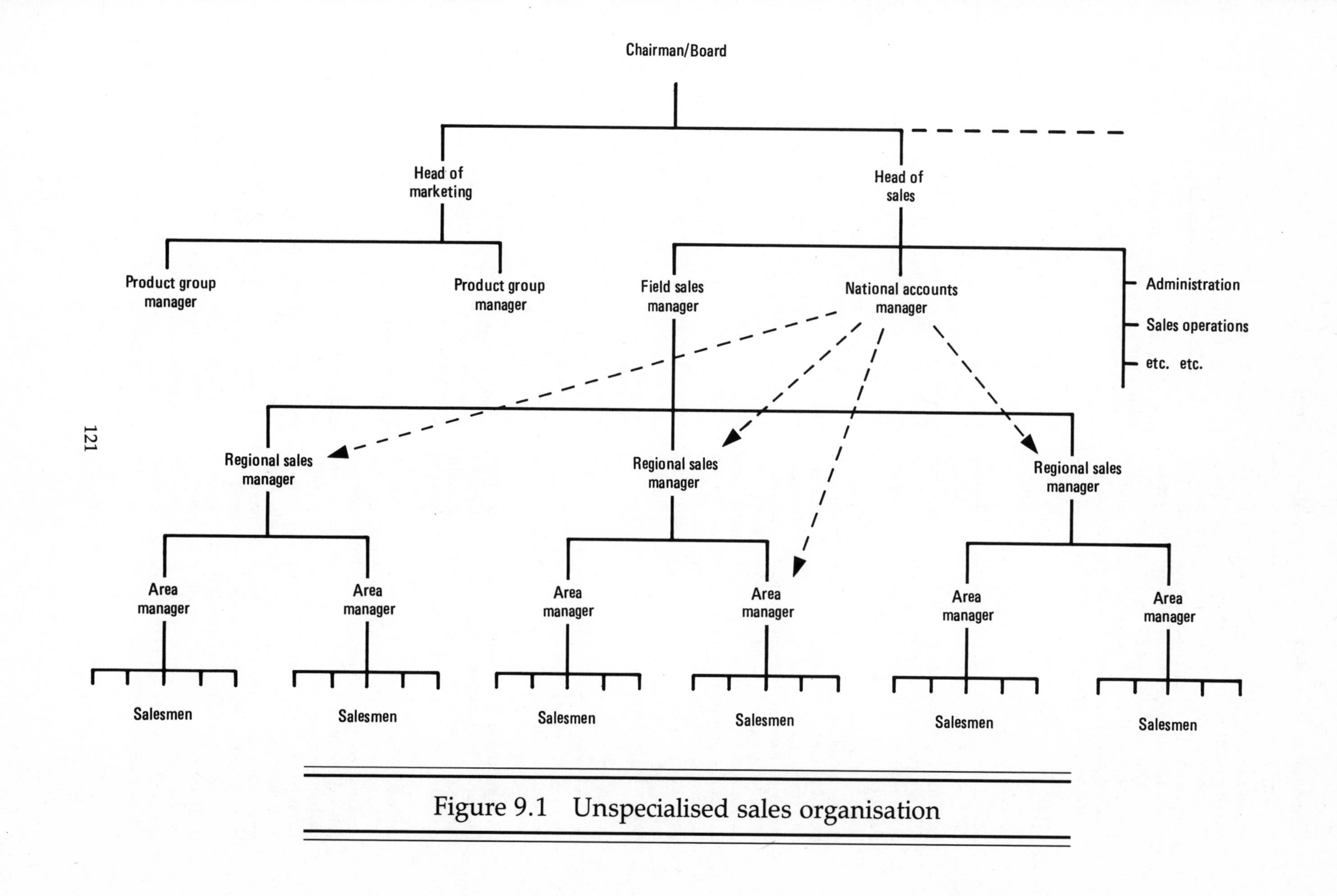

Figure 9.1 Unspecialised sales organisation

strategies should be co-ordinated in the person of one director, depends on the total size of the organisation. Either way, the organisation structure at its lower levels will be the same. In the examples of organisation structures which we shall be looking at, the functions of the 'head of sales' and the 'head of product marketing' will be the same whether or not they are also board members.

Other responsibilities

So much for the organisation of the field selling operation; it remains to consider what other direct responsibilities of the selling operation have to be covered. Depending on their importance, the functions of sales operations (promotions and tactics), sales planning and development, administration, recruitment and training, may all require full time management, or even whole departments. The head of trade marketing must also take responsibility for these, as well as for field selling. If the duties are onerous, he may no longer be able to control directly a number of regional managers, but may have to delegate the entire field selling operation to an overall field sales manager who will report to him personally.

National accounts

If major account management is an important function, and because of widespread operations cannot be handled by the regional managers in their own regions, a national accounts manager or managers will have have to be appointed. This introduces the first complication to an otherwise straightforward structure; the national accounts manager has to communicate directly with regional managers and perhaps area managers in order to tell them what has to be done resulting from his negotiations centrally with the major accounts. Regional and area managers therefore have to have a 'dotted line' relationship with the national accounts manager – their direct responsibility is to their immediate superior but they have a complementary duty to co-operate with national accounts as the need arises. All these relationships are illustrated in Figure 9.1.

Specialisation in the field

When specialisation is introduced to the field selling force, the crux of the matter is whether the whole of the sales organisation continues to follow the same selling programme, or not. If there are to be separate groups of specialists according to the selling function performed, such as first grade salesmen, assistants, merchandisers or display staff, but they still all deal with the same range of products as part of the same selling strategy, then there is no need for any great complication in the organisation structure. The only change need be at field level where, instead of supervising only one grade of selling staff, area managers will now have to control several grades, each going different ways and performing different tasks. But at the higher levels of the organisation nothing need change,since the different forces in the field are still all part of the one single operating plan. In exactly the same way, there can be specialised salesmen for different types of customers in each area, without this affecting the structure any higher up.

Figure 9.2 shows an organisation where the area manager has an assortment of this kind to look after. Obviously this will greatly increase his burdens, and might justify giving him an assistant, but he would not be greatly helped by the creation of a central function, say, to 'co-ordinate' the activity of sales assistants. Such central functions which advise rather than do should be looked at very critically. What area managers get their sales assistants to do should be laid down, like everything else, as part of the overall selling strategy and programme.

Product specialisation

Real complication arises when it is decided to have specialist selling groups for different parts of the product range. The first problem, as mentioned before, is that divisions between products and customers rarely coincide exactly. Some customers are going to be buyers of items from more than one product group. Either the specialist sales forces are going to have to duplicate one another's calls

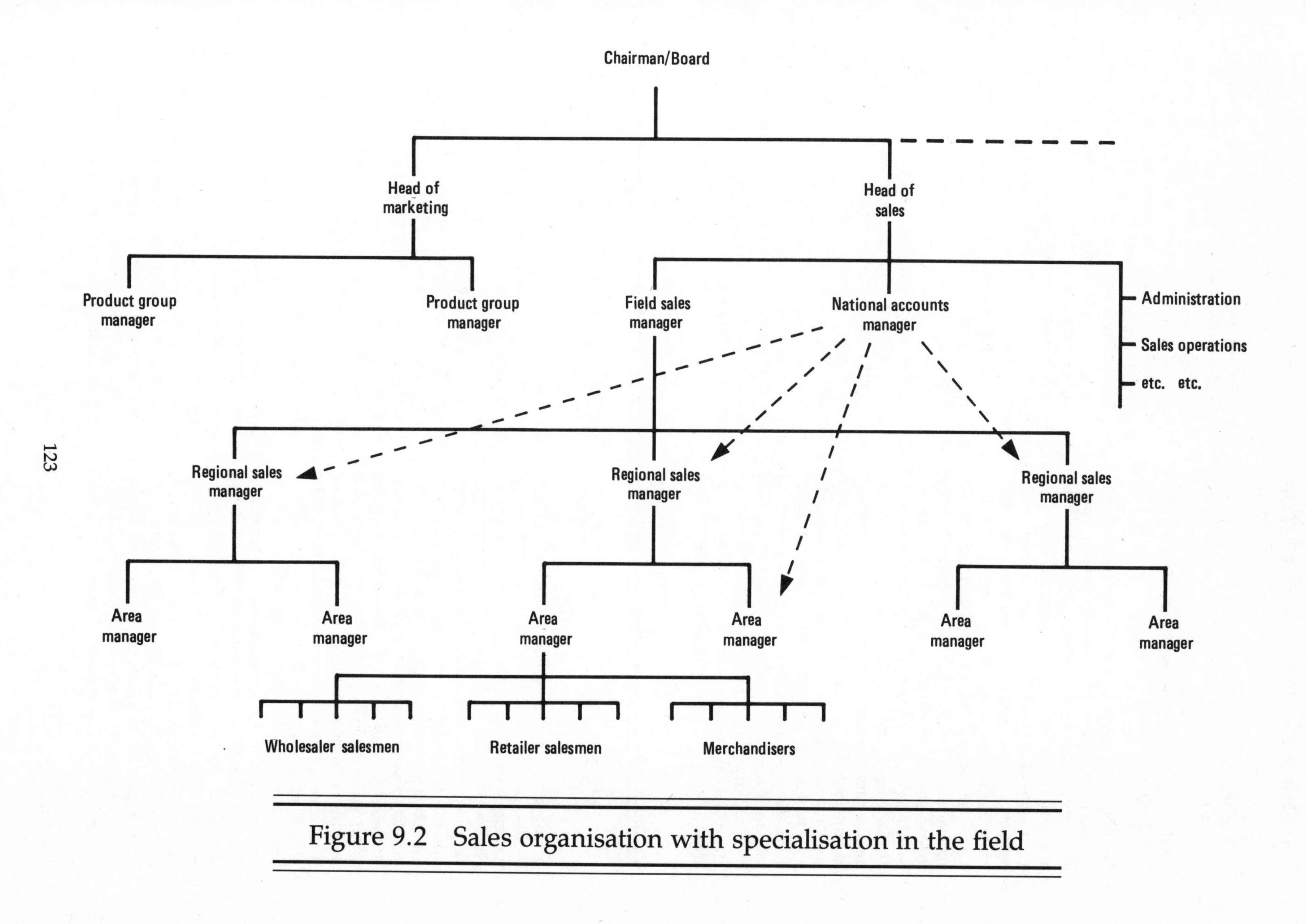

Figure 9.2 Sales organisation with specialisation in the field

on the same customers, or else strict specialisation cannot be preserved and some salesmen will have to handle more than one product group. Some working rule for this must be laid down.

The object of having product specialisation is so that each type of product can benefit from a different, tailor-made selling approach. This implies different selling programmes and even several quite different sales strategies to be worked out. Product marketing should logically be divided on exactly the same lines, and it will be natural for those specialised in the appeal of the product to the consumer to wish to communicate directly with those specialised in selling it to the trade. Communicating directly from the centre to salesmen in the field is rarely feasible, and the need grows up to have field management who are also specialised along product group lines, and who will be the points of contact with product marketing. At the same time, the numbers of salesmen required for each product group will be dissimilar and their territories will not coincide: it may be necessary to group them into areas which are also of different size so that the different area managers for the different product groups may not coincide geographically either. Add to this the overriding necessity for account management co-ordination as well, and a highly complicated structure results. Figure 9.3 shows how in such a set-up the dotted lines begin to multiply across and between functions, even when there are only two specialist groups. Field managers have to respond to their hierarchical superiors, while keeping contact with their product marketing specialists and with each other, on questions of shared customers. This is likely to be one of the most expensive forms of organisation, and its adoption has to be very fully justified.

Nevertheless, where the product groups really are different, to the extent that each must work out with its trade marketing colleagues a quite distinct strategy for its distribution through the trade, it may be a false economy to try to use one unified sales organisation to implement more than one strategy. Concentration of purpose can be lost, which is more vital to a business than some duplication of calls on customers.

A case study

In chapter 6 reference was made to the arguments for and against the extra complexity of having specialised sales groups for different classes of trade customer. It is superficially very reasonable to see one's business as falling into this kind of division, and to feel that there must be merit in giving specialised sales attention to these quite different kinds of customer. A real-life situation which illustrates the point occurred in the H & B company in Britain. H & B manufactures a range of toiletries, ranging from toothpaste to shampoos and hair sprays, which are not quite in the category of fashionable cosmetics but which nevertheless have to appeal as well as be functional. Several decades ago, such items insofar as they existed at all sold almost exclusively through pharmacies, and therefore H & B's sales organisation was originally completely devoted to selling directly to pharmacies. By degrees, the lines began to be taken up by general shops, but only in a small way which did not justify widespread sales callage. Instead, a small separate sales force was established to encourage stocking by wholesalers for indirect supply to general shops.

In due course the era of the supermarket arrived and before long supermarkets became the major outlet for H & B's products. Fewer people now go to a pharmacy to have a brand of toothpaste recommended, but instead choose it for themselves from the supermarket shelves along with the rest of the shopping. H & B therefore formed a third sales group to ensure good prominence in supermarkets.

Consequently, in recent years H & B operated three distinct sales forces throughout the country for pharmacies, wholesalers and supermarkets. Certainly each sales force dealt with its customers in completely different ways. Pharmacies responded to the professional approach, wholesalers were only interested in bulk terms and deals, while the main task in supermarkets was to fill the

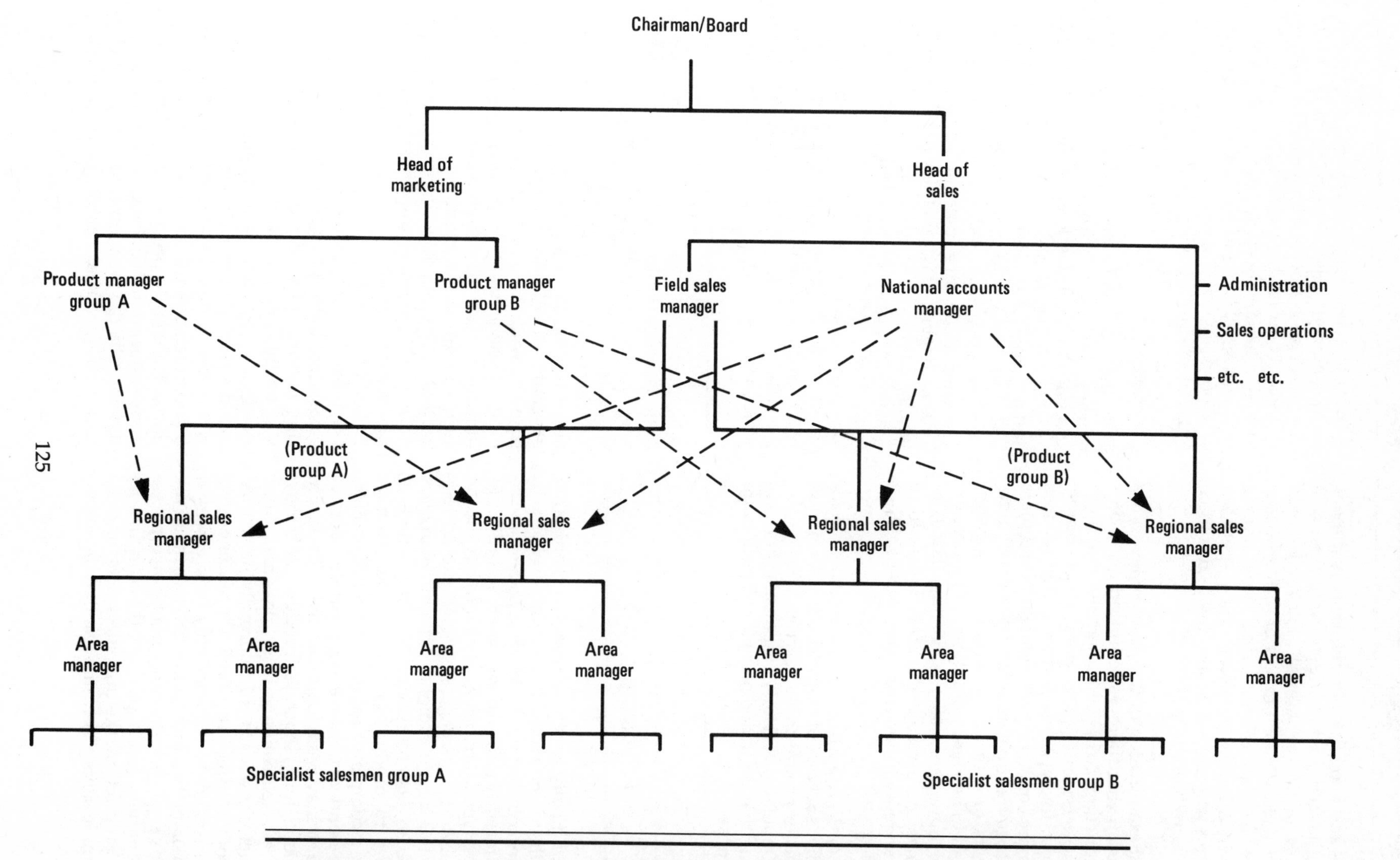

Figure 9.3 Sales organisation specialised by product group

shelves and keep the toiletries display fitment looking attractive when the store manager was too busy to do this himself. Each sales area contained different numbers of different representatives, all criss-crossing each other's routes in the same territory. Time spent on travelling was excessive, and total sales force numbers were high.

Careful examination of the problem led to the conclusion that there were indeed quite different functions to be performed, but that these did not necessarily correspond to the classic divisions in type of customer. Differences were more concerned with whether customers were large multiple operations, or small independents; or with what kinds of servicing support had to be given; and these differences extended throughout all the existing classes of customer. As a result, the H & B sales force has been reorganised into five different grades of selling staff:

1 Local group negotiators, responsible for the success of total dealings with all major groups in their areas.
2 Outlet supervisors, responsible for seeing that the action plans for all outlets are carried out.
3 Local order representatives, who make scheduled calls on all types of outlet to make sure stocks are maintained and to collect orders accordingly.
4 Merchandising staff, who advise on layouts in all types of shop, and design displays.
5 Sales support staff, part time workers who keep shelves filled and records up to date.

Only the local order representatives work to journey schedules, with the merchandising and sales support staff keeping to the tasks set by the representatives. The negotiator and outlet supervisor are more free ranging, making visits as specific needs arise. Total numbers have been reduced by 25 per cent. The integrated teams come directly under regional managers, of whom there are five for the whole country, so that specialisation by function applies only at field level. Results from the changeover are increased sales, lower costs, better distribution availability, a simpler organisation and improved teamwork. Analysis of real functional differences in the selling operation will generally yield such dividends.

Product divisions

The difficulty with a sales organisation specialised by product is to know where to stop in splitting the functions. There have to be different groups of salesmen according to product speciality; there probably have to be specialist area managers as well; should regional managers, national account managers and so on, also be duplicated or triplicated according to product group? At the extreme, where a company wishes to concentrate effort single-mindedly into each separate product group, it may seem logical to divide the entire company into separate product divisions, each as self-contained as possible. Such product divisions would normally be treated as profit centres, or practically autonomous businesses, held together only by a common board of management, and each sharing in the minimum of services provided by a corporate headquarters. Each product division has its own product marketing specialists and its own trade selling operation, so that the organisation structure in each product division once again becomes of the simplest 'non-specialised' variety. This is shown in Figure 9.4. Each selling operation selects its own target customers and pursues its own selling programme without regard to any overlapping with the customers of the other product divisions. Only very generalised functions, such as administration, training and so on, could continue to be shared between divisions. Most other support functions would have to be duplicated in each division separately.

Obviously this is a very expensive form of organisation, appropriate only to the largest of corporations. One of the skills of managing vast business empires is the judgement of the exact point at which it is more efficient to have independent groups, if necessary competing with one another, rather than one huge monolithic structure attempting to do everything. The unified organisation, with all functions concentrated and unduplicated, may be theoretically the more efficient, but in practice independent operations of manageable size,

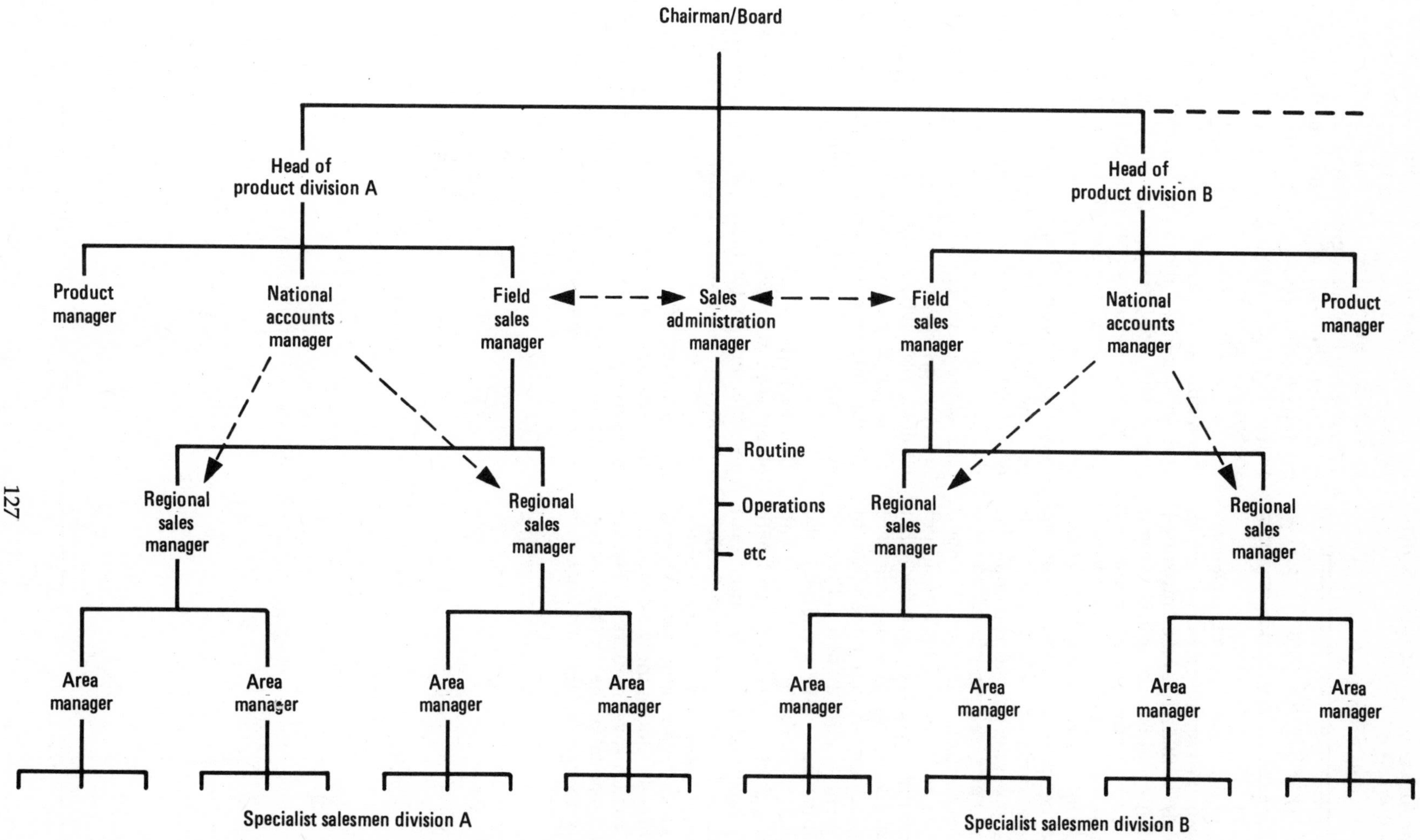

Figure 9.4 Company organised by product divisions

even with some functions sub-optimised, may give better results.

Matrix structures

The ideal way of organising people in a common enterprise is the hierarchical structure, or pyramid of levels, with each level commanded by the level above and each man following a single leader. Roman armies were organised in this way, and the method works now as it worked then. Unfortunately business enterprises tend to be more complex, consisting usually of several pyramids side by side, each contributing a separate part to the common objective – marketing, selling, production, research, financial control, and so on. Combining these separate efforts into one grand strategy only at the top of each pyramid, that is to say at board level, can give rise to lack of mutual understanding and co-operation at levels lower down. As already noted, the sales organisation must have effective liaison not only with product marketing but also with production on matters of planning, and with the financial departments as regards cash flow, credit control, and distribution service. Merely having 'dotted lines' between the pyramids to encourage communication may not be good enough. One of the most interesting attempts to improve matters is the so-called two-dimensional or matrix organisation structure. This recognises the fact that self-contained pyramids for each function are inadequate. Instead, operating responsibility is given to mixed teams consisting of representatives of each function, grouped around a common leader, but each at the same time upholding the objectives of his own specialism. One of the ways of arranging such a structure is shown in Figure 9.5.

It is assumed there are two market groups, A and B, although the same structure could apply with only one group, or with several. Each group is led by a member of the product marketing section, supported by members of the other functional departments. The board members in charge of each function control on the one hand their operating departments, each in the usual pyramid, and at the same time oversee their special representatives in each of the market groups. The market groups are responsible for working out an overall strategic plan which will have the support of all the functions involved, and also for securing the implementation of the plan by the appropriate action within each function.

This example is given mainly to show that other ways of structuring an organisation are possible, not that a matrix organisation will necessarily be more effective. It could be simply a recipe for confusion by committee, if the members of the groups are not practical men accustomed to achieving results. No organisation structure will be a substitute for commonsense among its members, coupled with the desire to work together as a team.

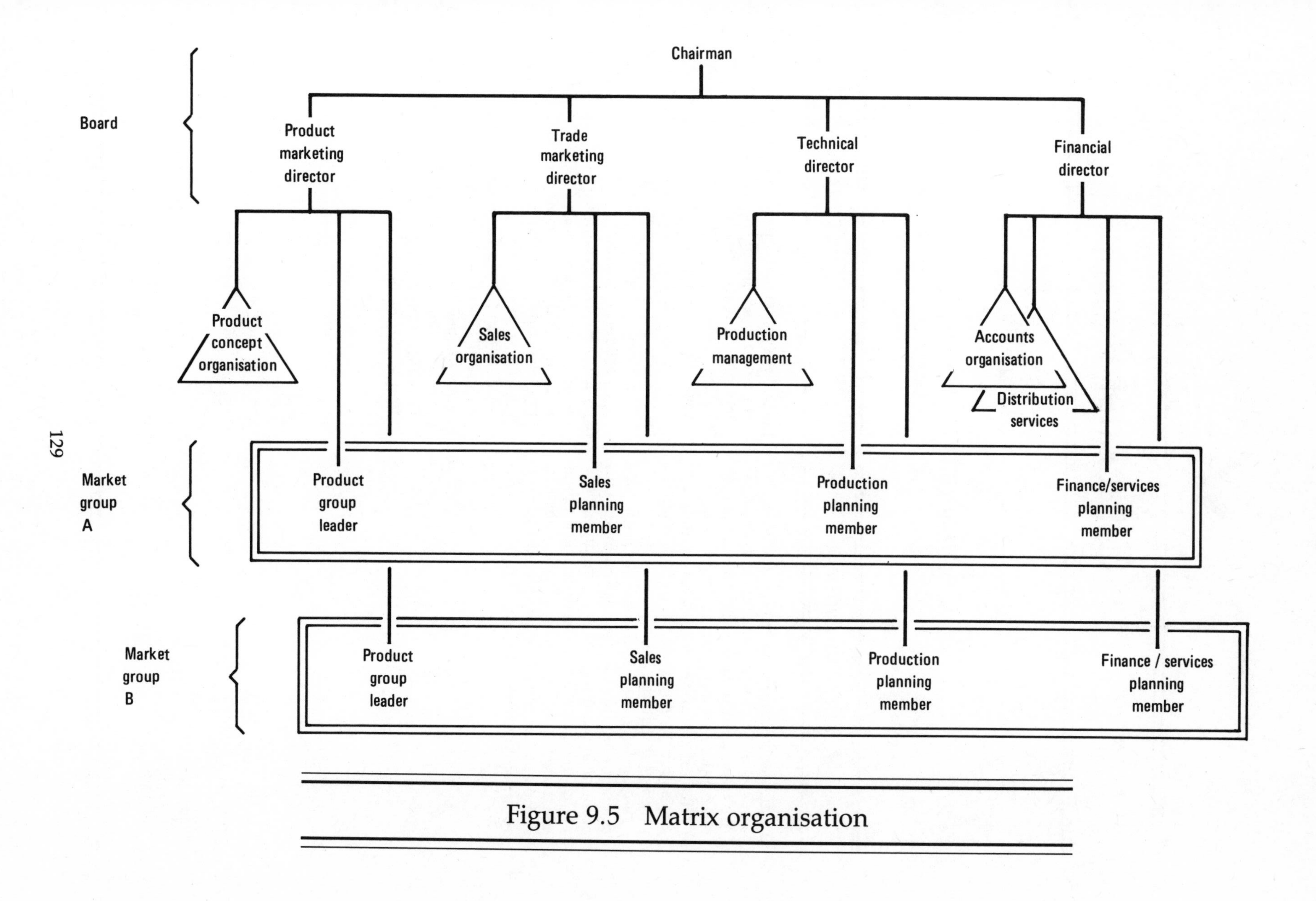

Figure 9.5 Matrix organisation

Checklist 9

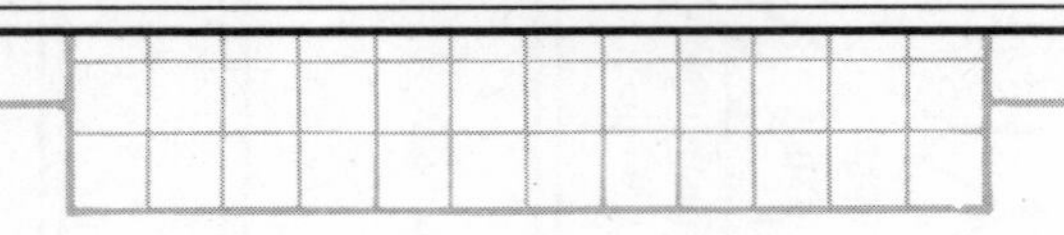

Organising the sales force

9.1 Responsibilities

(a) Are the functions for which the sales organisation is responsible clearly defined? Are these in turn specified in the written job descriptions of the appropriate people?
(b) What are the arrangements for the sales organisation having a say in the operation of physical distribution services?
(c) Does sales have regular liaison with production planning? Is production taken into account in planning selling campaigns?
(d) How are credit limits fixed? Is there a limit on trade debts as a whole? Are salesmen completely familiar with the credit control routine? Are they satisfied with it?

9.2 Structures

(a) Is there an official organisation diagram for the sales operation? Does it also show relationships with other departments?
(b) How are trade selling objectives represented at board level? At what level are they co-ordinated with product marketing?
(c) If there is a national accounts function, in what ways does it communicate with the field selling operation?
(d) What case is there, if any, for specialised selling staff at field level? What would be the lines of division? How would organisation structure be affected.
(e) Is there any need for specialisation by product, and if so how could this be organised? Would independent product divisions be justified?
(f) Are there any arrangements for multi- functional groups working together as teams? Would this be beneficial?

10

Information for control

Information is needed to control whether things have happened as planned. Information on its own, without a plan to measure it against, is merely confusing: while a plan without information as to how it is working can be a dangerous piece of self-deception. In the sales organisation, what management have to plan for and consequently control are:

1 The selection of customers to be serviced
2 The type of selling attention and service to be given
3 The conduct and cost of selling operations in the field
4 The sales performance actually achieved in the various sectors.

There is a further element against which it is highly desirable to measure the performance of the selling organisation, if it is at all possible to do so; and that is the profit contribution obtained from the various trade sectors. This will have to be left until last, as it involves a number of complex issues. The other areas, for which sales and trade marketing management have responsibility, are the ones where adequate information is going to be required, and the objective must be to capture and disseminate this information as efficiently and as economically as possible.

Customer information

Criteria for selecting target customers have already been discussed in chapter 7. Once the selection is made, the essential facts on all current customers and on all potential customers in whom there is an interest must be recorded and kept up to date. Apart from name and address, and any system of reference numbers, the essential information on customers is likely to comprise:

1 Customer location, in sales region, zone, or in any map reference system if used
2 Customer classification, as used in determining selling action
3 Trade terms and discounts allowed
4 Summary of sales performance to date
5 Estimated sales potential
6 Selling action planned
7 Call frequencies, standard call times
8 Credit limit

Linking with accounts

Every credit account customer of a business will have an account in the ledgers and will probably be indexed in the accounts department for the information they want to know. It is clearly desirable that information held by accounts and by sales should be integrated, or at least not self-contradictory (and it is surprising how often that happens). When accounting is computerised, there is every scope for maintaining comprehensive customer information files in the central computer with all the information needed by all parties. Sales performance figures can be summarised directly from the computerised ledger account. Once information is held in a computer in this way there is normally no difficulty in having it analysed and extracted in any way one chooses. The essential thing is to foresee all the items of information which have to be included, as it is generally much more difficult to extend these after the system is set up.

Cash customers and potential customers who

have not yet done any business will not appear in accounts department records. Profile information for these will have to be kept separately by the sales department, or else added specially to any central computer files even though there are no accounts to be kept.

Communicating with salesmen

It is vital for salesmen to have accurate and up-to-date information on the customers they visit, particularly as regards current performance – not only the value of sales, but exactly which items were last purchased and when, so as to plan the selling interview. How much of this latter detail should also be kept at head office is to some extent optional. If the analysis would have to be done separately by both salesman and head office, or if it would be a difficult task to keep either copied from the other, then it is more important that the record should be kept by the salesman, and made available to head office only when specially required. On the other hand, this kind of manual record keeping distracts the salesman from more productive work and is not likely to be done efficiently in any case. If the information is being generated in a computer in the first place – that is, if invoices to the customer are computerised – it will probably cost less in the long run to have the summary of sales history per customer produced at head office and sent out to the salesmen in convenient form. Assuming that salesmen are working to regular journey schedules, which is desirable in any case, an update for the relevant customers can be mailed to salesmen just in advance of the scheduled call day.

For those businesses which do not have the advantage of computers, a simple but effective system is the so-called 'shuttle card'. This is a card per customer, kept by the salesman, giving the customer details, and listing down one side all items in the product range. At each visit, the salesman notes in successive columns the quantities ordered of each item, and mails the card to head office. Head office extracts the order details from the last column, endorses it as accepted, and mails the card back to the salesman. An example of a shuttle card is given in Figure 10.1. By this means the salesman always has an up-to-date record of orders placed in time for the next call.

Selling interviews can very usefully be built around the record of customer purchases, or non-purchases, and even more so if, for a distributor, the record shows the current stock position as well. This would normally be filled in first by the salesman checking stocks before interviewing the buyer. Figure 10.2 illustrates a stock and order summary card for a customer which could either be a shuttle card or one kept solely by the salesman for information. A little mental arithmetic with the record of past purchases compared to remaining stock will provide convincing argument for a new order. Some customers keep such records for themselves, others expect the supplier's salesman to write them up for them. This may take a good deal of the salesman's time, but if it is persuasive in getting orders, it is time well spent. Conceivably, a supplier's computer could produce summary information of this kind which would be of service to the customer as well as to the salesman and could rank as part of the package of trade benefits.

The customer records kept by or for salesmen in whatever form must always be readily available for handover to another salesman who has to take over the customer for any reason.

Field operations

Salesmen will in the normal way be supervised by their immediate management to ensure that they go about their tasks properly and that they keep themselves busy. This will not however necessarily prove that all customers are being serviced as planned. To make sure that the planned selling programme is carried out, there must be a direct check that the individual customers have been attended to, and not merely that salesmen are fully occupied.

Salesmen must therefore positively report on calls made and calls not made against plan. The key to simple control is the laid-down journey plan, which was recommended earlier. If such a document is kept up to date for every salesman, all he has to do is send in a regular copy of it, marking any calls which were not made and adding any extra calls which were made. Unmade calls should be investigated, both to ensure follow-up and to

ORDER RECORD CARD

Customer Name: ABC Ltd
Address: London Road, Westchester

Reference No.: 23
Category: 4A
Call Programme: 1 x (40 + 13 mins)

Scheduled Day(s) for Call: Week 3 Wed.
Salesman: B. Jones

	Date Ordered	Order Quantities in Cases								
		7/5/XX	4/6/XX	2/7/XX	30/7/XX					
Product A	250 gm	50	30	40	35					
Product A	500 gm	10	15	10	15					
Product B		5		5	5					
Product C			12	~~6~~	10					
etc.										
Check Total Case Quantity		125	110	~~120~~	105					
Order Processed/Amended		9-5-XX	10-6-XX	(114) 4-7-XX	1-8-XX					
Comments				C not avail until next week						

Figure 10.1 'Shuttle card' for order transmission

STOCK/ORDER SUMMARY

Customer MAGNO LTD. | Ref. No. 14 | Sched. Day Friday

Address South Street | Category 2B

Norchester | Call Programe 4 x (65+8)

		Quantities in Cases									
	Date:–	4/7/XX		11/7/XX		18/7/XX					
		Stock	Order	Stock	Order	Stock	Order	Stock	Order	Stock	Order
Product A	250 gm	20	50	40	30	30	40				
Product A	500 gm	5	10	1	15	5	10				
Product B		5	5	8	–	6	5				
Product C		10	12	15	(6)	5	10				
etc. etc.											

Figure 10.2 Customer's stock and order card

discover whether there is anything genuinely impractical in the journey plan which needs amendment. It would of course be possible to keep a running record of calls made on each customer's file, to ensure no omissions, but this would be too elaborate unless for customers of quite exceptional importance. As long as journey plans are checked to ensure that they do include all customers, then a check that planned journeys were made is all that is required.

Completion of selling activity has to be reported by the salesman himself, since he is the only one who knows, but the accuracy of reports should be checked by irregular accompaniment, and by having supervisors check directly with customers that visits have indeed been received as reported. The knowledge that such checks are being made is enough to create respect in the selling staff and ensure reliable reporting.

Orders to calls

From the confirmation of calls that have been made, the next control by head office should be on the ratio of orders received to calls made. Where getting orders is in fact the primary purpose of sales calls on the distributive trade, the orders to calls ratio is a first indication of whether call frequencies are correct. A low ratio means that calls are being made more frequently than the trade requires replenishment. If the trade cannot be made to order more in total, there is no advantage in getting it to order more often, and it may be possible to do just as much business with fewer calls. Total weekly miles or kilometres travelled should also be reported by salesmen on their copy journey plans, and the average distance per call checked. Excessive travelling and calls left unmade usually go together.

Again, the journey plan should be checked to see whether routeing can be improved or whether the travelling time allowance should be increased.

Selling costs

The costs of the sales force operation will normally be reported in the regular financial accounting of the company. In the first instance, cost figures are required only against the item totals for which budget estimates have been prepared. A variance against budget can then be investigated in greater detail, to identify the actual items involved.

The ratio of selling costs to sales value should be kept under observation, being the crucial test of the entire trade marketing strategy. Remembering what was said in chapter 5, it is also necessary to check that the level of trade terms and discounts to the trade is not increasing either. These do not appear as an itemised set of costs in the financial accounts, although they reduce the net proceeds of sales made, and so adversely affect the costs to sales ratio. The ratio is in fact affected by three things: (a) a rise in costs, (b) a reduction in sales volume, and (c) a reduction in sales value, possibly through higher discounts to the trade. It is insufficient to control the costs of sales operations, if the cost of benefits to the trade is allowed to increase instead.

Achieved distribution

Finally, the immediate objective of all selling activity should also be continuously monitored. This is the level of trade penetration, and distribution availability from stock. Once availability in the trade has been achieved, a trade selling operation has effectively done all it can, and the subsequent rate of sale must depend on the appeal the product arouses in customers. Regular reporting from market research agencies may be available, or else specific survey checks on distribution availability may have to be carried out from time to time by the sales force itself.

A case study

An example of a high efficiency sales information system is one which was established some years ago by the SL company in Paris. SL markets food preparations throughout the French market from its offices on the Champs Elysees. Grocery distribution in France is mainly by indirect supply through a limited number of main distributors, and through the central depots of the major multiple chains. Direct ordering from and delivery to the actual retail outlets in relatively rare, even when these are large supermarkets and hypermarkets. The task for the field sales force is therefore principally to ensure that distribution and presentation in the retail outlets is maintained at the highest possible level, by encouragement, persuasion, and ensuring that replenishment orders are regularly placed through the proper channels for each outlet. At the same time the amount of shelf space allocated for display has to be carefully watched and recorded; retail prices checked, and information collected on competitors' activities, distribution and prices.

Few direct orders are taken by the sales force but it is essential for salesmen to be kept informed of orders received through indirect channels, and for the company to get information back from the salesmen on how the market is reacting. It was decided that the only way to do this was to take fullest advantage of what a computer system could offer, using what were then the latest techniques for data entry.

The field force operates to a very regular schedule of visits, with all journey plans and visit dates on file in the computer. Also on file is detailed information about every major retail outlet, of which there are some thousands rated as important by SL. Not only is all status information filed but also details such as the average rate of sale per company product, the amount of display space allocated per product, the retail prices currently charged, and similar information on key lines from competitors. Just in advance of the scheduled date for making a call, the salesman receives a computer printout giving a summary of the latest situation for each important customer. This gives him an updated reminder of what to look for. By counting stock and comparing it with the latest calculated figure of average sale per item, the salesman can convince the customer of the size of replenishment order needed from his central warehouse or wholesaler. If display facings have been reduced, the salesman can immediately see this from his printout and take the matter up with the customer.

Where any of the recorded information has altered, for example the retail prices charged, or the amount of space devoted to competitors, the salesman writes in the new figures in the appropriate spaces on the printout. He does this in carefully formed, hand written numerals using heavy pencil. The printout with the changes is mailed back to head office, where it is fed in through a special conveyor to the computer which is actually able to *read* the new figures as written in by the salesman. This technique is known as 'optical character reading' or OCR. Provided the hand written characters conform reasonably well to the laid down shapes and sizes, the computer can scan and recognise them without error. Only a short training period is necessary for salesmen to learn how to write the numerals correctly, and in practice the system works to a totally insignificant error rate.

By this means, the two-way exchange of information between head office and salesman takes place without any clerical intervention at all. The salesman does not have to write up any records for his own use, as he gets a fresh updated set from the computer each time: and the information he sends back is read in automatically to the computer without the need for transcription or keying-in. A system of this type is quite expensive, but where it is vital both to ensure that salesmen's information on customers is accurate, and to receive their input in return, it can readily pay for itself.

A minor feature of the SL system is that the salesman also writes on his printout in OCR figures the *actual time taken* for each call. This provides positive confirmation that the call has been made, and also gives an updated figure for time spent on each customer, for the eventual revision of standard time allowances.

New technology

It is always worthwhile to investigate the best method of actually transmitting orders from salesmen to head office, and getting information back to them. This may not always be the mail service. Mail is sadly becoming slower and less reliable, as well as not altogether cheap. The value to a company of getting orders in expeditiously, and of knowing that they are all in, with no stragglers still to arrive from the field, should not be underestimated. For example, if orders come in quickly it may be possible to manufacture against order and save on stockholdings, while still giving an acceptably prompt delivery. Many companies have been able to justify using courier services to collect orders from the regions, or telexing them in from regional depots, or even equipping salesmen with two-way radios for instant communication. A relatively inexpensive method is for salesmen to telephone their day's orders in the evenings (at cheaper rates) to a telephone answering machine at head office, for transcription the next morning. Each salesman can be given his own time slot to avoid congestion on the lines.

A drawback to all these methods is that transcription of the incoming message is required, in one form or another. If orders are being entered to a computer system, as is increasingly common, the order details have to be 'keyed-in' by special operators; giving rise to delay, extra cost, and the possibility of error. The latest technology in elecctronics, combined with automatic telephone networks, now makes it possible for the salesman in the field to communicate directly with the head office computer, giving a very significant improvement both in time and in accuracy.

Voice response systems

There are basically two rather different systems available. In the first of these, the salesman is equipped with a 'key pad', which is simply a miniature keyboard, carried in the hand, with keys for the digits 0 to 9. It looks exactly like the set of keys mounted on the latest push-button telephones; and indeed it performs the same function, since when the keys are pressed it converts each digit into a characteristic acoustic tone. The key pad is connected to a small loudspeaker mounted in a rubber cup, which can be fitted over the mouthpiece of an ordinary telephone. It is now possible to transmit numerical data over the telephone line by means of this 'acoustic coupler'.

To use the system, the salesman goes to any telephone, which can be a public pay-phone, and calls up a number which connects him directly to an answering device on the head office computer (or on a mini-computer specially installed for the purpose). This answering device is equipped for 'voice response'; that is, it has a synthetic voice producing mechanism which can put together a limited collection of words and phrases with which to respond to the inputs it receives. When the number is first called, the machine will respond by identifying itself, and saying something like 'Go ahead'. The salesman then connects his key pad to the telephone mouthpiece, and proceeds to key in, in coded form, the details of the order he wants to transmit. The machine will guide the salesman by 'saying' what it wants to be told next. Typically, a message will start with the salesman keying in a code number to identify himself; then a code for the customer; then a code for each item ordered, with the quantity in plain figures. At each stage, the computer will verify the figures received, and if they are not in the valid range will respond with a verbal message to that effect. If they appear to be valid, the machine can be programmed to 'repeat' them verbally in confirmation.

In this way the salesman can input all his day's orders directly to the computer in a form it can understand and act on, and he has the added assurance of having heard the computer itself acknowledge what it has been told, knowing that it will be processed immediately. As regards the equipment required, the system is not particularly expensive – the key pad is a simple device, and only one voice response machine can serve hundreds of salesmen. The drawback is that the telephone remains connected during the whole of the time that salesmen are keying in their coded orders; and unless they can become particularly speedy in doing this the system is liable to run up a very considerable telephone bill if it is used from all parts of the country.

Microterminals

With the second method of order transmission this difficulty is avoided. Salesmen are equipped with the very latest technology in the form of 'microterminals'. A microterminal is a completely portable, battery powered device, which looks like a rather large electronic calculator, with the same kind of keyboard and display panel. It can be carried in the pocket or in a brief case, but it is nevertheless a complete computer in its own right, with a substantial amount of memory store, and a built-in program to perform a whole variety of calculations and data handling.

The microterminal is designed to receive the input of data through its keyboard, and store it in memory until it is required. Unlike a tape recorder, it does not store data on a mechanical medium, but actually holds it in the electronic memory of the microchip itself, for as long as the power supply remains on. The rechargeable batteries therefore have to be kept topped up. Terminals are programmed specially to suit the particular application, prompting the user by means of the diplay panel to input coded data in the correct sequence. Code numbers for customers and for products can be checked for validity before being accepted; quantity figures can be totalled automatically for checking. By the end of the day the salesman will have entered to his terminal the coded details of all the orders taken during the day, using the terminal as a kind of electronic order book. For his own satisfaction, the salesman can call up on the display panel, line by line, everything which has been recorded,to check its correctness and amend it if necessary. When he gets home, he connects the terminal through a special adaptor (called a modem) to the telephone, and leaves it there all night. During the night, the computer at head office automatically calls the telephone number of each salesman in turn, activates the terminal, and causes it to transmit all its stored data in the form of a single very high speed 'burst'. Since the telephone line need only be connected for probably less than a minute, and at the cheapest overnight rate, the costs of telephoning are very much less than with the open line voice response system.

It is also possible for the head office computer to transmit new data *back* to each salesman's terminal. This could take the form of any urgent messages, which the salesman can call up and read from the display panel next morning; or it could be routine information on available stocks, latest prices, targets and quotas. Depending on capacity, microterminals can be programmed to serve as a complete guidance system for the salesman, prompting him with details of the complete product range and prices, calculating discount levels, keeping running totals of quantities per item sold and left to sell, or manipulating data in any other way which would be of service.

Such miniature computer systems are expensive, and unlike most other computers cannot normally be programmed and reprogrammed at will by the user. Since they have to be purpose built by the manufacturer for one particular routine sequence, their application has to be extremely carefully planned. Nevertheless, in very large selling operations they more than pay for themselves under three broad headings:

1 Rapid and reliable transmission of orders,already checked for valid coding, and input directly to the computer without the need for data preparation staff at head office.
2 Guidance and simplification of routine for the salesman.
3 Facility for the transmission of up to the minute data back to the salesman.

The information battle

The wider aspects of these new technology systems have to do with keeping the salesman better informed than the customer, and better equipped for closing the sale with him. Traditionally the retail trade has been particularly badly informed about the rates of sale of individual items – with a checkout system, there is no detailed record of items sold, so that the rate of sale has to be laboriously calculated from opening stock, plus quantities purchased, less remaining stock. Often the supplier's salesman comes to be relied on as a source of this information, which gives him invaluable influence over keeping stocks generously replenished. Nowadays, with the increasing use of electronic point of sale equipment, the distributive trade is rapidly improving its own information and presentation of the facts. Unless the salesman is also aided by the latest technology he is in danger of being left floundering in the face of the customer's superior insights. The selling interview of the future may increasingly become one where the buyer consults the computer video screen on his desk for an analysis of past performance and future sales prospects,while the salesman rapidly calls up on his hand held microterminal the counter assessment which was fed into it from his head office computer the night before.

Sales records

The figure of sales actually made is probably the most vital statistic there is for a company; yet it is surprising how often this figure seems to be different depending on which record is being looked at. The only valid figure for sales is that which represents quantities actually delivered and invoiced, less any returns, and for which payment is legally due. Many companies 'pre-invoice' their sales; that is, the invoice is typed out in one operation along with the order, or packing note to the warehouse or factory, on the assumption that the goods will be delivered as ordered. If something is out of stock, an adjusting credit note has to be raised. Thus, the corrected figure of sales in a given period may take some time to emerge, with some slight variations in the interim. As a check on current progress, many companies find it worthwhile to evaluate orders day by day as they are received. This figure will be subject to possible customer cancellation as well as to non-availability, and of course in a given period the value of orders received will differ from the value actually delivered and invoiced. Nevertheless it is a very useful advance statistic.

In fact it is highly desirable to make a regular comparison between the total value ordered in a period, and the total eventually supplied, as a check on the level of service, i.e. the in-stock availability being achieved. For this assessment to be valid, a fair amount of judgement is required. If an item is known to be out of stock, salesmen must be warned not to go on taking orders for it which cannot be supplied. Its absence will therefore not show up on the calculation of service level as above, but some allowance for it should be added back afterwards. Similarly a distinction may have to be made between items out of stock through unforeseeable production breakdowns, and those whose offtake was simply not predicted correctly.

How much analysis?

Once invoices less credits have been issued, they are on the one hand debited to the accounts of the individual customers, and on the other hand credited in total to the 'sales account' of the company. This much must always be done whatever the system, whether the simplest form of manual bookkeeping, or the latest in computer processing. Thereafter it is up to sales and marketing management to decide what additional analysis of the sales figures is desirable and justified. Product marketing management will almost certainly have made a case for sales to be analysed into totals per product group or even per product. Sales management invariably want to see total sales per salesman and per sales area. What need is there for anything else?

With manual methods of invoicing and bookkeeping, this question can often be left until a need actually arises. Copies of all the original invoices for each month or for each year will be filed away somewhere and can always be gone through again to extract manually whatever further analysis is required. The same amount of clerical labour is involved whether the analysis is planned in advance or decided on afterwards. If such special analysis is beyond the capacity of the existing staff, temporary assistance can probably be hired – at least the information is always available.

Computer limitations

It is of course possible to perform exactly the same kind of manual analysis even with a computer system, always provided the computer has actually produced file copies of all the invoices. However, it seems more than slightly ridiculous to have a highly expensive machine standing idle, and to perform a laborious clerical operation oneself – apart from the fact that, if a computer has been installed, the volume of invoices is likely to be enormous anyway. In living with computer systems, an essential working rule is that, unless you have specified in advance to the computer people everything that you are going to want, you are unlikely to be able to get it. This is because, as well as having a formidable memory, a computer also has a unique capacity for forgetting. In a typical invoicing system, the computer will evaluate and print out the invoice, transfer the total value to the accounts, and perform any other analysis and posting that was programmed into it – and then instantly clear its memory of all record of the transaction. It is impossible to call back for any further processing the original details of the invoice it has just printed, unless specific arrangements are made to keep a record of them in a form that the computer can read. This will usually mean on magnetic tape.

If, therefore, there is any likelihood of further analysis being required, it is very worthwhile to discuss with the computer people the feasibility of keeping all original invoice details on tape, say for at least a year. This gives the possibility of having a special program written at any time to extract whatever information is required – for example, sub-totals of sales for particular types of customer; or sales per item to any one customer. If customer profitability is going to be examined, this last analysis will be essential.

Customer profitability

As long as a company is making enough profit, there may be no need to worry too much about where it is coming from. Few companies however can maintain such a lofty detachment, without wanting to check how each part of the business is doing individually, to see which parts are below par, and whether any could be improved.

Contribution per product

Since businesses are usually subdivided, if at all, by product group, it is typical for the profit of each *product group* to be analysed separately as far as possible. Total sales in each product group can be extracted from invoices, as suggested in the previous section; production costs per product are known (and controlled); while advertising normally relates to one product at a time, or else can be fairly allocated between them. Thus, it is reasonably easy to calculate for each product the 'contribution' it makes towards overheads after these direct costs. Table 10.1 shows a specimen presenta-

Table 10.1
Product profitability analysis

£000s

	Product Group A	Product Group B	Product Group C	Total
Sales at net selling price	8,500	5,000	6,500	20,000
Cost of goods sold	4,675	3,000	3,575	11,250
Advertising costs	1,275	1,000	975	3,250
Sales promotion costs	–	300	250	550
Total direct costs	5,950	4,300	4,800	15,050
Contribution before indirect expenses	2,550	700	1,700	4,950
(Contribution as percentage of sales)	30%	14%	26.1%	24.75%
Indirects:				
Distribution costs				998
Selling costs				1,020
Management costs				640
Rents, rates, depreciation and other overheads				1,210
Total indirect costs				3,868
Net profit before interest and tax				1,082
(Net profit as percentage of sales)				5.4%

tion of a year's profit and loss account for a business with three product groups.

The costs of distribution, selling, management, etc. have to be treated as 'indirects' since it is impossible to estimate exactly how far they are incurred in respect of individual products. Such costs can therefore only be put against the business as a whole, not against products. Even so, it is easy to see from the table that product group B is making less contribution than the others, both in total and as a percentage of sales value, and it must be valuable to the company to know this.

Note at this stage that it would be perfectly easy to 'allocate' the indirect costs to the different product groups according to any system the company likes, whether equally to all three, or pro rata to turnover, or pro rata to anything else; but that this information would not prove anything on its own. If a cost is factually related to a particular item, then it is most helpful to relate the two in the accounts. If costs are not factually related it is much better to leave them unallocated altogether. Sooner or later a financial figure based on an allocation of costs will be taken as factual, and some conclusion drawn from it; which will almost inevitably be wrong.

Contribution per customer

Just examining profits,or the lack of them, will not of itself improve matters. However, in the same way as it is prudent to check on the relative performance of the major product groups, there is an equally good case to be made for analysing the profit contribution of the major *customer groups* – or even of single large customers. The object is exactly the same as with products: to see which groups or which individual customers are less profitable than others, what scope there is for making improvements, and whether extra costs incurred in one direction are really being offset by savings elsewhere. Analysing the costs and profit contribution by customer is, however, a great deal more complex than by product. There is no point in doing it at all unless at least three conditions are known to exist:

1. There is liable to be considerable variation in prices, margins and costs as between customers.
2. It is going to be possible to do something about this.
3. Costs can be discovered accurately, without relying on arbitrary allocations.

Differences in the profit contributions obtained from customers arise principally from variations in prices and discounts; or variations in gross margins of the products supplied; or variations in the costs of selling and distribution; or all of them at once. If there is only one factor involved, for instance if some customers get bigger discounts than others while everything else remains the same for all customers, then it is perfectly easy to deduce that these customers make a lower contribution, without having to do a complex analysis. But when several factors are at work, a detailed analysis is the only way of discovering what is really happening.

What is the use?

There is no point in making this kind of analysis at considerable trouble and expense if there is nothing that can be done about the results anyway. Sales management are often pessimistic about this. We get the best prices we can, they say; we give no more discount than we have to, and we keep selling costs to a minimum. What is the point of doing all these calculations merely to tell us what we already know? The answer of course is that management do *not* already know exactly how all these costs are working out, and once they do know there is invariably something they can find to do to make matters a little better. In negotiations with major customers, it is essential to know exactly what level of contribution is being achieved before making any further concessions; and to be able to judge how far a concession on one point could be balanced by a saving on another. Profitability information on the different groups of customers, e.g. pharmacies versus grocers, is of the greatest importance in judging where to apply greater support.

Need for accuracy

Customer profitability analysis can be carried out regularly, or only as often as required,

A case study

A case in point arose some years ago in the marketing of a washing powder in a European country. In continental markets, domestic washing powder is typically sold in supermarkets in quite large multi-kilo fibre drums rather than in packets – the housewife likes to buy in bulk when shopping by car. When buying in bulk she expects and is given a lower price per kilo. But the product itself costs no less per kilo to produce, and in fact the packing in drums costs rather more per kilo than in packets – the latter are filled automatically by machine whereas the drums have to be filled and the lids stuck down by hand. Washing powder in drums is sold mainly through the largest supermarkets and hypermarkets, and these naturally benefit from the highest levels of discount because of the size of their purchases. At the same time, they receive the greatest amount of attention from the sales force. Salesmen call weekly if not daily, special deliveries are made at all hours, and teams of merchandisers help with layout and display.

Each group of management responsible for these separate activities was convinced it was giving encouragement to a profitable business – indeed this was supposed to be the most important sector of business the company had. Only when the profit contribution from major supermarkets was carefully analysed was it revealed that this sector was in fact incurring a net loss. Higher product cost at lower selling prices with bigger discounts and greater selling costs produced this inevitable result; but only customer profitability analysis brought all the facts together for the first time.

---

perhaps once or twice a year, or when some planning decision has to be taken. But unless really accurate figures can be obtained it is far better not to do it all. In particular it is useless to make an analysis using *average* figures for any element – average product margins or average discounts or average cost of distribution. The whole point of the exercise is to discover variances from the average in particular cases, and there is nothing for it but to try to get to the actual costs wherever they are more than trivial. To do a customer profit analysis properly, the following information will be required for the period in question:

1. Actual quantities supplied of each product
2. For each product, the actual net price paid, after discounts and credits
3. For each product, the actual costs of production at the relevant time
4. Actual costs of any campaigns, promotions or special allowances for this customer
5. Actual costs of selling and providing sales support, based on records or estimates of time spent
6. Actual costs of physical supply and delivery, either from transporters' invoices or from a realistic 'cost model' of own transport and warehouse costs.

It will now be apparent how desirable it is to have a record of all past invoice details preserved on computer tape. For whichever customer or group of customers is being analysed, a quite simple program can read through the tape, summarise the quantities of each product supplied and the prices invoiced, and multiply out the total value at selling price less the given unit cost at the time. This is the *only* way to arrive at a true figure for the gross margin realised from any particular customer. Using average margins would of course conceal exactly what we are trying to discover. Detailed analysis of this kind is particularly easy with a well organised computer system, and to be realistic is really only feasible with such a system. Making a manual analysis to this degree of detail would rarely be something to contemplate.

The next most difficult part is to model the costs of distribution. This is in fact an exercise in cost allocation, but where the allocation is made according to the elements which 'really' caused the costs to be incurred. For example, it might be decided that delivery costs arose so much in respect of distance, so much in respect of quantity supplied, and so much as a fixed overhead for each delivery made. The balance between each element would have to be a matter for very careful calculation and judgement. Whatever the ratios, it is absolutely vital to double check that when they are applied to *all* the deliveries that were actually made over the period, the total comes back as near as makes no difference to actual costs for the period. The ratios can then be applied to the transactions of any one customer in the assurance that the allocation is at least correct arithmetically.

Customer profitability format

Figure 10.3 shows the basic format for the calculation of customer profit contribution. In the same way as when calculating profit per product group, only costs which can be 'directly' charged are included. Costs which cannot be factually related to particular customers are best left as 'indirect' overheads, to be met out of the profit contribution from all customers. Thus marketing services, management, and general overheads are not included. It is arguable whether advertising costs should be included or not. From one point of view these can be considered part of the 'cost' of each product, just as much as the cost of production, and therefore should be added to the cost of goods sold. A contrary view would be that the amount spent on advertising has nothing to do with the trade customer, and that therefore it should not be charged against the profit contribution he makes. When first launching a product, a company might easily spend more than its total revenue on advertising as an investment for the future, but thereby making the item a net loss in current accounting terms. Any trade customer who supported the campaign by stocking the product would therefore apparently also show a loss. To avoid confusions of this kind it is perhaps better on balance to keep advertising as a general overhead and not include it in the analysis of profitability per trade customer.

The profitability of a customer depends very much on the mix of products he buys, given their varying margins; and the profitability of a product depends very much on the mix of customers who buy it, given their varying rates of discounts and costs. Trade marketing and product marketing management must therefore do their planning jointly to ensure that neither makes the wrong assumptions about which products will be bought and who will buy them.

Customer profitability analysis

Period covered . . . . Date of analysis . . . .

Customer or customer group . . . .

	£	%	Notes
1 Total sales @ invoice value		100	From invoice records
2 Total ex-factory cost of sales			Quantity per product x standard cost, including materials, production and factory services
3 Gross margin on sales			1 minus 2
4 Special allowances and credits			Any credits or payments to the customer not deducted from invoice
5 Cost of selling			Estimated from records of calls made
6 Cost of distribution			From transporters' invoices, or from distribution cost model
7 Customer contribution to overheads and profit			3 minus (4 + 5 + 6)

Figure 10.3 Format for the analysis of customer contribution

Checklist 10

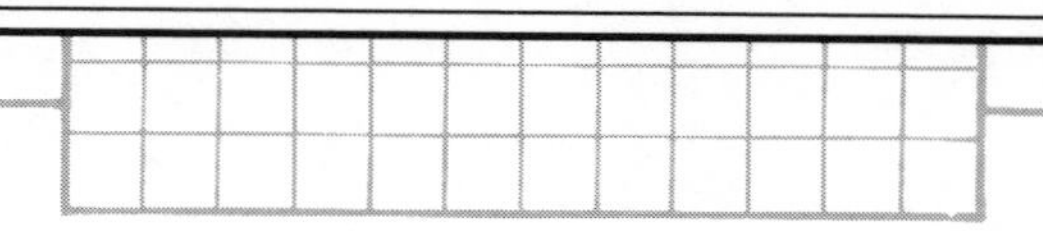

Information for control

10.1 The information base

(a) Is all necessary information on present and potential customers complete, up-to-date, and rapidly accessible in one place? Does it cross-check with accounts records?

(b) What arrangements are there for this information to be shared with salesmen? Could manual record-keeping be reduced? Could information be made of positive assistance to the customer as well as to the salesman?

(c) Is there a control that selling calls are being made as planned? Are orders to calls and travelling distances analysed? Is distribution in the trade regularly monitored?

10.2 Techniques and systems

(a) Have all alternative methods of communication to and from the field been evaluated for cost effectiveness? What value can be set on time saved in receiving orders?

(b) Under local conditions, would it be possible to use electronic/computer/telephone systems? Is a feasibility study worthwhile?

10.3 Sales analysis

(a) In how many ways are sales figures analysed and published at present? Are these sufficient? Are they all useful?

(b) Can supplementary analyses be obtained if required? If there is a computer system, does it appear sufficiently flexible?

(c) Is there reason to suppose that profit contribution may vary significantly between different types of customer? Could this be analysed accurately? Would it be possible to improve results given better information?

11

Promotions and display

Throughout this book it has been emphasised that sales (or trade marketing) management is in the main responsible for achieving distribution of the product in the trade; while their product marketing colleagues are concerned with making the appeal to the consumer. There are however two aspects of the product marketing plan for appeal to the consumer which require the direct involvement of the sales organisation. These are: the implementation of consumer promotions; and the achievement of display at the point of sale. In both of these areas the sales organisation acts as it were as an agent of product marketing management, executing plans on their behalf, rather than developing plans of its own.

Consumer promotions

By consumer promotions we mean any kind of extra benefit or special activity tied in to the product itself and designed to appeal to the consumer directly. The activity can of course also be tied into media advertising at the same time, but unlike a purely advertising campaign, there will be some feature associated with the item itself at the point of sale at the same time. Consumer promotions are not applicable only to the general public; the technique can be employed very effectively with commercial and industrial buyers as well. The essence of a promotion is that it should be temporary. Otherwise the action loses all impact and becomes merely a routine characteristic of the product, which buyers come to expect.

Since there is going to be something special about the item itself or the way it is sold, it follows that the distributive trade is likely to have some part to play in putting the promotion across. Trade co-operation will be required; and it is the function of the sales organisation to know how to go about securing this, and what kind of price may have to be paid for it. In order to achieve their purpose of motivating the consumer, promotions require at least the passive consent of the distributor. A well thought-out promotion is one where, instead of this consent being only grudgingly given, or having to be paid for, the distributor becomes an enthusiastic participant, even to the extent of contributing money of his own to make the scheme a success. Achieving this is the role of a skilful sales organisation.

Consumer promotions promote specific products; therefore the cost of them is clearly chargeable to the product marketing budget. While the promotions budget is therefore held by product marketing management, it should however be made a rule that it must not be *spent* except as part of a joint plan endorsed by trade marketing or sales management in every case. Product management have sole discretion in spending the media advertising budget, since whether well spent or badly, this makes no demands on anyone else. Promotions spending however does make large assumptions about what other people will or can do, and joint planning is essential.

Trade promotions

Alongside consumer promotions aimed at the retail customer, there can also be special promotions aimed at the distributive trade. These may also take the form of free gifts and so on offered to the distributor, which can be viewed on the one side as public relations and the general entertainment of trade customers, and on the other side as outright bribery of customers' employees.

The question of gifts to employees can be a very tricky one for suppliers. That such gifts are expected goes without saying. Giving away a pin-up calendar or a ballpoint pen is totally innocuous; it can also arouse quite fierce resentment as being insufficient or even insulting. The attitude of employers also varies widely. Some are very happy that suppliers should contribute to the living standards of their staff – as long as they all do it equally, and so gain no advantage. Two guiding rules for suppliers should be: make sure that employers are aware of what is being given and do not object; and make offerings as far as possible as prizes, in return for specific performance, as best salesman or something of the kind.

Less controversial are trade promotions which consist of a special temporary price benefit on the product, or supplying an extra quantity free. The common objective of all trade promotions is to provide an inducement to the trade to put more support behind the distribution of the product, without it being intended that any particular benefit should be passed on to the consumer (other than perhaps a better in-stock availability). A good name for trade promotions is trade stimulants, since the function is to brighten up sales figures which have become a little jaded, and get more product into the trade. Since the objective is improved distribution, it would be proper for the budget for such activity, if any, to be under the control of trade marketing management. In practice, in drawing up their total budget for the achievement of distribution through the trade, trade marketing management might be wise to allow a small contingency element for the cost of extra inducement in any sector which is falling behind. No special policy decision is then needed to bring it into use.

As a corollary to consumer promotions which have to be implemented through the trade, trade stimulants may have to be implemented through special deals on particular products. Clearly then there should be consultation between trade marketing management and their product marketing colleagues on the possible effects of such deals to the trade. It could be highly embarrassing to try to improve overall trade figures by making a special deal on one particular product, in ignorance of some other impending plans for it, or of some limitations on production capacity.

Two birds, one stone

Rather than keeping consumer promotions and trade stimulants in separate compartments, the real challenge is to see how far the two sets of objectives can be combined. Anything which motivates the consumer to buy more is a most direct form of encouragement to the trade. Anything which induces the trade to give the product more support will result in increased sales to consumers. Thus by very judicious joint planning, it should be possible to marry the objectives for consumer and for trade, and to make one budget serve two purposes. This could be said to be the ultimate in joint product/sales co-operation.

A similar position arises with media advertising, where one budget must jointly influence both the consumer directly, and the trade indirectly. Before contributing its support in providing distribution the trade must be impressed with the seriousness and the effectiveness of efforts to win the consumer franchise for the product. Joint planning between product management and trade marketing management again has a part to play. It is the function of trade marketing management to provide input both on the level of advertising budget and on the ways in which it can best be spent to carry conviction in the trade and indeed to provide the most effective support. Advertising which involves or invokes the trade in some way, or which is run jointly with the trade, need have no less impact on the consumer, while serving the dual role of winning trade support.

As major retailers grow more important, they begin to demand special deals exclusive to themselves, which will enable them to offer a benefit to their customers not available from their competitors, and which will therefore benefit themselves indirectly. Thus instead of being able to run their own programme of consumer promotions throughout the year, available through all distributors at the same time, manufacturers find themselves having to devise individual promotions for major customers and spend their product promotions budget selectively in the trade. In these circumstances it is the national accounts managers who increasingly have the job of proposing how product promotional money shall be spent. Very careful appraisal becomes necessary to ensure that it is still the product, rather than the major account, which benefits the more from whatever deal is struck. If special offers and promotional activity are allowed to become concentrated only in the major distributors, with little ever on offer elsewhere, it is the major distributor who will tend to get the credit for having an enterprising sales policy, rather than the product being recognised as a particularly good buy.

Profit contribution again

On this point it is relevant to refer to the last chapter, where customer profitability was discussed. It was said there that on balance product advertising costs were best left out of account when comparing profit contributions between trade customers, if only because the effect, whatever it is, applies to all distributors equally. The same would hold good for product promotional costs, *when the promotion applies equally to all sales of the product through all outlets.* When promotions are made available selectively through particular customers, the situation is altogether different. The cost of the promotion of a given product should now most definitely be charged against the calculated profit contribution from each distributor who actually benefitted. If product X is supplied at 10 pence off only when sold through retailer A, then the cost of the rebate should be treated as a product cost against A's profitability. Analysis of customer profitability thus becomes a very potent method of checking how promotional benefit is being distributed.

Sales involvement

Sales involvement in the actual implementation of promotions will include the following aspects:

1 To check the appropriateness of the proposed promotional scheme. This is not to say that sales should set themselves up to be authorities on what is not their business, namely how to appeal most effectively to consumers, but neither should they acquiesce in a scheme which they have reason to think is not going to work. They would be right to insist that every promotion has clearly quantified objectives, related both to product strategy and to trade strategy, and indeed to company strategy as a whole. Once they know what they are supposed to be achieving, they are half way to achieving it.

2 Sales must prove their record of being the experts on what can be achieved in the trade, at what cost and with what results. They must be able to judge how far the trade can be persuaded to participate actively in a scheme, giving material support where necessary, with no extra reward beyond the prospect of increased sales; or if reward is required, what is the minimum that can be negotiated; or even whether the trade could be got to contribute to the value of a scheme from its own normal margins. They must be able to judge how a promotion aimed primarily at the consumer can be turned into an equally effective stimulant to the trade at the same time.

3 To assess the workload for the sales force in selling a proposed promotion to the trade, and in making any physical arrangements for its implementation. This might include arranging display material, or counting stocks before and after, or applying price reduction stickers or counting coupons. Auxiliary sales support staff can often be used for these tasks, and might have to be hired temporarily for the purpose. Sales management must in any case be able to provide an accurate costing for whatever is involved.

4 To schedule promotional workload for the sales force so that it can be properly carried out and so that product management can be informed well in advance of capabilities.

5 Prior to the launching of a promotion, to collect relevant market information; such as the actual retail prices being practised, if the point of the promotion is to achieve a reduction; or to get news of any forth-

coming competitor activity which might cause a clash.

6 To give advice on any proposed point of sale material, as to its suitability for its purpose, and as to the quantities required. The sales force must also take the responsibility for the distribution of point of sale material, and for its being put to proper use.
7 To supervise implementation in the trade, with whatever policing and auditing may be necessary.
8 When the promotion is ended, to collect information on the results achieved: the extent to which it was implemented, the sales achieved, residual stocks, total costs, and an evaluation of benefits.

Some of these aspects are worth looking at more closely.

Promotional workload

Selling in a promotion to the trade requires additional time, both on the part of the salesman to make his presentation and on the part of the trade customer to understand the proposition and to respond. The amount of time required depends on:

1 The complexity of the scheme, particularly as regards the participation required from the trade customer, and the benefits he stands to gain.
2 Whether the promotion has already been agreed to in principle by the head office of a multiple distributor, and the salesman has only to confirm the details at branch level.

Actual times required for selling in different forms of promotion in different circumstances are a matter for further observation and time study of the sales force. If promotions are a regular feature of the selling programme, an average allowance for promotional selling can be built into the standard times for every type of call. Where they are less regular, some contingency allowance should nevertheless be made in calculating the salesman's total workload. Otherwise, if promotional activity is quite exceptional and has not been allowed for, it can only be done by requiring overtime work from salesmen, or by temporarily cutting out some lower priority scheduled work. A sales organisation which has properly calculated its scheduled work, and worked out its salesmen's deployment accordingly, is in a much better position to adapt rapidly to a change of priorities of this kind. If customer records have been kept up to date and readily accessible, revised call plans with the promotional work substituted can quickly be drawn up and issued to salesmen, rather than it being left to them to make what changes they choose.

As well as the time element involved in selling in promotions, there is the question of how many separate promotions a salesman can be expected to sell effectively in the course of one interview, and how many the customer will have the patience to listen to. Planning for more than two or at the most three promotions in the course of one interview would be very suspect. The promotional schedule that can be accommodated by a sales force therefore becomes quite limited, and priorities for its use should be agreed with product management as far ahead as possible, leaving perhaps a small reserve capacity for last minute tactical actions. At the same time it should be checked that promotions for less important products have not been made so complicated as to require more time spent on them than on the major items.

Types of promotion

What the sales force will actually have to do towards mounting and supervising a promotion of course depends on the form it takes. Promotions for this purpose can be broken down into no more than about four principal variations.

The 'on-pack' offer

This is the form of promotion where some kind of 'giveaway' is attached to the product itself. The extra benefit may either be material, or in the form of a written promise – that is, it might be an extra quantity of the product itself, or another article given away with it; or else it could be some kind of voucher or token for claiming a benefit or prize elsewhere, or for entering a lottery or competition. There are innumerable sub-varieties, but from the sales force point of view the common feature is that the benefit is integral with the product itself and so passes straight through to the consumer without requiring any direct intervention by the distributor. For the distributor, the product is still the same stock item as before, with buying and selling prices presumably unchanged. When stocks incorporating the promotion reach him, he will pass them on to consumers for as long as they last. As a matter of good customer relations the sales force will inform distributors in advance of the form the promotion will take, and for how long special stocks will be supplied; salesmen will make the most of the increased demand which the promotion will bring to sell in extra promotional stocks to the trade. Special effort will be needed to get orders from all distributors for stocks carrying the offer so that availability is complete when the promotion is due to start. But as far as passing on the benefit to the consumer is concerned, the distributor has no extra function to perform – unless the 'giveaway' makes the article bulkier and it requires more storage and display space.

Usually all physical preparations for this form of product promotion can be carried out at source, by modifying the pack or the packing process in the factory. If the objective of the promotion is to move stocks which are already in the hands of distributors, the sales force might be called on to prepare the promotional packs in the field – by sticking on the gift vouchers or banding the giveaway article to the packs. This is likely to be a long drawn out, messy and uneconomical process which will completely wreck the normal work schedule of a sales force. Putting through a special price offer on existing stocks is likely to be much more cost-effective in these circumstances.

The redemption coupon

A redemption coupon is one which a consumer can present to a distributor to claim money off a purchase of the promoted article. Coupons may be printed for cutting out in newspapers and magazines, or given away door to door, or else printed on the pack of the article for use with the next purchase. These different methods of course have quite different consumer objectives – whether to encourage an initial trial purchase or to retain loyalty for a repeat purchase – but in the end they make the same demands on the distributor's co-operation in accepting the coupons in lieu of money, for eventual redemption by the supplier. When the coupons are printed on pack there are really two stages to the promotion; first getting distribution for stocks carrying the on-pack offer, and secondly arranging for redemption of the coupons themselves.

Distributor co-operation is needed in two senses; both in accepting the coupons in lieu of money at all, but more importantly in ensuring that they are exchanged only against the article being promoted. A redemption coupon offer is very vulnerable to abuse and surveys done in the United States, where coupons are a favourite means of promotion, suggest that abuse is in fact very rife. Coupons will have to be printed in numbers representing in face value a vast amount of money, and if these can be exchanged other than against purchases of the product, a supplier can run into a very serious net loss. A redemption rate of around 5 per cent is all that a supplier would bargain for in making a coupon offer, so the degree of vulnerability is obvious. The sales force will have the task of persuading distributors to co-operate, and judging how far they are likely to instruct and supervise their staff effectively; as well as making spot checks of its own. The first reaction of distributors will be to require payment for the extra inconvenience, against which sales must argue the extra revenue which the promotion will bring. A more insidious response is for distributors to gratify their own customers by exchanging coupons freely against any purchase, at the expense of the supplier who is trying to promote his own product.

Since prior commitment from distributors is required before coupons can be distributed, it is almost imperative for this kind of promotion to be negotiated first at major account level and then made selectively available only through the branches of those accounts which have agreed to redeem the coupons selectively. Committing distributors at large to doing so before they have all been asked is to risk a most embarrassing (and public) repudiation; or else to become the victim of unregulated redemption.

The bargain pack

In this type of promotion, the original article is offered in a new and what is intended to be more attractive form or pack. It differs from the simple on-pack offer in that the promotional variant is now a quite different item of merchandise from the original unpromoted article, and one which both the consumer and the distributor have to be persuaded to purchase instead. The commonest example would be the 'banded pack', where, say, three of the items are banded together and offered for the price of two. A crucial distinction is whether the promoted pack and the ordinary pack can go on selling side by side. If the promoted pack merely replaces the ordinary pack, at no greater cost – for instance, it is put in a fancy wrapper for Christmas – the distributor can continue to regard it as the same stock line, with the new supplies replacing the old. But where a promoted pack has a greater total price, even if it is a better bargain for a larger quantity, the distributor has to treat it as a new stock line and decide whether or not to carry it, depending on his assessment of offtake and the margin it offers. He may well wish to go on stocking the normal item in any case.

The task of the sales force is to convince distributors that the bargain pack will command sales largely additional to the normal and persuade them to adopt it as an extra line while not totally stopping purchases of the old. Getting a new line adopted even temporarily becomes more difficult, the more highly organised the distributor's business. For modern supermarket chains with computerised inventories it entails opening a new item file in the computer and advising all branches, as well as probably revising an entire shelf layout to introduce new facings. Major accounts management know only too well what is involved in getting a new item 'listed' in this way by the headquarters of a multiple.

As a means of promotion bargain packs are clearly of considerable appeal to consumers, but the difficulty of introducing them makes them more suitable for permanent inclusion in the stock range rather than as a purely temporary special offer. Temporary offers are better made through price reductions.

The special price offer

This is the form of promotion which is at the same time most directly appealing to consumers, and most demanding of co-operation from distributors. In essence it is simple enough: for a given period, or for a given quantity of stock, the standard article is to be sold to consumers at a specially reduced price. The net price to the distributor will be reduced as well, but not necessarily so as to leave him with percentually the same margin as before. Very occasionally, it might be thought justifiable to *increase* his margin, so as to give an extra incentive to him, as well as to the consumer. More usually, the aim will be to persuade him that his reward will come from the increased sales brought by the promotion, even at a lower percentage margin. Getting distributors to make a contribution in this way to the cost of special price offers is one of the prime objectives of trade marketing negotiation.

A price reduction can be handled in two ways: either by having the reduction prominently printed on a specific quantity of stock (known as 'flash packs'); or by merely publicising a reduction on normal stock which remains unmarked. In the first case, the quantity and therefore the total cost of the promotion is fixed, but the time it will take for all promoted stock to sell is unknown. With unmarked stock, the promotion may be either on a specific quantity or for a specific period, but it is the quantity actually sold at a discount which is the variable.

In some countries there are legal objections to marking packs with the actual reduced consumer price, since this is reminiscent of 'RPM' or resale price maintenance. Marking the amount of the proposed reduction ('10 pence off') can be confusing if it is not clear what it is to be reduced from. In either case marked packs are not popular with distributors. Not only does the marked pack restrict their pricing freedom, but in many cases the marked stock will have to be treated as a separate stock line for inventory purposes. Both before and after the promotion, marked and unmarked stocks are likely to be in the pipeline at the same time, at different prices. Depending on the stock and value control system being practised, the two may have to be recorded separately as different items.

From the sales force point of view, handling a 'flash pack' promotion is relatively straightforward. A planned quantity of the promoted pack has to be sold, of which each major account manager and each salesman will probably be given a quota. Normal negotiation and salesmanship have to be used to get these quantities taken up by the trade, largely in substitution for the unpromoted item. A distributor who will not accept the (reduced margin) deal on promoted stock can go on having normal priced supplies instead, but of course will not be able to offer the reduced price of his competitors. Once the marked stock has been sold in to the trade at its special price the trade is more or less constrained to sell it on according to the price marking, and no further control is needed.

With unmarked stock, the situation is more complicated. As before, the basic proposition on reduced prices has to be negotiated with distributors. But this time, the supplier has to rely on the distributor as an honest agent in passing on the reduction to his own customers at the levels agreed. The supplier may make the reduction on a particular quantity ordered, in which case the distributor undertakes to keep that parcel separately identified and sell it all in turn at a reduced consumer price. Alternatively, the distributor may undertake to sell at a reduced price for a specified period, noting the quantity sold, and claiming a retrospective rebate from the supplier accordingly.

Either way, the distributor, particularly if a large scale multiple operation, is undertaking quite a considerable administrative task. All this counting and checking of stock has to be delegated out through staff in the branches where, in a large retailing operation, hundreds of such promotions may be going on at the same time. Mistakes can easily be made. On top of this, there is a very considerable temptation for branch staffs to delay the introduction of reduced prices and to return them to normal ahead of time. By so doing, they can realise for their branch a greater value for the promoted stock than the amount due according to the control system, and so help to balance any stock losses elsewhere. The supplier's sales force will therefore have the additional onerous task of policing the arrangements made, spot checking that consumer prices are reduced to the correct level and trying to verify the stock quantities involved. When the promotion is being planned and negotiated, the extent of auditing by the sales force should be made very clear, both to make proper allowance for the workload entailed, and to ensure co-operation from distributors at branch level.

Control of promotions

Some distributors on the other hand may be only too keen to participate in promotions. When a company runs a regular programme of promotions, some parts of the trade can often see promotions coming and arrange to buy only when a special price offer is available. By ringing the changes between alternative suppliers, such distributors may be able to keep quite a comprehensive stock range going, all of it at discounted prices, so gaining for themselves a reputation for cheapness, at the expense of regular availability of particular products. When this occurs, it is a signal that promotions are no longer fulfilling their original purpose, but are merely being taken advantage of by the trade as a form of speculation. It may be necessary to make promoted stocks available only as a limited quota of purchases made at normal price.

Display and merchandising

The sales organisation also carries responsibility for the most important promotional activity of all – ensuring that the product range is attractively and widely displayed in all the outlets where the consumer should be able to buy it. The product is usually its own best advertisement. It has to be seen, and seen in sufficient quantity and in sufficient contrast with its surroundings to create an impact. This is what is meant by 'display'. Additional material may be introduced as well, but the product itself should be designed or packed so as to be the main feature. Display material, being both product specific and related to advertising, will normally be the responsibility of product management, but sales management must also have a say in its design, practicality and quantity to ensure it is entirely suitable for use at the point of sale.

'Display' is the generic term for the end effect. In the same way 'merchandising' has come to be something of a generic term for the whole operation of achieving display, particularly in self-service outlets. Merchandising may cover anything from bringing stock forward out of the back room and filing the shelves with it, to building special display sites or even redecorating a shop front. Most of the work involved in merchandising can be and very largely should be done by the distributor himself. It is part of his trade function of achieving distribution aimed at the consumer, in return for which he earns his reward from the supplier. Sending in staff to do the work for him at the supplier's expense is something of an admission of failure in getting the distributor to honour his side of the bargain. Ideally, the supplier's contribution should be limited to those aspects which he can do best – the provision of ideas, layouts, special materials, and, where really necessary, expert staff such as shopfitters or signwriters. But for ordinary stock shifting and housekeeping tasks the distributor can provide labour much more economically than the supplier can.

Negotiations with distributors must stick on this point, that if the supplier is going to have to provide manual labour at the point of sale, the sharing of reward with the distributor will have to be altered, and disproportionately to the real value of the work. Distributors must be induced and persuaded to produce display for themselves, by negotiation, example, exhortation, training – anything short of giving in and doing the whole job for them. Merchandising means getting display. It does not have to mean employing merchandisers.

One of the most depressing situations is where both a supplier and all his competitors each employ full time merchandising staff to fill distributors' shelves for them, when in the end no one gets a display advantage and the only gainer is the distributor whose store labour has been supplied free. The dilemma for the manufacturer is great, but he has to remember that the provision of merchandising assistance is practically irreversible. Once granted, the arrangement cannot be withdrawn without *loss* of display.

For the minimum of direct assistance which has to be provided, sales management must still seek the cheapest way of providing it. It may be more cost-effective to use semi-skilled, possibly part time staff, rather than divert salesmen from their proper task of selling. This issue was already discussed in chapter 6.

Display as media

In developing countries, where the normal media like TV, cinema, press, posters and even radio, make little or no impact, the role of display has to be an even wider one. To put over a message to potential consumers in such conditions, particularly in rural areas, a manufacturer may have to expand his display function to the point where it replaces every other kind of media. In other words, as well as supplying the product, the manufacturer has to supply the media to carry the message as well.

Ordinary shop display of the product will of course be used to the full, but in addition a supplier may have to organise his own putting-up of posters and signs, demonstrations of the product in villages and market places, and even free cinema shows from mobile vans by way of publicity. When operations get to this level, there is a very considerable extra function for a field force to perform. Either this must be formed as a specialist department within the trade marketing sales organisation, or, if it is set up independently, liaison with the sales organisation must be of the closest. Clearly, running a media service cannot be made merely an incidental task of a regionally organised sales force, and at the very least a specialist division would be required. On the other hand all its operations must be very closely tied into the rest of the field selling campaign, and none are better placed than the field sales force to advise on how and where an own-media operation should be mounted. At the same time, it will be the sales force's task to ensure that full distribution availability is achieved in the appropriate areas to back up the media efforts. As an advertising medium, even although set up by the manufacturer himself, the content of a field display campaign should be the responsibility of product management since it is directed at the consumer; but as a field operation it poses the same problems of deployment and supervision as the rest of the field sales force. Sales management will certainly have a contribution to make.

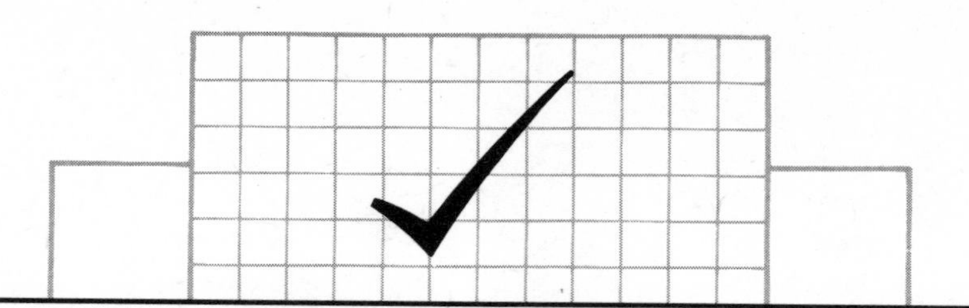

Checklist 11

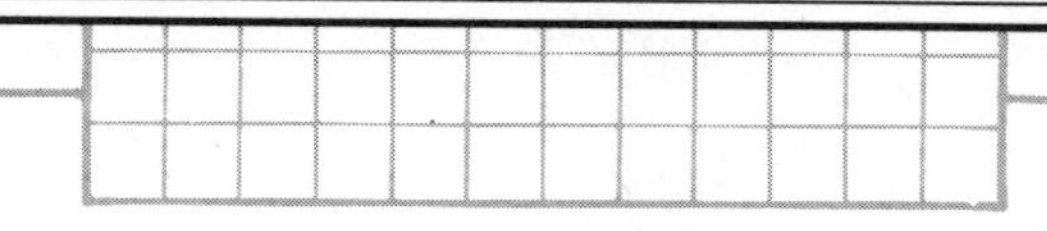

Promotions and display

11.1 Promotional policy

(a) Are promotions aimed at the consumer a regular part of marketing policy? Is there a budget for them, and who controls it?
(b) Is there a separate policy of promotions or stimulants addressed solely to the distributive trade? Are these budgetted for?
(c) Is sales management consulted on the planning of consumer promotions? Are the responses of distributors taken into account?
(d) Are consumer promotions seen by the trade as a benefit to them? Can they be persuaded to contribute financially? Can one budget be used to motivate both consumer and distributor?
(e) Are consumer promotions applied in common through all distributors, or on a selective basis among distributors? What control is there on the sharing of benefit between distributors?

11.2 Promotional administration

(a) Is work connected with promotions allowed for in sales force workload calculations? Is there an advance schedule of how many promotions can be handled?
(b) If redemption coupons are used, does the sales force have a role to play in spot checking for invalid redemptions?
(c) On special price offers, is it acceptable both legally and to the trade to mark reductions or reduced prices on packs?
(d) On unmarked price offers, what arrangements are there to ensure that reductions are passed on to consumers in full, for the agreed quantity or for the agreed period? Does the sales force have to check stocks?
(e) Are sales of promoted stock limited to a quota of normal sales per distributor?

11.3 Merchandising

(a) Does the sales force undertake shelf filling or display building for distributors? Or are special staff employed for this?
(b) Are distributors doing their own fair share of such work? Is there a clear policy on what assistance, if any, may be given?
(c) Would it be worthwhile to operate a direct-to-the-customer publicity service? Anything from putting up signs, or product demonstrations, or even mobile exhibitions?

12

The destiny of the business

An effective sales or trade marketing organisation can exercise a fundamental influence on the progress of a business well beyond its own immediate orbit. Its functional role is already vital enough; without the efficient channelling of the product to consumers through the distributive trade, everything else comes to a halt. The selling department must not, however, let itself become merely a service for carrying out the plans of other people. As a dynamic trade marketing department which is more than the traditional idea of a sales department, the more expert it is in its own field, the more title it has to contribute positively to what the business as a whole should be doing.

Decision points

In arriving at its own strategy for selling through the trade, the trade marketing organisation has only a limited mix of methods to rely on. These are: the choice of trade channel; the fixing of trade reward; the employment of field selling; the arrangements for logistics and support; and the use of merchandising for display. Throughout this book the theme has been how these elements should be marshalled into a strategy which is not only coherent but also fully complementary to the plans of product marketing management. Continuing review is called for in the light of changing circumstances, and the cycle of planning followed by control may have to be entered upon at whichever point first demands attention. Nevertheless, it is important to remember that the strategic plan does consist of an interdependent sequence of choices and the revision of one may have repercussions among the others. To recapitulate, the principal decision making stages are:

1. Assessing the product range, in regard to its target consumers, who they are, where they are, and how they are most likely to be reached through the distributive trade;
2. Assessing the market structure of the trade, its characteristics and its behaviour, and the ways in which competitors make use of it;
3. Reviewing the product marketing plans, for whatever implications they hold for trade distribution, with the aim of achieving fully integrated plans for trade and for product;
4. Reviewing and re-selecting the trade channels to be used for distribution, reconciling the conflicting interests of different levels in the trade, and achieving distribution agreements where necessary;
5. Making allowance for the concentration of distributors and the growth of major accounts;
6. Planning the levels and mechanisms of reward to distributors while maintaining a strong influence on consumer prices;
7. Determining the types of selling and support effort required, and the corresponding costs;
8. Planning and quantifying the selling effort to distributors;
9. Planning and deploying selling forces accordingly;
10. Organising these forces according to function and ensuring harmonious working;
11. Organising information appropriate to the elements to be controlled, and for use in well informed negotiations;

12 Allowing for involvement in direct appeal to consumers through promotional and display activities.

Strategic thinking

Pulling all these elements together into one consistent plan produces a trade marketing operation which can be said to be in control of events, rather than controlled by them. At the same time, a very definite contribution is made to the strategic thinking of the business as a whole. The most direct involvement is in the corporate decision on the total sales volume to go for, to produce the optimum profit. Extra volume can probably always be obtained, at a price. Perhaps the major contribution to be made by an effective trade marketing operation is the ability to say accurately what the price of obtaining sales will be, so enabling the most profitable level to be planned for. The financial objective of a business must be the return on capital employed, not just maximum sales. Higher sales will demand greater resources, and the most profitable level may not be the maximum. Forecasting the resources required for each level of result is the function of trade marketing management.

Other incidental contributions to the business strategy will include input on the level of consumer prices to be aimed at, after allowing for trade reward and the costs of selling which will be necessary. Trade marketing will offer a very valid view on the product range itself, in the light of the special needs of the distributive trade, and not least as regards the trade's own opinion of what consumers really want. Promotional needs and methods must be advised on. Trade marketing also has a vital contribution to make to production planning, in accurately forecasting not only total sales volume, but also the fluctuation month to month in the rate at which it will have to be supplied ex-factory into the trade. As well as seasonal variation in consumer demand, this must take into account the custom of the trade as regards stockholding, and the extent to which fluctuations in demand can be smoothed out. It clearly has the greatest bearing on the maximum production capacity to be planned for, and so again on the optimum level of investment in resources.

Prediction, forecasting, targets

A very large part of the trade marketing function thus consists of making accurate predictions of how sales figures will turn out. All objectives have to be converted to specific forward planning by means of forecasts and it is on trade marketing management that this duty mainly falls.

Judgemental flair

In cases where there is no really relevant previous performance to go on, forward planning requires what might be described as a facility for judgemental prediction. Other names for this would be instinct, hunch or inspired guesswork. It is a flair for this kind of thing that marks out the successful tycoon from mere worthy businessmen, and it is unlikely to be learned by precept. In our context the process must however start from some assessment of demand for a product, at a price. Someone in a business becomes convinced: 'There must be a million people who would buy this'. Or else: 'A product at this price should take 10 per cent of the market'. Judgement of this kind may often be tempered by other practical considerations: 'We could only produce half that quantity in the first year in any case, so we must be safe in going for that'.

Prediction of this kind belongs most naturally to product marketing management, being concerned with consumer response to a product concept. Of course market research techniques and test marketing can be used to assist the process, and initial judgements will be revised as quickly as feedback can be obtained from the market place. The role of trade marketing management is to translate such assessments of consumer reaction into terms of the trade response to it. Here some relevant previous experience already begins to be applicable. While the product itself may be new and unknown, the trade's reaction to the introduction of a new product is not. In theory, the trade is ready to welcome any new product which will generate new consumer demand; in practice each new item is regarded with suspicion until it proves itself. There is a great deal of self-fulfilling prophecy in the adoption of a new line by the trade. Belief in its success will cause it to be given exposure, which is indeed likely to bring success. Encouraging this process is an essential skill of trade marketing management, and one where the process of predicting results against a given level of resource expenditure is already very relevant.

Forecasting

Forecasting is the process of prediction based on information, however incomplete this may be. In weather forecasting, the winds and clouds which are known about today are used to predict whether or not it will rain tomorrow. Projecting known and recognised patterns of events into the future is a valid process only if these patterns represent some underlying cause. Where patterns are merely random, projecting them forward is like fortune telling from tea leaves. Forecasting therefore must be a combination of identifying what are the reflections of real events, and projecting forward the patterns which these produce. Two different approaches result: the 'micro' or small scale analysis of the situation, and the 'macro' or broad sweep review. The two must be conducted independently, and reconciled. If the pattern viewed as a whole suggests a particular figure for the total forecast, when it is broken down into its component parts does this produce a reasonable figure for each part when considered individually? When added together, do the forecasts for individual sectors, individual customers or individual salesmen come to a reasonable figure in total? A common cause of error may be that each individual predicts a performance for himself in isolation, ignoring what his neighbours or competitors may be going to do. Only when individual forecasts are added together does it become apparent that the total is too large for realism. In making sales forecasts, all members of the selling organisation must be made to participate, putting forward their own best estimates for the area for which they are responsible, to be considered against the overall view formed by top management. When the finalised targets for each area and for each individual are eventually passed back (preferably with a word of explanation for any changes which have been considered necessary) these will receive a far greater degree of commitment from staff than targets which were merely handed down in the first place. Not only will these be respected less, they are more likely to be wrong.

Targets

Targets are a prediction of what could be achieved; forecasts are the best estimate of what will actually happen. Ideally the two should be the same, but as time goes on, while keeping the original targets, it may be necessary to forecast that they will not be completely realised – or perhaps even exceeded. Setting unrealistic targets in the first place is not to be recommended. While initially such targets may do something to summon extra effort from all concerned, they will soon come to be discounted in everyone's mind but in the meantime may actually lead to wrong action through being taken too literally. Keeping clocks deliberately fast does not make people any more punctual in the long run and leaves no one knowing what the right time is.

At any one time there may therefore have to be two sets of figures in an operating business: the targets as originally fixed for the current year, and updated forecasts at intervals, which will be used for the planning of stocks and production, and also for any remedial action that may be necessary. Both sets of figures will be broken down in the same way, by period and by trade sector, region, area and salesman – sometimes even by customer. Targets and forecasts for growth must above all be realistic. Investment plans based on over optimistic estimates can prove to be disastrous.

Forecasting methods

Insofar as they are based on past performance, forecasting methods involve the manipulation of numbers, and there are endless ways in which this can be done. Numbers on a page do not project a picture which makes itself readily comprehended by most people. Figures all on a line or in a column are just figures, and no pattern or shape emerges. All crucial figures should therefore be converted to chart form, so that the eye can immediately take in the proportions of one result against another. Incidentally, sales figures and forecasts should, whenever possible, represent quantities not monetary values. That way, inflation does not have to be allowed for.

Graphs and charts

The continuous line graph is traditionally used to show the fluctuations of sales from one period to another, and this is usually convenient enough, but it has to be remembered that it too is not a strictly accurate representation of what has been happening. A continuous line graph should only be used to show the *continuous* state of something in relation to the two axes, which usually represent a quantity of something and the passage of time. Thus, it is appropriate for a barograph to record the change of atmospheric pressures over time, or for registering the rate of output of something. The level that existed at any instant can be read directly off the graph. But a sales graph does not show the *rate* at which sales were being made, minute by minute; it purports to show the sales that were made in total, period by period. For this purpose it is far better to use a bar chart, with a column for each period.

Figure 12.1 shows a year's sales figures in bar chart form, with a traditional sales graph of the same figures superimposed. In the bar chart, each column is proportional to sales in the period, and if added end to end all the bars would be proportional to total sales for the year. The continuous line however does not add up to anything, and it suggests a rate of *movement* which is not strictly true. Both increases and declines are made to appear gradual from one period end to the next, which may not have been the case at all. They may have occurred during the period, not after it, and they may not have been gradual. Perhaps more dangerous is the fact that a moving line suggests it is going to continue

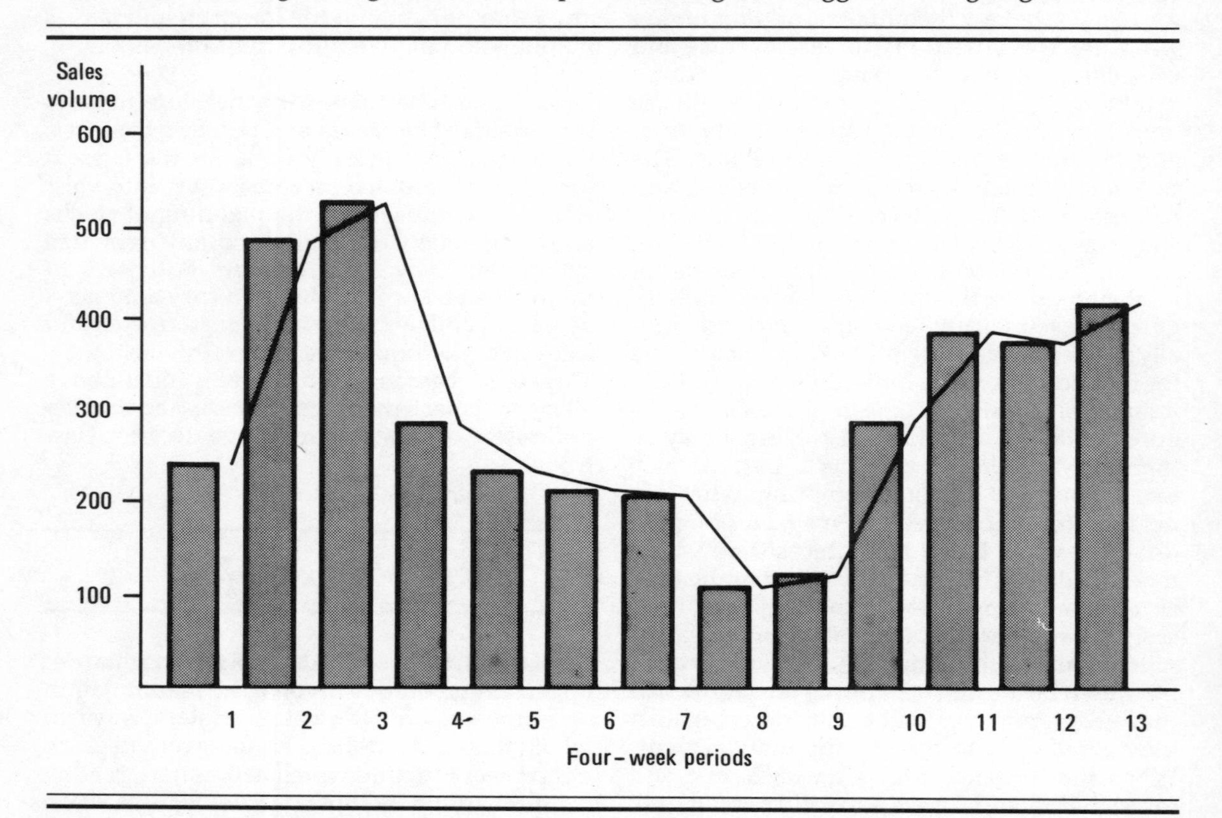

Figure 12.1 Sales volume as bar chart and as graph

moving in the same direction, when there is absolutely no reason why it should. With a bar chart, the size of one bar is much less suggestive of how big the next one is going to be, which is much closer to reality.

Arithmetic mean

Returning to numbers, there are many inferences to be drawn from them which cannot be shown on charts, and arithmetical processes have to be used instead. The thing most commonly done with a string of numbers is to take their simple average, more correctly known as their arithmetic mean. All the values are added, and divided by the total number of them. This is the same thing as taking an equal proportion of each of them or, in the case of previous sales figures, giving equal 'weight' to all past periods, however distant or distorted by extraneous events. A simple average of all past periods is therefore unlikely to be much of a guide to what will happen next. The figure of average rainfall for a place is not a lot of help in deciding whether it will rain tomorrow – some, but not a lot. It is worth remembering that there is much more chance that the average will not happen, than that it will. Often the average is something which never happens at all, like the average family with 2.5 children.

Seasonality

Seasonal fluctuation in sales of a given product is very common, and when it happens it can be a most useful guide to expectations. The average rainfall for this month in past years is already a much better predictor of the amount of rain in this month this year. First there has to be a reasonable explanation for the seasonal fluctuation. If it cannot be explained, it might be just coincidence, or else there will be no knowing if and when the undiscovered reason should disappear again. In the first place, the cause of the seasonality itself has to be predicted, if there is any uncertainty about it – for example, Christmas will certainly occur on December 25th, but it is anyone's guess whether it will be a hard winter. Thereafter the effects on sales of such a prediction have to be extrapolated from the pattern of past years when such conditions actually occurred. The best way of doing this is to take the sales figures for the same seasonal period in all *relevant* past years, take their simple average, and convert this to an *index* of seasonality for the period.

To illustrate this point, Table 12.1 shows sales figures for two successive years, divided into 13 equal four-weekly periods. If each of these years' sales are drawn in bar chart form, it is immediately obvious that there is a fairly regular seasonal pattern. (The values for Year 2 are already shown in Figure 12.1. The reader can try superimposing the values for Year 1.) To define the pattern, the average for each period over the two years is expressed as a percentage of the average for a whole year. Thus the average for period 1 is (198 + 250) divided by 2, giving 224, which is 6.6 per cent of the average for a whole year at 3412. The seasonality index for period 1 is therefore 6.6 per cent, and so on. However annual sales develop in total, these proportions for each period are likely to remain relatively stable.

Growth and MAT

Any overall rate of growth (or decline) tends to be obscured by seasonality. In order to eliminate it, the total of sales for a whole year past should be calculated again at each period. This is known as a moving annual total, or MAT. At each new period, the sales figure for the latest period is added on to the last MAT, and the figure for the corresponding period last year is dropped off. Using the values in Table 12.1, the MAT at the end of Year 1 was 2922. At the end of period 1 in Year 2 the MAT becomes:

$$2922 + 250 - 198 = 2974$$

and at the end of Period 2 it becomes:

$$2974 + 491 - 545 = 2920$$

Thus each new MAT figure covers one full year, with all the different seasons represented (assuming that all seasonal effects are in fact annual). A MAT figure can of course only be calculated after at least one year's history of a given product has accumulated, and a good deal of judgement may be needed to decide if it should be discontinued again because the product has been so altered that

Table 12.1
Annual sales figures

Period	Year 1	Year 2	Average	Seasonal Index	Year 2 MAT
1	198	250	224	6.6	2974
2	545	491	518	15.2	2920
3	252	525	388.5	11.4	3193
4	167	282	224.5	6.6	3308
5	155	235	195	5.7	3388
6	112	213	162.5	4.8	3489
7	97	205	151	4.4	3597
8	129	110	119.5	3.5	3578
9	147	125	136	4.0	3556
10	168	287	227.5	6.7	3675
11	252	380	316	9.2	3803
12	277	374	325.5	9.5	3900
13	423	425	424	12.4	3902
Total	2922	3902	3412	100.0	

the previous sales history is no longer relevant to it. For as long as successive MAT figures are available they should be scrutinised for signs of any continuing trend, expressed as percentage growth, positive or negative, over a period. The figures in Table 12.1 demonstrate a fairly steady growth rate throughout Year 2 of the order of 30 per cent.

Exponential smoothing

If sales figures are computerised, it is more than likely that the computer system treats them to a process known as 'exponential smoothing'. This is a method of calculating a 'weighted' average of past results which is particularly suited to computer processing and is therefore much used. Instead of adding all previous results and dividing by their number, this method produces a new average by adding a fraction of the latest result to a complementary fraction of the previous average. The fraction used is always denoted by the Greek letter α (alpha) and has a decimal value between 0 and 1. Expressed in this way:

$$\text{new average} = \alpha\ (\text{latest result}) + (1 - \alpha)\ (\text{previous average})$$

This can be rewritten as:

$$\text{new average} = \text{previous average} + \alpha\ (\text{latest result} - \text{previous average})$$

or:

$$\text{new average} = \text{previous average} + \alpha\ (\text{error})$$

Thus to calculate an average by exponential smoothing, it is only necessary to find the 'error' between the latest result and the previous average, multiply this by α, and add the previous average again. This is particularly convenient for the computer, as it is not necessary to store a record of all actual previous sales by period, but only one figure of the last previous average.

The higher the value given to α, the greater the 'weight' given to the latest result compared to earlier results in forming the new average. All previous results contribute to the new average, but in proportions which diminish ever more slowly until the earlier ones become quite insignificant (which is why the process is called exponential). With an α value of 0.2, the new average contains 20 per cent of the previous result, but only 1 per cent of the result from 14 periods ago. With an α value of 0.1, only 10 per cent of the latest result is taken into account, but 1 per cent of the result from 22 periods ago is still included.

Exponential smoothing always needs a 'previous average' to start from. Thus with a new product having no past history it is necessary to make an initial estimate of sales from which the process can start, and depending on the α value used the effects of this initial estimate will linger for quite a long time in each new average. The calculation reflects any continuing trend of growth or decline, but always with a time lag; therefore it never fully projects any trend which may be occurring. Seasonality is not taken into account at all, in the basic formula. The method is therefore not a substitute for keeping a record of all actual past sales by period, and it does not, as is sometimes implied, provide an 'automatic' forecast of sales.

Other processes

Much more complex computer analysis of past sales can of course be made, to take account of these and other points. Many such systems consist essentially of analysing the pattern of past sales figures to find a mathematical formula which most closely matches this pattern, and then projecting this into the future. The drawback is that as such methods become more sophisticated, ever more emphasis is given to the numerical aspects of the past, in ways which are harder for the layman to follow. This makes it even more difficult to apply 'judgement' in modifying the calculation which has been made, that is to say by taking account of some knowledge which is not conveyed in the past figures but which is going to be relevant to the future. Complex mathematical methods of forecasting tend to be self-defeating, as the user is unsure of what has been taken into account and what has not.

Repetitive forecasting

Forecasting the sales of a given product is usually a repetitive process, with a new estimate required for each planning period. Forecasts should always be made for more than just one period ahead, and preferably for a whole year at a time. In this way, when making an estimate for each new period, all the earlier estimates that were made for that period can also be looked at, to review exactly what considerations have caused a change of mind over time, if there has been one. This kind of input can be just as valid in influencing a final decision as all the more factual evidence.

It goes without saying that if planning periods are going to be compared with one another, they must at least be of equal length to start with. Calendar months are very unsatisfactory in this respect as the number of working days in each can vary by 20 per cent – which would be considered a very significant fluctuation in sales. The most equal way in which a year can be divided up is into 13 four-week periods, which is what will be used for purposes of example.

The object then is to make a new forecast every four-week period for all 13 ensuing periods. To do this, the following aspects should be taken into account for each period considered:

1. Sales in the same period in previous years;
2. The growth trend, positive or negative, as a percentage figure year on year, taken from the MAT figures;
3. Coming the other way, *along* the year: the seasonality pattern predicted for the current year, expressed as a percentage index for each period;
4. The trend of error in previous forecasts this year, whether consistently over or under;
5. Cumulative sales compared to the original target for the current accounting year;
6. All previous forecasts for the period being considered;
7. Any special circumstances, such as promotions, new products or stock shortages, which may have affected sales in previous periods;
8. Any similar special circumstances which are foreseen for future periods.

Items 1 to 6 in this list could undoubtedly be reduced to a numerical formula specifying exactly what weight to give to all the different factors, so that analysis could be done automatically by computer. The difficulty would be in deciding what weights to use. In making such forecasts manually, or mentally, it is very useful to have all these relevant figures brought together on one sheet of paper for each item, and a specimen of a suitable format is given in Figure 12.2.

This begins by listing across the top the actual sales per period in past years. All businesses must have a fixed year for planning and budgeting purposes, whether this runs from January to December or over any other period. In Figure 12.2 we are displaying results per planning year, although we shall also be trying to make forecasts for 13 four-weekly periods at a time, irrespective of which planning year they are in. So across the top go the results for (preferably) two or three past planning years, plus the results for the current planning year so far, updated each period.

The next line shows the original target figures for each period this year, for ready comparison with the actuals in the line above. Similarly, the next two lines show the cumulative actuals against the cumulative target figures. At the end of the line a note is made of the growth trend which is being assumed in these target figures; for example, a steady growth of so much per cent, or else an intial growth followed by a levelling off. Finally, there is a line showing the seasonal percentage index for each period, i.e. the proportions in which the year's turnover is expected to be split by period.

In the bottom half of the form, successive series of forecasts are made at each of the 13 periods. Each forecast should itself be made for all 13 ensuing periods; that is, at the end of the line, the forecast figures are brought back round again to the beginning of the line. The figures below the 'step' dividing line are therefore forward estimates for the *next* planning year. At the bottom of the page is a line to show the error between each final forecast for a period (the figure in the box) and the actual sales achieved. A minus figure denotes sales *below* forecast, a plus figure is sales *over* forecast.

Working forward 13 periods at a time means that for the last period there have been 13 previous estimates, including the original target figure, before the final one. This may seem a wholly unnecessary repetition, but if forecasting is to be taken seriously, the only way to improve is to practise, and to check whether later attempts have been more accurate than the earlier ones. It is also very undesirable to get into the habit of working only within the confines of the current planning year. When annual targets are set, forecasts have to be made for a year ahead, and possibly for longer, if planning is being done much in advance. At the beginning of the year, it is usual to take a view right to the end of it, but as the year goes on, this would mean looking only one or two months ahead. The end of a planning year can come to hypnotise managers into behaving as if the current year was enough to worry about for the moment, with next year somehow being held in abeyance. Working consistently up to 13 periods ahead means that a global view of a whole year is always being taken, and by the time a new planning year comes round a great deal of the forward estimating for it has been done already.

Profit responsibility

In all the preoccupation with sales volume, it is easy for management to lose sight of their responsibility for ultimate profit. Excuses for doing so lie ready to hand, since no one department of a business can control all the elements involved and can always disclaim liability for the end result. Rather than shying away from involvement in profit, an effective trade marketing department should try to become increasingly profit conscious and to seek out the opportunity to have a voice in ways of generating profit. Major accounts managers and field sales managers must be encouraged to develop their profit awareness and instil it in all staff for whom they are responsible, in respect of all those cost elements which they can influence.

Trade marketing management are responsible for two vital areas of cost and therefore for the consequences of these costs on the ultimate trading profit of the business. These are:

1 The overall level of trade reward in return for providing distribution availabil-

Period	1	2	3	4	5	6	7	8	9	10	11	12	13	
Previous years: 1)	198	545	252	167	155	112	97	129	147	168	252	277	423	2922
2)	250	491	525	282	235	213	205	110	125	287	380	374	425	3902
Present year	325	563	530											
Target	330	760	570	330	285	240	220	175	200	330	465	475	620	
Actual cumulative	325	888	1418											
Target cumulative	330	1090	1660	1990	2275	2515	2735	2910	3110	3440	3905	4380	5000	Projected growth 28%
Seasonal index	6.6	15.2	11.4	6.6	5.7	4.8	4.4	3.5	4.0	6.7	9.2	9.5	12.4	Total for this year:-
Forecast 1	320	670	600	375	320	250	230	175	220	320	450	500	620	5050
2 →	400	700	600	375	320	250	230	175	220	320	450	500	620	5085
3 →	400	700	550	340	320	240	220	175	220	320	465	500	620	4858
4														
12														
13														
Forecast error	+5	−137	−20											

Figure 12.2 Period forecasting

ity, and thence the level of gross margin on sales which can be achieved.

2 The costs of selling and supplying to the trade at a volume commensurate with product marketing plans, and thence the levels of indirect costs and net trading profit which can be achieved.

Product management cannot plan for the gross profit which their marketing strategy will generate without making assumptions about the trade channels which will have to be used and therefore the net selling value into the trade which can be realised. The corporate plan for net trading profit and thence return on total investment must accept these assumptions and add others, on the level of indirect overheads in selling and logistics which will be necessary to sustain them. It is the function of trade marketing management, which aims to be more than just a sales management, to provide input to these assumptions and ensure a coherent plan for the business as a whole. Trade marketing management thereby become co-signatories to the corporate strategic plan, and effective partners in controlling the destiny of the business.

The strategy document

At the end of all earlier chapters a checklist has been given of the topics covered, designed to encourage thinking about the issues which have to be decided in arriving at a coherent strategy for achieving market distribution. Such a strategy must not only be arrived at, it should also be committed to paper, both so as to force clear thinking on every issue, and also to serve as a policy statement and plan for the business. The strategy document should be updated regularly and should not be departed from without due debate and a formal board decision.

This final checklist outlines a suggested format for such a document, which will summarise all the factors which have been taken into account, and the operating policy which has been chosen.

1. *Factual information*

1.1 Background

A summary of any facts related to the country or the market as a whole which have a bearing on strategy at this time; for instance:

Economic situation and outlook
Population development and living standards
Geographic or climatic considerations
Communications and transport facilities
Technological developments

(Since these will affect other strategies besides that of market distribution, they may already be summarised in the overall corporate strategy document.)

1.2 The product range

Types of product to be distributed, numbers of items in each category, different pack sizes; consumer categories aimed at, new products planned. Any features of the product marketing strategies which bear on distribution through the trade.

1.3 The trade structure

Total numbers of outlets in each relevant trade category, with any inter-relationships, special characteristics, etc; broken down by size and by geographic region. Current figures of penetration, distribution availability and sales volume in each category.

1.4 Competitors' operations

The main competitors per product group, their relative market shares and volume, their methods of market distribution, and their terms to the trade.

2. *Operating policy*

2.1 Distribution method

The selected channels for market distribution; intended numbers of distributors for direct selling, and as indirect stockists; target levels of distribution availability. Basis of distributor agreements, if any. Degree of concentration of sales to major accounts.

2.2 Trade terms and arrangements

The total pricing and reward structure intended for each trade sector; how consumer prices are to be supervised; mechanisms for discounts and bonuses; basis for any trade differentials.

2.3 Selling and servicing

Type, intensity and extent of selling and servicing in each trade sector; thence numbers, grades, organisation and deployment of selling and support staff. Arrangements for account management and negotiation. Total costs.

2.4 Sales objectives

Planned volume for coming year through each trade sector; related to complementary marketing plans for products.

2.5 Physical distribution

Jointly with any other departments responsible: implications of planned volume on physical distribution; needs for warehousing, order processing, transport and delivery. Service levels and stockholdings required.

2.6 Costs

Planned costs of obtaining distribution, as variable costs (trade reward) and fixed costs (sales force). Percentual costs per trade sector at planned volume levels. Reconciliation with financial and product marketing plans: gross margins attainable per product group/trade sector; remaining indirect costs. Promotional budgets and contingencies if any.

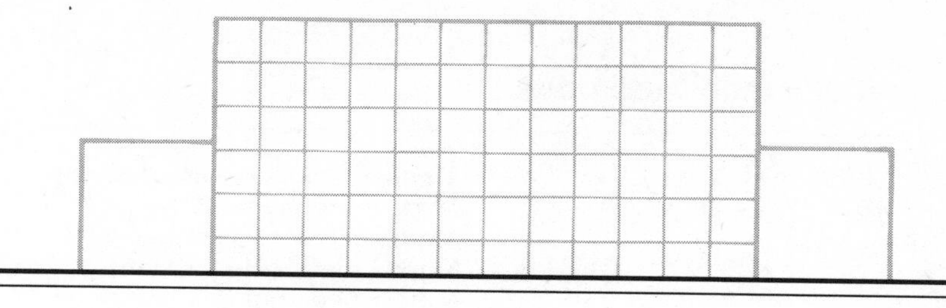

Index